SARAH BROWN'S
·HEALTHY LIVING·
COOKBOOK

SARAH BROWN'S
· HEALTHY LIVING ·
COOKBOOK

DK

DORLING KINDERSLEY
· LONDON ·

Senior Editor Fiona MacIntyre
Art Editor Anita Ruddell

Senior Art Editor Anne-Marie Bulat
Managing Editor Daphne Razazan

Photography Philip Dowell

First published in Great Britain in 1985
by Dorling Kindersley Publishers Limited,
9 Henrietta Street,
London WC2E 8PS
First paperback edition 1991

British Library Cataloguing in Publication Data
Brown, Sarah
  Sarah Brown's healthy living cookbook.
  1. Vegetarian cookery
  I. Title
  641.5'636   TX837

  ISBN 0-86318-114-7

Printed in Italy by Arnoldo Mondadori, Verona

· CONTENTS ·

GOOD SOURCES OF
· NUTRIENTS ·

· INTRODUCTION ·

F*at is bad for you . . . polyunsaturated fats lower cholesterol levels . . . take more exercise . . . jogging can kill . . . bananas are fattening . . . have plenty of fresh vegetables . . . carrot juice is poisonous . . .* These are just some of the many contradictory warnings and dictates that we are exposed to every day. The 1980s—with their marathons, workouts, F-Plan and microdiets—may have brought an awareness of the importance of health, but as awareness increases it gets harder and harder to sort out all the advice and differing opinions. When is something really good for you and when is it just a fad or a clever piece of marketing? This confusion even extends to the actual foods available—there's a vast range of foods from which to choose nowadays, many tempting us with their brightly coloured packaging and words like "full of natural goodness", "wholesome" or "energy-building". They look so good, but do they really offer anything beyond this? Are they nutritionally sound or are they, yet again, the product of clever marketing? In this book I've explained what your body needs in order to be healthy, showing you how to provide the essentials by buying the right ingredients and cooking them with care.

Health, diet and fitness are inextricably linked. You won't retain good health without a sensible approach to both diet and exercise. Unfortunately, good health is often something we don't think about until we no longer have it. When we are young we take good health for granted and don't bother to develop sensible eating patterns which will stand us in good stead in later life.

Taking care of your health through diet and exercise isn't just a matter of adding a couple more years to a rosy retirement. One in three deaths in people over 35 could be postponed by making changes in the diet. Many of the so-called diseases of civilisation such as cancer, heart disease, high blood pressure, obesity and diverticulitis are becoming increasingly linked with diet—more specifically to diets which are high in refined sugar, fat and salt, and low in fibre. As long ago as 1916, studies comparing the low-fat diets of the Japanese to the cholesterol-rich diets of northern Europe and America found a high correlation between high-fat, low-fibre Western diets and cancer and heart disease.

Increasingly, we are being advised to adapt our eating patterns and our attitude towards exercise. These changes have been clearly outlined by the recent COMA and NACNE reports on food and health in Britain. Prepared by doctors, nutritionists and scientists, their message is quite clear, not cranky or faddy, and it provides a guideline for a healthy diet for us all. Simply, it is this: eat less fat, particularly saturated fats, which come mainly from animal and dairy products, eat less sugar, eat less salt and eat more whole, fresh and fibre-rich

foods, particularly cereals, fresh fruit and vegetables. This book follows those guidelines, outlining the nutrients that are essential for your body and explaining what the good foods are and what to use as alternatives for those that you should avoid (see page 172).

Does this mean a diet of carrot juice with a uniform of leotard and track suit? Are the days of gourmet dinner parties long gone? Far from it. Food doesn't taste any the less delicious just because it's good for you. There is a wealth of tasty recipes to try in this book, so you don't have to miss out on the pleasure of well-cooked, interestingly seasoned food. What is more, one's concept of what is delicious eventually changes so that if you used to enjoy sweet, sugary things they will come to taste sickly, while rich, high-fat foods will seem heavy and indigestible.

So follow the principles outlined here, take exercise regularly and enjoy your food and your health. I do!

Sarah Brown

◆ THE WAY TO GOOD HEALTH ◆

Pages 50-168 contain my recipe suggestions to help you towards good health. Based on the high-fibre, high-protein, low-fat principle, each recipe is accompanied by a nutritional profile (see page 10). This will help you to understand exactly what nutrients are contained in each dish, and in what quantity.

Interspersed among the recipes are six ideas for balanced meals, that is, meals which are high in fibre and protein but low in saturated fat, and which provide a good source of vitamins and minerals. Further ideas for recipe combinations, and advice on meal planning, are given on pages 182-183.

For the main nutrients, apart from carbohydrates, there are recommended daily intakes. These may vary slightly from country to country, but the levels most commonly recommended are listed with the essential nutrients—fibre, protein, vitamins, minerals, fats and carbohydrates—illustrated on pages 18-28. Remember, it's more important to be aware of what you eat over the course of several days rather than become obsessive about ensuring that every meal within a single day is perfectly balanced. On pages 172-177 you will find advice and information about foods to avoid or cut down on, with suggestions for healthier alternatives.

◆ NUTRITIONAL PROFILES ◆

Each recipe has its own nutritional profile, so that you can see exactly how much protein, fibre, polyunsaturated and saturated fat each portion provides, as well as the number of calories it contains. The profile also indicates which vitamins and minerals are found in significant quantities in each recipe.

Nutrients

The amount of protein, fibre, polyunsaturated and saturated fat per portion is given in grams. Should you want to keep a conscientious check on your daily intake, total up the nutrients in everything that you eat, to make sure that it tallies with the recommended daily intake.

NUTRITIONAL PROFILE	per portion
Total calories	205
Protein	13g ✓✓✓
Fibre	14g ✓✓✓
Polyunsaturated fats	1g ✓✓
Saturated fats	0.5g ✓✓✓
Vitamins	Good source of:
	B1, B2, B6, C, FA, N
Minerals	Good source of:
	Ca, Cu, Fe, Mg, Zn

Calories

The total number of calories per portion is given to help those on calorie-controlled or restrictive diets.

Vitamins & minerals

All dishes contain some minerals and vitamins, but if the dish is an exceptionally good source of a particular vitamin or mineral, these are listed individually. The abbreviations used are listed, right. A dash indicates that a dish is not exceptionally high in any particular vitamin or mineral.

Key to abbreviations used

Vitamins
N   Niacin (B3)
FA   Folic acid

Minerals
Ca   Calcium
Cu   Copper
Fe   Iron
K   Potassium
Mg   Magnesium
Zn   Zinc

Understanding the tick system

Perhaps of more immediate use in understanding the nutritional make-up of a meal are these ticks. They allow you to see, at a glance, what each recipe is a good source of, and what nutrient it is high in. In protein, fibre and polyunsaturated fat, three ticks indicate an excellent source, two that it is a very good source and one that it is a good source. In the case of saturated fats, three ticks indicate that a dish is exceptionally low in saturated fats; two ticks indicate that the saturated fat level is low and one tick that it is moderately low.

GOOD
SOURCES
OF
· NUTRIENTS ·

·THE ESSENTIALS·

Which foods are essential to us, and what are we better off not eating at all? Here is a brief guide to the essential, and not-so-essential, components of our diet. For a guide to the recommended daily intakes, see pages 16 to 28.

·PROTEIN·

Proteins have two main functions. Firstly, they promote growth and form the framework of different body structures such as skin, nails and hair. A constant supply of protein is needed for the maintenance of body structures and to repair worn-out tissues. Secondly, proteins maintain supplies of enzymes, hormones and antibodies. These regulate many of the body's most important functions, such as the ability to digest food. Protein in excess of the body's requirements is either changed to fat and stored, or used to produce heat and energy.

Proteins are made up of amino acids, which consist of carbon, hydrogen and oxygen groups, together with nitrogen, which enables the amino acids to string together forming long, complex molecules. Some 20 or so amino acids act like building blocks, and can combine in different ways to produce a wide variety of proteins. Eight amino acids are called "essential", because the body cannot do without them and cannot synthesize them for itself. These are isoleucine, leucine, lysine, methionine, phenylalanine, threonine, tryptophan and valine. Growing children also need arginine and histidine.

Protein from animal sources—meat, milk and eggs—contain all the essential amino acids in roughly the proportions that the body needs, hence they are called first class proteins. No single vegetable food contains amino acids in the proportions the body needs, so they are referred to as second class proteins. A mixture of vegetable proteins is needed to provide an adequate level of the essential amino acids in the total diet. For example, wheat is low in lysine but contains adequate methionine; beans are low in methionine but contain adequate lysine. Eat the two foods together and the amino acid requirements are met—the combination of the protein sources gives a high-quality protein supply. The ability of proteins to make up for each other's deficiencies is known as their supplementary or complementary value. The traditional cuisines of most cultures have recipes based on protein's ability to do this. For example, rice and dhal (lentils) are combined, tortillas and refried beans, pasta (wheat) and chick peas.

We are currently advised to eat fewer saturated fats and increase our intake of dietary fibre. Meat and dairy products, although good sources of protein, are also high in saturated fats and lacking in fibre. Plant proteins can easily be combined to provide good proteins while containing little fat (in the case of pulses and grains), as well as being a plentiful supply of fibre. The soya bean is exceptional in being a source of high-quality protein in itself, since it contains good proportions of all eight essential amino acids.

Complementary proteins

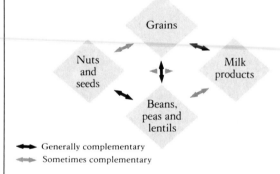

Grains

Nuts and seeds

Milk products

Beans, peas and lentils

⬌ Generally complementary
⬌ Sometimes complementary

·FIBRE·

Dietary fibre is the term used to describe a group of substances which are not broken down by the digestive enzymes. There are five kinds of fibre: cellulose, hemicellulose, gum, pectin and lignin. Each plays a different role in improving health and preventing disease.

Cellulose

This comes from the tough outer walls of plant cells. In the gut it takes up water and increases the bulk of partly-digested foods. Bulkier food moves more quickly through the body, and takes with it toxins that may have accumulated in the lower intestine.

Hemicelluloses

These come from the cell walls of plants. These too help bulk out food, making it pass more quickly through the body.

Gums

These are sticky substances exuded by plants. Like pectin, gum reduces cholesterol uptake. Gums also line the stomach and slow down the absorption of sugar, which is especially useful for diabetics.

Pectins

These are found in the soft tissues of fruits. In the gut they bind some of the bile salts produced by the gall bladder. This may reduce the digestion and absorption of fats and cholesterol, which may thus help to prevent heart disease.

Lignin

This is a woody substance, found mainly in root vegetables. Like cellulose it adds bulk to stools, making them easier to pass, and may help to prevent haemorrhoids, varicose veins and possibly cancer of the rectum.

All fibres make food chewy, so that you eat less, and more slowly. This is good exercise for the jaws and stimulates saliva production, which helps neutralize acid formed on the teeth, reducing dental decay. Fibre also swells up in your stomach, making you feel more satisfied after eating.

For a range of fibre intake you should eat beans, whole grains, and fresh fruit and vegetables. Meat and dairy products contain no fibre. Merely sprinkling bran on top of other food is not the best way to increase fibre intake. An acid in bran called phytate combines with minerals, reducing their absorption. It is best to eat fibre as part of a complete food, such as wholewheat bread, as this contains a greater quantity of these minerals than is found in refined grains.

◆ VITAMINS ◆

Vitamins are chemicals required by the body in very small quantities. Since the body cannot produce them, they must be supplied by food.

Vitamins fall into two distinct groups: water-soluble (the vitamin B group, vitamin C and folic acid), and fat-soluble (vitamins A, D, E, K). Water-soluble vitamins dissolve in the blood and tissue fluids; they cannot be stored in the body for long. Any excess is excreted in the urine. In contrast, fat-soluble vitamins can be stored by the body in the liver and fatty tissues.

The amount of any vitamin required each day varies according to age, sex and occupation. Growing children, pregnant and lactating mothers all need more vitamins, as do the elderly and those recovering from illness. Other factors, such as diet or lifestyle, also influence vitamin requirements.

Chemicals contained in many widely-consumed substances—alcohol, cigarettes, coffee, aspirins, the Pill—use up much of the body's vitamin resources, so people who smoke, drink or take regular medication need to be sure their food is rich in vitamins.

Vitamins can be destroyed during processing, storing or cooking. Refined foods such as white flour have relatively few vitamins. Water-soluble vitamins are vulnerable to heat; a large amount can be destroyed during cooking, especially in water, since the vitamins escape into the cooking liquid. Fat-soluble vitamins are generally more stable but can be sensitive to light and air. Freezing does little damage to most vitamins.

The prime functions of each vitamin are as follows:

Vitamin A

This keeps skin and mucous membranes (linings of the stomach, intestines, bladder, nose, throat and respiratory passageways) healthy. It is essential for vision in dim light.

The B-group vitamins

These are important in the metabolism of carbohydrates, fats and proteins in the body. They keep the hair, skin, eyes, mouth and liver healthy. They are needed for proper functioning of the brain, nervous and circulatory systems, and for red blood cell formation.

Vitamin C

This is necessary for healthy connective tissues such as bone cartilage and collagen. It promotes the healing of wounds, helps fight against infection, and increases the absorption of iron.

Vitamin D

This is essential for maintaining normal levels of calcium and phosphorus in the blood, and enhances the absorption of calcium, ensuring sound formation of bones and teeth; thus, vitamin D is especially important for pregnant women and young children.

Vitamin E

This is a component of all cell membranes. It acts in a similar way to antioxidants (used to prevent food going rancid), and so prevents damage to the components of the cell membranes. It protects unsaturated fats in the body from damage and protects vitamin A from destruction.

Vitamin K

This is needed to prevent haemorrhaging.

Folic acid

This, along with vitamin B_{12} is needed for the successful formation of genetic material in DNA (which is why it's important in early pregnancy). It also helps in the formation of proteins.

◆ MINERALS ◆

Four per cent of our body is made up of one hundred or so different minerals, of which about 20 are known or suspected to be essential. Six are present in the body in large quantities: sodium, potassium, chlorine, calcium, phosphorus and magnesium. The body usually obtains a sufficient supply of sodium and phosphorus from most foods. The other fourteen are called trace elements, making up less than 1/10,000th part of our body. As yet the function of some trace elements, such as tin, vanadium and nickel, is not well understood.

Plants are the main source of minerals, as they absorb them from the soil. Minerals are part of the structural framework of the body, being present in bones and teeth, as well as in muscle fibres and nerve cells. They enable muscles to contract and relax, and impulses to be transmitted through the nerves. As soluble salts, they contribute to the composition and balance of body fluids. Minerals are constituents of enzymes, vitamins and hormones and they enable many chemical reactions to take place which break down and utilize food.

Apart from their individual functions, minerals also work in groups. A balanced relationship is important between, for example, sodium and potassium, or calcium, phosphorus and magnesium. Taking supplements of only one mineral may cause a deficiency of another.

Balance is the key word, and the relationship between minerals can be easily upset.

Modern agricultural and food processing techniques can distort the mineral balance. For example, phosphates are used extensively by farmers as fertilizers. A high intake of phosphorus increases the body's need for calcium. Another example is salt. Our intake of sodium is some eight to ten times our requirement due to the salt contained in processed foods and added in cooking; this may upset the sodium/potassium balance.

Pollution from car exhausts, cigarette smoke and drugs such as antibiotics, the Pill, alcohol and caffeine all affect our mineral needs.

A varied diet of wholefoods, fresh fruit and vegetables and nuts should provide an ample supply of all the essential elements, particularly if the food is grown on healthy, composted soil.

The functions of individual minerals are as follows:

Sodium, Potassium and Chlorine

These are responsible in different ways for the mechanisms that ensure a constant volume of body fluids. Chlorine (in the form of chloride) is necessary for making hydrochloric acid in the gastric juices of the stomach. This is required for the digestion of proteins. Potassium is required for muscle cells and blood corpuscles. Sodium is essential for balancing the quantities of fluids inside and outside each cell.

Calcium, Phosphorus and Magnesium

Calcium is a major component of the bones and teeth and is necessary for their maintenance. It is also needed for blood clotting, maintenance of cell membranes and for proper functioning of the nervous system. Phosphorus teams up with calcium to maintain healthy bones and is also important for energy release. Magnesium is necessary for the utilization of calcium and potassium and for nerve functioning.

Iron, Zinc and Copper

Iron is necessary for the formation of haemoglobin, which carries oxygen in the blood. Vitamin C enhances iron absorption, and a trace of copper is needed for the correct functioning of iron in the body. Zinc is essential for growth and for the synthesis of proteins. It is necessary for wound healing, sexual maturation, and the maintenance of skin, hair, nails and mucous membranes.

An adequate supply of iron, zinc and copper is particularly important for those who eat little or no meat, since a supply of these minerals is usually obtained from liver and meat.

Iodine
Very small quantities of iodine are required for the normal functioning of the thyroid gland which regulates the rate of metabolism in the body.

◆ FATS ◆

There are three main types of fat: saturated, monounsaturated and polyunsaturated. The type depends on the number of free "links" in the chemical structure. Saturated fats have hydrogen atoms attached to all of their links; monounsaturated fats have a few links free, and polyunsaturated fats have many free links.

Saturated fats are generally of animal origin, with the exceptions of coconut and palm oil, and hydrogenated (artificially hardened) vegetable fats. The more saturated a fat, the more solid it is. Polyunsaturated fats tend to be liquid at room temperature, and are found mainly in plants and in fish. Monounsaturated fats are found particularly in nuts and fruit.

No single food contains only one sort of fat; what distinguishes foods is the proportions in which different fats are present. Meat, for example, contains ten times as much saturated fat as polyunsaturated fat, whereas wholewheat bread has twice as much polyunsaturated fat as saturated fat.

Apart from being a concentrated source of energy, fat has several other functions. Food containing fat is more palatable, since fats help the flavours to mingle and facilitate swallowing. Fats satisfy the appetite, not only because they are high in calories, but also because they slow down digestion, keeping the stomach full for longer. The fatty tissues store the fat-soluble vitamins A, D, E and K. Fat is stored in layers under the skin to help keep the body warm, and it cushions the vital organs to protect them against impact and hold them in place. Stored fat can be used for fuel if the body is deprived of food.

Polyunsaturated fats provide essential fatty acids (EFA)—linoleic, linolenic and arachidonic. These are vital constituents of the capillaries and membranes, and are used to regulate blood flow. Linoleic acid needs to come from the food we eat; the other EFAs can be synthesized by the body but this process is slow and it is better to obtain them from food.

For more about the different types of fat and their effect on health, see page 172.

◆ CARBOHYDRATES ◆

Carbohydrates are compounds of carbon, hydrogen and oxygen. The two main types of digestible carbohydrates are sugars (simple carbohydrates) and starches (complex carbohydrates); they are our most important source of energy.

The chief sugars are simple sugars or monosaccharides, consisting of glucose, fructose and galactose, and double sugars or disaccharides, comprising sucrose, maltose and lactose. Sucrose is by far the most commonly eaten sugar, and yet, apart from calories, it provides no nutrients at all.

Starches are an example of polysaccharides, or complex carbohydrates. It is recommended that we should eat more starches (contained in potatoes, wholewheat bread and flour products) and fewer simple carbohydrates.

Before being used by the body, carbohydrates must be broken down into simple sugars, which can then be absorbed through the walls of the small intestine into the bloodstream. They are then either broken down to produce energy, or stored in the liver as glycogen. This forms a reserve to help maintain blood sugar levels between meals or during exercise. Excess carbohydrate is stored as fat.

Apart from giving us energy, carbohydrates are needed to metabolize protein so that it can be used to build and repair body tissues. The central nervous system also requires a steady supply of carbohydrates.

To release the energy stored in carbohydrates, the body requires sufficient quantities of vitamins. Especially important in this respect are vitamins in the B complex group, used to regulate the production of energy from glucose.

USING THIS BOOK FOR A HEALTHIER DIET
The following thirteen pages give an easy-to-use photographic guide to some of the best sources of essential nutrients available in some common foods. For each food item illustrated, the weight of the sample is shown and the quantity of protein, vitamin, and so on, stated.

GOOD SOURCES OF
• PROTEIN •

Proteins are made up of amino acids, and it is these that the body needs for
growth and the maintenance of healthy muscles and tissues. Of the 20
different types of amino acid, 8 have to be obtained from protein-containing food.
Some of the best sources are yeast extract, cheese, peanuts and chick peas.
Recommended daily intake: 65-90 g (men), 55-63 g (women)

EXTRACTS AND GRAINS

Yeast extract
Protein per 100 g: 39.7 g
Weight shown: 15 g
Protein content: 6 g

Soya flour
Protein per 100 g: 36.8 g
Weight shown: 7 g
Protein content: 2.6 g

Wheatgerm
Protein per 100 g: 26.5 g
Weight shown: 7 g
Protein content: 1.9 g

Bran
Protein per 100 g: 14.1 g
Weight shown: 2 g
Protein content: 0.3 g

Wholewheat flour
Protein per 100 g: 13.2 g
Weight shown: 5 g
Protein content: 0.7 g

Oatmeal
Protein per 100 g: 12. 4g
Weight shown: 8 g
Protein content: 1 g

Semolina
Protein per 100 g: 10.7 g
Weight shown: 8 g
Protein content: 0.9 g

Wholewheat bread
Protein per 100 g: 8.8 g; Weight
shown: 80g; Protein content: 7 g

Rye flour
Protein per 100 g: 8.2 g
Weight shown: 6 g
Protein content: 0.5 g

DAIRY PRODUCTS AND EGGS

Parmesan
Protein per 100 g: 35.1 g
Weight shown: 200 g
Protein content: 70.2 g

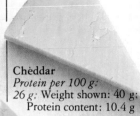

Cheddar
*Protein per 100 g:
26 g:* Weight shown: 40 g;
Protein content: 10.4 g

Double Gloucester
Protein per 100 g: 26 g
Weight shown: 80 g
Protein content: 20.8 g

Brie
Protein per 100 g: 22.8 g
Weight shown: 100 g
Protein content: 22.8 g

Coulommiers
Protein per 100 g: 22.8 g
Weight shown: 60 g
Protein content: 13.7 g

Cottage cheese
Protein per 100 g: 13.6 g
Weight shown: 20 g
Protein content: 2.7 g

Eggs
Protein per 100 g: 12.3 g
Weight shown: 100 g
Protein content: 12.3 g

Yogurt
Protein per 100 g: 5 g
Weight shown: 20 g
Protein content: 1 g

Soya milk
Protein per 100 g: 3.6 g
Weight shown: 20 g
Protein content: 0.7 g

Skimmed milk
Protein per 100 g: 3.4 g
Weight shown: 20 g
Protein content: 0.7 g

Whole cow's milk
Protein per 100 g: 3.3 g
Weight shown: 20 g
Protein content: 0.7 g

Whole goat's milk
Protein per 100 g: 3.3 g
Weight shown: 20 g
Protein content: 0.7 g

NUTS

Peanuts
Protein per 100 g: 24.3 g
Weight shown: 12 g
Protein content: 2.9 g

Pistachios
Protein per 100 g: 19.3 g
Weight shown: 12 g
Protein content: 2.3 g

Almonds
Protein per 100 g: 16.9 g
Weight shown: 15 g
Protein content: 2.5 g

Walnuts
Protein per 100 g: 20.5 g
Weight shown: 30 g
Protein content: 6.2 g

Brazils
Protein per 100 g: 12 g
Weight shown: 20 g
Protein content: 2.4 g

PULSES

Chick peas
Protein per 100 g: 8 g
Weight shown: 15 g
Protein content: 1.2 g

Lentils
Protein per 100 g: 7.6 g
Weight shown: 10 g
Protein content: 0.8 g

Tofu
Protein per 100 g: 7.4 g
Weight shown: 14 g
Protein content: 1 g

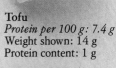

Split peas
Protein per 100 g: 7.1 g
Weight shown: 20 g
Protein content: 1.4 g

Haricot beans
Protein per 100 g: 6.6 g
Weight shown: 12 g
Protein content: 0.8 g

GOOD SOURCES OF
· FIBRE ·

Fibre, which makes up the cell walls of the plants which we eat, is a form of carbohydrate. It is essential for the efficient working of the digestive system, although it is not actually digested by the body. Among the best sources of fibre are bran, apricots, prunes and wholewheat bread.
Recommended daily intake: 25-30 g

GRAINS AND PULSES

Bran
Fibre per 100 g: 44 g
Weight shown: 4 g
Fibre content: 1.8 g

Soya flour
Fibre per 100 g: 11.9 g
Weight shown: 6 g
Fibre content: 0.7 g

Wholewheat flour
Fibre per 100 g: 9.6 g
Weight shown: 20 g
Fibre content: 1.9 g

Wholewheat bread
Fibre per 100 g: 8.5 g
Weight shown: 60 g
Fibre content: 5.1 g

Haricot beans
Fibre per 100 g: 7.4 g
Weight shown: 20 g
Fibre content: 1.5 g

Oatmeal
Fibre per 100 g: 7 g
Weight shown: 20 g
Fibre content: 1.4 g

Pot barley
Fibre per 100 g: 6.5 g
Weight shown: 20 g
Fibre content: 1.3 g

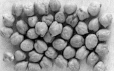

Chick peas
Fibre per 100 g: 6 g; Weight shown: 20 g Fibre content: 1.2 g

FRUIT

Dried apricots
Fibre per 100 g: 24 g
Weight shown: 25 g
Fibre content: 6.0 g

Dried figs
Fibre per 100 g: 18.5 g
Weight shown: 25 g
Fibre content: 4.6 g

Prunes
Fibre per 100 g: 16.1 g
Weight shown: 40 g
Fibre content: 6.4 g

Dried peaches
Fibre per 100 g: 14.3 g; Weight shown: 25 g Fibre content: 3.6 g

Blackcurrants
Fibre per 100 g: 8.7 g
Weight shown: 20 g
Fibre content: 1.7 g

Dates
Fibre per 100 g: 8.7 g
Weight shown: 40 g
Fibre content: 3.5 g

Raspberries
Fibre per 100 g: 7.4 g
Weight shown: 20 g
Fibre content: 1.5 g

Blackberries
Fibre per 100 g: 7.3 g
Weight shown: 20 g
Fibre content: 1.5 g

Sultanas
Fibre per 100 g: 7 g; Weight shown: 20 g Fibre content: 1.4 g

NUTS VEGETABLES

Passion fruit
Fibre per 100 g: 6.7 g
Weight shown: 80 g
Fibre content 5.4 g

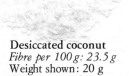

Desiccated coconut
Fibre per 100 g: 23.5 g
Weight shown: 20 g
Fibre content: 4.7 g

Peas
Fibre per 100 g: 12 g
Weight shown: 20 g
Fibre content: 2.4 g

Sweetcorn
Fibre per 100 g: 5.7 g
Weight shown: 20 g
Fibre content: 1.1 g

Currants
Fibre per 100 g: 6.5 g
Weight shown: 20 g
Fibre content: 1.3 g

Almonds
Fibre per 100 g: 14.3 g
Weight shown: 20 g
Fibre content: 2.9 g

Parsley
Fibre per 100 g: 9.1 g
Weight shown: 1 g
Fibre content: 0.1 g

Raisins
Fibre per 100 g: 6.4 g
Weight shown: 20 g
Fibre content: 1.3 g

Fresh coconut
Fibre per 100 g: 13.6 g
Weight shown: 80 g
Fibre content: 10.9 g

Brazil nuts
Fibre per 100 g: 9 g
Weight shown: 25 g
Fibre content: 2.3 g

Plantain
Fibre per 100 g: 6.4 g
Weight shown: 300 g
Fibre content: 19.2 g

Peanuts
Fibre per 100 g: 8.1 g
Weight shown: 20 g
Fibre content: 1.6 g

Spinach
Fibre per 100 g: 6.3 g
Weight shown: 14 g
Fibre content: 0.9 g

Celery
Fibre per 100 g: 4.9 g
Weight shown: 40 g
Fibre content: 2.0 g

GOOD SOURCES OF
• B VITAMINS •

Vitamins are used in minute quantities by the body but they are essential
for its proper functioning. The best sources include yeast extract, nuts,
bran and egg yolk.

Recommended daily intake:
B_1: 0.9-1.4 mg B_2: 1.3-1.7 mg B_3: 15-18 mg B_6: 2 mg B_{12}: 1-2 µg

VITAMIN B_1

Yeast extract
Vitamin per 100 g: 3.10 mg
Weight shown: 12 g
Vitamin content: 0.37 mg

Bran
Vitamin per 100 g: 0.89 mg
Weight shown: 4 g
Vitamin content: 0.04 mg

Almonds
Vitamin per 100 g: 0.92 mg
Weight shown: 15 g
Vitamin content: 0.14 mg

Parmesan
Vitamin per 100 g: 0.50 mg
Weight shown: 80 g
Vitamin content: 0.40 mg

Wheatgerm
Vitamin per 100 g: 1.45 mg
Weight shown: 5 g
Vitamin content: 0.07 mg

Soya flour
Vitamin per 100 g: 0.75 mg
Weight shown: 5 g
Vitamin content: 0.04 mg

Wheatgerm
Vitamin per 100 g: 0.61 mg
Weight shown: 3 g
Vitamin content: 0.02 mg

Egg yolk

Vitamin per 100 g: 0.47 mg
Weight shown: 20 g
Vitamin content: 0.09 mg

VITAMIN B_3

Brazil nuts
Vitamin per 100 g: 1 mg
Weight shown: 20 g
Vitamin content: 0.20 mg

Millet
Vitamin per 100 g: 0.73 mg
Weight shown: 8 g
Vitamin content: 0.06 mg

VITAMIN B_2

Brie
Vitamin per 100 g: 0.60 mg
Weight shown: 80 g
Vitamin content: 0.48 mg

Yeast extract
Vitamin per 100 g: 58 mg
Weight shown: 7 g
Vitamin content: 12 mg

Cheddar

Peanuts
Vitamin per 100 g: 0.90 mg
Weight shown: 8 g
Vitamin content: 0.07 mg

Yeast extract
Vitamin per 100 g: 11 mg
Weight shown: 12 g
Vitamin content: 1.3 mg

Vitamin per 100 g: 0.50 mg
Weight shown: 40 g
Vitamin content: 0.20 mg

Bran
Vitamin per 100 g: 29.6 mg
Weight shown: 2 g
Vitamin content: 0.59 mg

Peanuts
Vitamin per 100 g: 16 mg
Weight shown: 8 g
Vitamin content: 1.28 mg

VITAMIN B₆

Bran
Vitamin per 100 g: 1.38 mg
Weight shown: 5 g
Vitamin content: 0.07 mg

Hazelnuts
Vitamin per 100 g: 0.55 mg
Weight shown: 18 g
Vitamin content: 0.10 mg

Parmesan
Vitamin per 100 g: 1.5 µg
Weight shown: 20 g
Vitamin content: 0.30 µg

Wheatgerm
Vitamin per 100 g: 5.8 mg
Weight shown: 5 g
Vitamin content: 0.29 mg

Yeast extract
Vitamin per 100 g: 1.30 mg
Weight shown: 10 g
Vitamin content: 0.13 mg

Wholewheat flour
Vitamin per 100 g: 5.6 mg
Weight shown: 10 g
Vitamin content: 0.56 mg

Wheatgerm
Vitamin per 100 g: 0.93 mg
Weight shown: 5 g
Vitamin content: 0.05 mg

Banana
*Vitamin per
100 g: 0.51 mg*
Weight shown: 100 g
Vitamin content: 0.51 mg

Brie
Vitamin per 100 g: 1.2 µg
Weight shown: 140 g
Vitamin content: 1.68 µg

VITAMIN B₁₂

Dried peaches
Vitamin per 100 g: 5.3 mg
Weight shown: 20 g
Vitamin content: 1.06 mg

Walnuts
Vitamin per 100 g: 0.73 mg
Weight shown: 20 g
Vitamin content: 0.15 mg

Egg yolk
Vitamin per 100 g: 4.9 µg
Weight shown: 20 g
Vitamin content: 0.98 µg

Yeast extract
Vitamin per 100 g: 0.5 µg
Weight shown: 20 g
Vitamin content: 0.10 µg

Button mushrooms
Vitamin per 100 g: 4 mg
Weight shown: 20 g
Vitamin content: 0.80 mg

Soya flour
Vitamin per 100g: 0.57 mg
Weight shown: 5 g
Vitamin content: 0.03 mg

Cheddar
Vitamin per 100 g: 1.7 µg
Weight shown: 40 g
Vitamin content: 0.68 µg

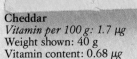

Cottage cheese
Vitamin per 100 g: 0.5 µg
Weight shown: 20 g
Vitamin content: 0.10 µg

GOOD SOURCES OF
• OTHER VITAMINS •

A daily supply of vitamins is necessary for the proper functioning of the
body. Among the best source of vitamins shown here are egg yolk,
hazelnuts and cabbage.

Recommended daily intake: Vitamin A: 750 μg   Vitamin C: 30 mg   Vitamin D: 2.5 μg
Vitamin E: 11 mg   Vitamin K: 70-104 μg   Folic Acid: 200 μg

VITAMIN A

Sorrel

*Vitamin per
100 g: 2,150 μg*
Weight shown: 1 g
Vitamin content: 21.5 μg

Carrots
Vitamin per 100 g: 2,000 μg
Weight shown: 50 g
Vitamin content: 1000 μg

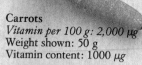

Parsley
*Vitamin per
100 g: 1,166 μg*
Weight shown: 2 g
Vitamin content: 23.32 μg

Margarine
Vitamin per 100 g: 200 μg
Weight shown: 20 g
Vitamin content: 40 μg

Spring cabbage
Vitamin per 100 g: 83 μg
Weight shown: 20 g
Vitamin content: 16.7 μg

VITAMIN C

Red pepper

*Vitamin
per 100 g:
204 mg;* Weight shown: 120 g
Vitamin content: 244.8 mg

Blackcurrants
Vitamin per 100 g: 200 mg
Weight shown: 10 g
Vitamin content: 20 mg

Parsley
*Vitamin per
100 g: 150 mg*
Weight shown: 2 g
Vitamin content: 3 mg

Sorrel

Vitamin per 100 g: 119 mg
Weight shown: 1 g
Vitamin content: 1.19 mg

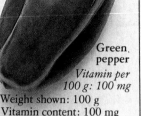

**Green
pepper**
*Vitamin per
100 g: 100 mg*
Weight shown: 100 g
Vitamin content: 100 mg

Lemon
Vitamin per 100 g: 80 mg
Weight shown: 100 g
Vitamin content: 80 mg

VITAMIN D

Margarine
Vitamin per 100 g: 7.94 μg
Weight shown: 20 g
Vitamin content: 1.60 μg

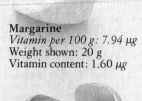

Egg yolk
Vitamin per 100 g: 5.00 μg
Weight shown: 1.75 g
Vitamin content: 0.09 μg

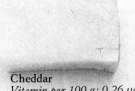

Cheddar
Vitamin per 100 g: 0.26 µg
Weight shown: 100 g
Vitamin content: 0.26 µg

Peanuts
*Vitamins per
100 g: 8.1 mg*
Weight shown: 20 g
Vitamin content: 1.6 mg

Cabbage
Vitamin per 100 g: 100 µg
Weight shown: 20 g
Vitamin content: .03 µg

Watercress
Folic acid per 100 g: 200 µg
Weight shown: 3 g
Vitamin content: 6 µg

Margarine
Vitamin per 100 g: 8 mg
Weight shown: 40 g
Vitamin content: 3.2 mg

Brie
Vitamin per 100 g: 0.18 µg
Weight shown: 120 g
Vitamin content: 0.22 µg

Bran
Folic acid per 100 g: 130 µg
Weight shown: 2 g
Vitamin content: 2.6 µg

VITAMIN E

Lettuce
Vitamin per 100 g: 200 µg
Weight shown: 10 g
Vitamin content: .02 µg

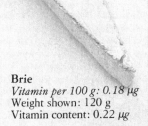

Hazelnuts
Vitamin per 100 g: 21 mg
Weight shown: 20 g
Vitamin content: 4.2 mg

Brazil nuts
Vitamin per 100 g: 6.5 mg
Weight shown: 20 g
Vitamin content: 1.3 mg

Soya beans
Vitamin per 100 g: 190 µg
Weight shown: 4 g
Vitamin content: 7.6 µg

Yeast extract
Folic acid per 100 g: 83 µg
Weight shown: 20 g
Vitamin content: 16.6 µg

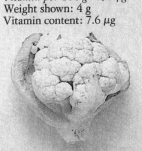

Almonds
Vitamin per 100 g: 20 mg
Weight shown: 20 g
Vitamin content: 4 mg

Egg yolk
Vitamin per 100 g: 4.6 mg
Weight shown: 1.75 g
Vitamin content: 0.08 mg

Cauliflower
Vitamin per 100 g: 150 µg
Weight shown: 60 g
Vitamin content: .18 mg

Wheatgerm
Folic acid per 100 g: 62 µg
Weight shown: 10 g
Vitamin content: 16.6 µg

GOOD SOURCES OF
· MINERALS ·

Like vitamins, minerals are required by the body in small or trace quantities.
Since the body cannot manufacture them, a daily supply has to be obtained
from food. Among the best sources are bran, cheese and nuts.

Recommended daily intake: Magnesium: 250 mg   Calcium: 500 mg   Potassium: 3 g

MAGNESIUM

Bran
Mineral per 100 g: 520 mg
Weight shown: 4 g
Mineral content: 21 mg

Soya flour
Mineral per 100 g: 240 mg
Weight shown: 6g
Mineral content: 14 mg

Peanuts
Mineral per 100 g: 180 mg
Weight shown: 10 g
Mineral content: 18 mg

Brazil nuts
Mineral per 100 g: 410 mg
Weight shown: 20 g
Mineral content: 82 mg

Millet
Mineral per 100 g: 162 mg
Weight shown: 17 g
Mineral content: 28 mg

Wheatgerm
Mineral per 100 g: 300 mg
Weight shown: 7 g
Mineral content: 21 mg

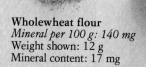

Almonds
Mineral per 100 g: 260 mg
Weight shown: 10 g
Mineral content: 26 mg

Wholewheat flour
Mineral per 100 g: 140 mg
Weight shown: 12 g
Mineral content: 17 mg

Walnuts
Mineral per 100 g: 130 mg
Weight shown: 38 g
Mineral content: 49 mg

Oatmeal
Mineral per 100 g: 110 mg
Weight shown: 10 g
Mineral·content: 11 mg

CALCIUM

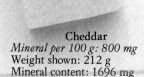

Cheddar
Mineral per 100 g: 800 mg
Weight shown: 212 g
Mineral content: 1696 mg

Spinach
*Mineral per 100 g:
600 mg*
Weight shown: 4 g
Mineral content: 24 mg

Parmesan
Mineral per 100 g: 1,200 mg
Weight shown: 210 g
Mineral content: 2562 mg

Brie
Mineral per 100 g: 380 mg
Weight shown: 190 g
Mineral content: 722 mg

Watercress
Mineral per 100 g: 220 mg
Weight shown: 3 g
Mineral content: 7 mg

Soya flour
Mineral per 100 g: 210 mg
Weight shown: 7 g
Mineral content: 15 g

Brazil nuts
Mineral per 100 g: 180 mg
Weight shown: 28 g
Mineral content: 50 mg

POTASSIUM

Parsley
Mineral per 100 g: 330 mg
Weight shown: 3 g
Mineral content: 10 mg

Dried figs
Mineral per 100 g: 280 mg
Weight shown: 42 g
Mineral content: 118 mg

Dried apricots
Mineral per 100 g: 1,880 mg
Weight shown: 26 g
Mineral content: 489 mg

Soya flour
Mineral per 100 g: 1,660 mg
Weight shown: 12 g
Mineral content: 200 mg

Blackstrap molasses
Mineral per 100 g: 2,927 mg
Weight shown: 20 g
Mineral content: 585 mg

Yeast extract
Mineral per 100 g: 2,600 mg
Weight shown: 10 g
Mineral content: 260 mg

Bran
Mineral per 100 g: 1,160 mg
Weight shown: 5 g
Mineral content: 58 mg

Dried peaches
Mineral per 100 g: 1,100 mg
Weight shown: 38 g
Mineral content: 418 mg

Parsley
Mineral per 100 g: 1,080 mg
Weight shown: 2 g
Mineral content: 22 mg

Dried figs
Mineral per 100 g: 1,010 mg
Weight shown: 46 g
Mineral content: 465 mg

Wheatgerm
Mineral per 100 g: 1,000 mg
Weight shown: 8 g
Mineral content: 80 mg

Sultanas
Minerals per 100 g: 860 mg
Weight shown: 10 g
Mineral content: 86 mg

Almonds
Mineral per 100 g: 250 mg
Weight shown: 10 g
Mineral content: 25 mg

GOOD SOURCES OF
•MINERALS•

A balanced intake of minerals is required and of the mineral-containing foods shown here the best sources are molasses, bran and fresh yeast.

Recommended daily intake: Iron: 10-12 mg   Zinc: 12 mg   Copper: 2-3 mg

IRON

Blackstrap molasses
Mineral per 100 g: 16.1 mg
Weight shown: 15 g
Mineral content: 2.4 mg

Parsley
Mineral per 100 g: 8 mg
Weight shown: 2 g
Mineral content: 0.16 mg

Millet
Mineral per 100 g: 6.8 mg
Weight shown: 14 g
Mineral content: 0.9 mg

ZINC

Bran
Mineral per 100 g: 16.2 mg
Weight shown: 6 g
Mineral content: 0.9 mg

Egg yolk
Mineral per 100 g: 6.1 mg
Weight shown: 20 g
Mineral content: 1.2 mg

Bran
Mineral per 100 g: 12.9 mg
Weight shown: 6 g
Mineral content: 0.8 mg

Soya flour
Mineral per 100 g: 6.9 mg
Weight shown: 11 g
Mineral content: 0.8 mg

Fresh yeast
Mineral per 100 g: 5 mg
Weight shown: 12 g
Mineral content: 0.6 mg

Brazil nuts
Mineral per 100 g: 4.2 mg
Weight shown: 44 g
Mineral content: 1.8 mg

Wheatgerm
Mineral per 100 g: 10 mg
Weight shown: 10 g
Mineral content: 1 mg

Dried peaches
Mineral per 100 g: 6.8 mg
Weight shown: 40 g
Mineral content: 2.7 mg

Dried figs
Mineral per 100 g: 4.2 mg
Weight shown: 56 g
Mineral content: 2.4 mg

Parmesan
Mineral per 100 g: 4 mg
Weight shown: 110 g
Mineral content: 4.4 mg

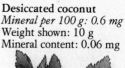

Wholewheat flour
Mineral per 100 g: 3 mg
Weight shown: 15 g
Mineral content: 0.45 mg

Bran
Mineral per 100 g: 1.3 mg
Weight shown: 4 g
Mineral content: 0.05 mg

Desiccated coconut
Mineral per 100 g: 0.6 mg
Weight shown: 10 g
Mineral content: 0.06 mg

Parsley
Mineral per 100 g: 0.5 mg
Weight shown: 2 g
Mineral content: 0.01 mg

Cheddar
Mineral per 100 g: 4 mg
Weight shown: 260 g
Mineral content: 10.4 mg

Oatmeal
Mineral per 100 g: 3 mg
Weight shown: 30 g
Mineral content: 0.9 mg

Brazil nuts
Mineral per 100 g: 1.1 mg
Weight shown: 37 g
Mineral content: 0.41 mg

Almonds
Mineral per 100 g: 3.1 mg
Weight shown: 12 g
Mineral content: 0.4 mg

Currants
Mineral per 100 g: 0.5 mg
Weight shown: 12 g
Mineral content: 0.06 mg

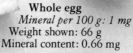

Peanuts
Mineral per 100 g: 3 mg
Weight shown: 10 g
Mineral content: 0.3 mg

Whole egg
Mineral per 100 g: 1 mg
Weight shown: 66 g
Mineral content: 0.66 mg

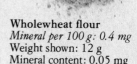

Brie
Mineral per 100 g: 3 mg
Weight shown: 215 g
Mineral content: 6.5 mg

Wholewheat flour
Mineral per 100 g: 0.4 mg
Weight shown: 12 g
Mineral content: 0.05 mg

COPPER

Walnuts
Mineral per 100 g: 3 mg
Weight shown: 50 g
Mineral content: 1.5 mg

Fresh yeast
Mineral per 100 g: 5 mg
Weight shown: 13 g
Mineral content: 0.65 mg

Dried peaches
Mineral per 100 g: 0.6 mg
Weight shown: 42 g
Mineral content: 0.25 mg

Broad beans
Mineral per 100 g: 0.4 mg
Weight shown: 15 g
Mineral content: 0.06 mg

GOOD SOURCES OF
· FATS & CARBOHYDRATES ·

The body needs carbohydrates to supply energy; it also needs fats in
moderation. The best sources of polyunsaturated fats (PUFA) are safflower
oil and soya bean oil; the best sources of carbohydrates are rice and pot barley.
Recommended daily intake: none in UK

POLYUNSATURATED FATS

Safflower seed oil
PUFA per 100 g: 72.11 g
Weight shown: 25 g
PUFA content: 18.03 g

Soya bean oil
PUFA per 100 g: 56.73 g
Weight shown: 25 g
PUFA content: 14.18 g

Sunflower seed oil
PUFA per 100 g: 49.95 g
Weight shown: 25 g
PUFA content: 12.49 g

Walnuts
PUFA per 100 g: 35.15 g
Weight shown: 30 g
PUFA content: 10.55 g

Brazil nuts
PUFA per 100 g: 22.93 g
Weight shown: 20 g
PUFA content: 4.59 g

Peanuts
PUFA per 100 g: 13.95 g
Weight shown: 12 g
PUFA content: 1.67 g

Soya flour
PUFA per 100 g: 13.34 g
Weight shown: 10 g
PUFA content: 1.33 g

CARBOHYDRATES

Rice
Carbohydrate per 100 g: 86.8 g
Weight shown: 10 g
Carbohydrate content: 8.68 g

Pot Barley
Carbohydrate per 100 g: 83.6 g
Weight shown: 15 g
Carbohydrate content: 12.54 g

Rye flour
Carbohydrate per 100 g: 75.9 g
Weight shown: 10 g
Carbohydrate content: 7.59 g

Oatmeal

Carbohydrate per 100 g: 72.8 g
Weight shown: 10 g
Carbohydrate content: 7.28 g

Wholewheat flour
Carbohydrate per 100 g: 63.5 g
Weight shown: 10 g
Carbohydrate content: 6.35 g

Split peas
Carbohydrate per 100 g: 54.7 g
Weight shown: 10 g
Carbohydrate content: 5.47 g

Lentils
Carbohydrate per 100 g: 50.8 g
Weight shown: 14 g
Carbohydrate content: 7.11 g

Butter beans

Carbohydrate per 100 g: 46.2 g
Weight shown: 17 g
Carbohydrate content: 7.85 g

·TECHNIQUES·

MAKING
• BREAD •

It is worth making your own bread, as many of the so-called wholesome and healthy brown loaves available in the shops are neither. Often the flour used is wheatmeal, which contains only 85 per cent of the whole grain, so many of the nutrients and much of the fibre are lost. Even the distinctive brown colouring may come from caramel. Such loaves often have as many additives as white bread, and are manufactured in much the same way, having no real fermentation time to enhance the flavour.

When making your own bread, choose a strong, stoneground 100 per cent wholewheat or wholemeal flour. Strong or hard flours, usually made from American or Canadian wheat, have a high gluten content, thus ensuring a strong, elastic dough which is needed for good results. I add a soft, low-gluten flour like soya for extra flavour and protein which the dough might otherwise lack. You can also add a little oil as this will improve the texture.

Once you've got used to making the basic loaf, try a variety of flours, also adding nuts, seeds or wheatgerm, cooked grains or even beansprouts for different flavours and textures. Richer bread doughs can be made using milk, yogurt or eggs as part of the mixing liquid. For naturally sweet loaves, use honey, molasses or dried fruits. If you are on a strictly salt-free diet, you can leave out the salt but the taste and texture of the loaf will be quite different.

·WHOLEWHEAT· BREAD

Along with grains and pulses, wholewheat bread is one of the staples of a vegetarian diet—it is high in protein, fibre, vitamins and minerals. It is also very easy to make at home. Bake in a preheated oven gas mark 7, 220° C (425° F) for 35-40 minutes. Once cooked, the bread should sound hollow when tapped on its base.

INGREDIENTS
700 g (1½lb) wholewheat flour
up to 5 ml (1 tsp) salt
25 g (1 oz) fresh yeast
25 g (1 oz) soya flour
425 ml (¾ pint) warm water
Makes two 450 g (1 lb) loaves

1 Whisk the yeast and soya flour with 150 ml (¼ pint) warm water. Leave in a warm place for 5 minutes or until frothy.

2 Mix flour and salt in a large bowl. Pour in the yeast mixture and add the remaining flour.

3 Mix the liquids in with a wooden spoon, then draw up the flour with your hands to form a dough.

4 Turn on to a floured surface and knead thoroughly until the dough has a smooth, velvety surface.

5 Put into a clean bowl and leave covered in a warm place for one hour to rise. This process is called "proving". It also enhances the flavour of the bread.

6 Turn the dough on to a floured surface, punch your fist into the dough and knead it again.

7 Divide the dough and shape into two loaves. Put into two greased tins and leave to prove for 10 minutes before baking.

• RYE BREAD •

A characteristic of rye bread is its close, moist texture and in this recipe this is achieved by adding buckwheat flour and yogurt to the ingredients. In the batter method of making bread used here, the wholewheat flour is mixed with the yeast first to start the dough rising. The low-gluten rye flour (which doesn't rise as easily) is then beaten into the risen mixture. Bake in a preheated oven gas mark 7, 220° C (425° F) for 35 minutes. The bread is cooked if it sounds hollow when tapped on the base.

INGREDIENTS
25 g (1 oz) fresh yeast
10 ml (2 tsp) molasses
300 ml (½ pint) lukewarm water
450 g (1 lb) wholewheat flour
pinch of salt
175 g (6 oz) rye flour
50 g (2 oz) buckwheat flour
10 ml (2 tsp) anise seeds
up to 150 ml (¼ pint) yogurt or buttermilk
Makes two 575 g (1¼ lb) loaves

1 Mix together the yeast, molasses and water in a large bowl. Leave in a warm place for 10 minutes until frothy.

2 Add half the wholewheat flour and beat in thoroughly. Cover and leave to rise for 45 minutes.

3 Beat in the remaining ingredients, adding enough yogurt or buttermilk to make a soft dough.

4 Turn out on to a floured surface and knead thoroughly until the dough feels smooth, adding more flour or liquid as necessary.

• SOURDOUGH •

This delicious sharp-tasting continental bread tastes better if kept for one day.

INGREDIENTS
For the sourdough starter
100 g (4 oz) rye flour
100 ml (4 fl oz) milk
2.5 ml (½ tsp) salt
For the dough
50 g (2 oz) yeast
500 ml (17 fl oz) warm water
450 g (1 lb) rye flour
10-15 ml (2-3 tsp) salt
225-300 g (8-10 oz) wholewheat flour
Makes one 1 kg (2.2 lb) loaf

Mix together the rye flour, milk and salt. Leave at room temperature for 48 hours. Blend the yeast with half the water and the sourdough starter. Mix in half the rye flour and leave overnight at room temperature. Mix the remaining rye flour with the salt. Add to the dough with the remaining water, then add the wholewheat flour and knead well. The dough should be moist but not sticky. Add more flour if necessary. Form into a loaf and prick all over. Place on a floured baking sheet. Leave to rise for 45 minutes. Bake at gas 6 400°F (200°C) for 1¼-1½ hours.

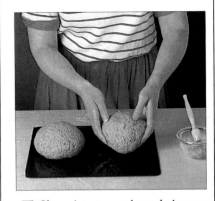

5 Shape into two cobs and place on lightly oiled baking sheets or in 450 g (1 lb) tins. Leave to prove for 30 minutes before putting in the oven.

MAKING ·YOGURT·

Yogurt can be made from any milk—cow, goat, sheep or soya, skimmed or whole, long-life or fresh—in either a wide-necked thermos flask or a special yogurt maker.

I prefer yogurt made from skimmed, long-life (UHT) milk. It has a thicker consistency than yogurt made from whole milk, and because it has already been heat-treated there's no need to scald it before adding the culture. Yogurt can be made even thicker by adding 15 ml (1 tbsp) of skimmed milk powder to the milk (basically, the more powder you add, the thicker the yogurt).

To start your first batch of home-made yogurt you will have to use either a commercially made natural yogurt, or a culture powder (the latter is advisable for anyone with an allergy to milk). For successive batches you can just keep back 30 ml (2 tbsp) of the yogurt each time.

INGREDIENTS
600 ml (1 pint) long-life skimmed milk,
or fresh skimmed milk
30 ml (2 tbsp) natural yogurt
15-30 ml (1-2 tbsp) skimmed milk powder
(optional)
Makes 600 ml (1 pint) yogurt

USING A THERMOS FLASK

1 Bring the long-life milk to a temperature of 43-44°C (110°-115°F), or scald the skimmed milk and cool to this temperature.

2 Stir in the yogurt starter and add the required amount of skimmed milk powder if using.

3 Pour into a clean, warmed thermos flask, preferably one with a wide neck or you may find it difficult to get the finished yogurt out. Leave overnight, or until set.

4 Transfer to a clean container and refrigerate. The mixture will thicken slightly as it cools.

USING A YOGURT MAKER

1 Bring long-life milk to a temperature of 43-44°C (110-115°F), or scald the skimmed milk and cool to this temperature.

2 Pour into clean yogurt pots, screw on the lids and switch on the machine. Leave to set according to the manufacturer's instructions.

MAKING HUNG · YOGURT ·

By hanging fresh yogurt in muslin it is possible to drain off excess whey, leaving a thick, creamy-textured yogurt similar to curd cheese. 600 ml (1 pint) fresh yogurt will make about 175 g (6 oz) hung yogurt.

1 Suspend a muslin cloth or jelly bag over a clean bowl. Pour the fresh yogurt into it.

2 Leave for at least 4 hours. The longer the yogurt is left, the thicker it will be. Turn it out into a clean container and keep in the refrigerator.

MAKING ·SMETANA·

Smetana is a low-fat soured cream made from skimmed milk and cream. Two types are available commerically—smetana and creamed smetana—and these can be bought from larger supermarkets and delicatessens. When making smetana yourself you'll need to use a commercial brand as a starter for your first batch, using half single cream and half long-life skimmed milk. Make sure that you bring the milk to the correct temperature and incubate it for slightly longer than you would for yogurt.

INGREDIENTS
300 ml (½ pint) long-life skimmed milk
300 ml (½ pint) single cream
30-45 ml (2-3 tbsp) smetana
Makes 600 ml (1 pint)

1 Put the milk into a saucepan and stir in the single cream. Heat gently to 43-44°C (110-115°F).

2 Add the smetana, and mix in thoroughly.

3 Transfer to a clean, warm, wide-necked thermos flask and leave for 12 hours or until set.

4 Transfer to a clean container and keep refrigerated for up to a week.

MAKING CURD
• CHEESE •

Like yogurt, curd cheese is a versatile ingredient in healthy eating—it can be used as a thickener, a garnish or a main ingredient. One of the best things about this low-fat, soft cheese is its freshness and creaminess—it makes commercially produced soft cheese seem cloying in comparison. Although the taste is mild, it gives plenty of scope for flavouring: add chopped chives, sage, paprika, coriander or garlic for a savoury cheese, and dried or fresh fruit for a sweet one. Once made, keep refrigerated in a sealed container for up to a week. This cheese also freezes successfully, but once it is thawed you should beat it well in a liquidizer or blender to ensure a smooth texture.

INGREDIENTS
600 ml (1 pint) whole milk
150 ml (¼ pint) cultured buttermilk
15 ml (1 tbsp) lemon juice
Makes 150 g (5 oz) curd cheese

1 Put the milk into a saucepan and then scald it.

2 Place a thermometer in the pan, and allow the mixture to cool to 21°C (70°F).

3 Mix in the buttermilk and gently heat the mixture to a temperature of not more than 77°C (170°F).

4 Stir the mixture every 5 minutes, being careful not to break up the curds. These may form at a temperature of 49-60°C (120-140°F). Keep mixture at separating temperature until curds have clearly separated from whey. Add juice if curds don't separate with heat alone.

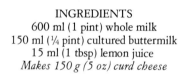

5 Put a colander inside a large bowl and line it with two or three thicknesses of muslin. Use a slotted spoon to scoop the curds into the muslin.

6 When most have been removed, gently pour the remaining curds and whey down the side of the muslin so as not to break up the curds.

7 Allow the curds to drain for 2 hours or until quite firm. Turn out into a clean bowl and keep refrigerated.

MAKING
• TOFU •

Also known as bean curd, tofu is made from a ground soya bean and water mixture which is then strained and pressed to form firm, off-white cakes. It is richer in protein than any other food of equivalent weight and is therefore a useful addition to a vegetarian diet. It is, however, more notable for its texture than its taste, which is rather bland, so dishes using it should always be well flavoured. Tofu can be bought from most Chinese supermarkets, and will keep for up to three days in the refrigerator.

INGREDIENTS
200 g (7 oz) soya beans
juice of 2 lemons
*Makes 275 g (10 oz) okara,
275 g (10 oz) tofu*

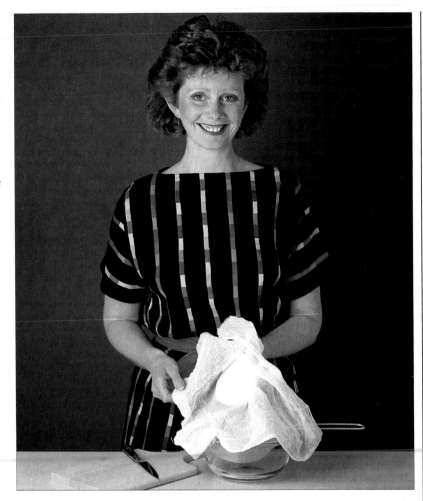

1 Put the beans in a bowl, cover with water and leave overnight in a cool place. Don't leave anywhere warm or the beans may start to ferment.

2 Drain and rinse thoroughly. Liquidize the beans to a creamy consistency, using one cup of water for each cup of beans. This mixture is called Go.

3 Bring 6 cups of water to the boil in a large saucepan or preserving pan. When boiling, add the liquidized soya beans.

4 Bring back to the boil. When the mixture boils up to the top of the pan sprinkle cold water over it. This will stop the boiling and the liquid will sink back.

5 Repeat this 3 times, stirring occasionally. This stage is very important as it destroys any toxins in the bean skin.

6 Line a colander with muslin and place over a clean bowl. Strain the mixture into it.

7 The crumbly residue in the muslin is called okara or soya bran. The liquid is soya milk.

8 Return the soya milk to a clean pan and bring to the boil. Pour into a clean bowl.

9 Add the juice of 2 lemons. Stir very gently then leave the mixture to curdle. If it doesn't, bring the liquid back to the boil and add more lemon juice.

10 Using a fine sieve, press lightly against the curds in the bowl and scoop out the liquid with a ladle.

11 Very gently tip the curds into a colander lined with muslin. Allow the moisture to drain off. This is soft or silken tofu.

12 For a firmer tofu, wrap the curds in muslin and weigh them down. The heavier the weight and the longer it is left, the more solid the tofu will be.

MAKING
· PASTRY ·

Pastry in general is not very nutritious—it is high in calories due to the fat content (hence, unfortunately, its mouthwatering appeal), and, when made with white flour, is low in fibre, vitamins and minerals. However, there are healthier ways of making pastry, using fewer fats. By switching to wholewheat flour, you can improve the nutritional content of your pastry. This is because wholewheat flour is higher in protein, fibre, vitamins and minerals than refined flour, and is also free from additives. Until you have had some practice with wholewheat pastry you may find it slightly difficult to handle. Due to its fibre content, you will need to add more liquid (whether water, skimmed milk, oil or eggs) than you would for refined flour, and you should allow a resting period of 30 minutes. This will give the fibre a chance to absorb the liquid and to swell. Another point to bear in mind is that wholewheat pastry has a much denser texture than refined pastry.

To guarantee a lighter effect I encourage beginners to add baking powder to the flour until they get used to handling the dough. Always roll out the pastry thinly as a little wholewheat pastry goes a long way.

· SHORTCRUST · PASTRY

This pastry has a nuttier taste and more ingredients than white-flour pastry.

INGREDIENTS
100 g (4 oz) wholewheat flour
pinch salt
up to 5 ml (1 tsp) baking powder
50 g (2 oz) fat (butter, solid vegetable fat, margarine or a mixture)
10 ml (2 tsp) oil
30-45 ml (2-3 tbsp) water
squeeze of lemon juice
Makes enough for a 23-25.5cm (9-10 in) flan case

1 Mix the flour and salt in a bowl and add the baking powder.

2 Using the tips of your fingers, rub the fat into the flour.

3 Mix together the oil, water and lemon juice. Sprinkle two-thirds of this over the rubbed-in mixture.

4 Draw the dough together. If it is not wet enough to hold together, add the rest of the liquid.

5 Wrap the pastry in polythene and leave for 30 minutes in a cool place before rolling out.

· LOW-FAT · PASTRY

This alternative to shortcrust uses oil not fat to provide richness.

INGREDIENTS
175 g (6 oz) wholewheat flour
15 ml (1 tbsp) soya flour
pinch of salt
6.5 ml (1½ tsp) baking powder
15 ml (1 tbsp) sunflower oil
skimmed milk to mix
Makes enough for a 23-25 cm (9-10 in) flan case.

1 Sift the flours, salt and baking powder together into a mixing bowl.

2 Add the oil and milk and mix to a soft dough. Let the dough rest for at least 10 minutes in a cool place before rolling out.

· YEASTED · PASTRY

This yeasted pastry, which is a cross between a bread and a pastry, has a good, light texture as long as it is rolled out thinly. For an egg-free variation, use 100 ml (4 fl oz) milk and add 15 ml (1 tbsp) soya flour to the fermenting yeast mixture. Then proceed as for the main recipe.

INGREDIENTS
75 ml (3 fl oz) skimmed milk, warmed
5 ml (1 tsp) honey
5 ml (1 tsp) fresh yeast
175 g (6 oz) wholewheat flour
pinch of salt
25 g (1 oz) butter, melted,
1 egg, beaten
Makes enough for a 23-25 cm (9-10 in) flan case.

1 Mix the milk and the honey together. Crumble the yeast into a separate bowl.

2 Pour the milk mixture on to the yeast and whisk together to blend.

3 Add half the flour to the bowl and stir in thoroughly.

4 Cover with a cloth and set aside for 30 minutes.

5 Add the remaining flour, salt, melted butter and egg.

6 Mix to a dough and then knead on a floured surface for 5-7 minutes. Leave to rest for 10 minutes before rolling out.

· STRUDEL · PASTRY

This is a versatile wholewheat alternative to the Greek filo pastry, and it can be served with both sweet and savoury fillings. With practice, strudel pastry is not hard to make. The secret is to knead the dough thoroughly so that it becomes very elastic. If this is done properly, you will be able to pull and stretch it out very thinly. When stretching the dough, work on a well-floured cloth as this helps to grip the dough and prevents it from shrinking back once stretched out. Once the dough is stretched out, leave it to dry slightly before covering with the filling and rolling up.

INGREDIENTS
150 g (5 oz) wholewheat flour
pinch of salt
10 ml (2 tsp) sunflower oil
100 ml (4 fl oz) water
oil for brushing
*Makes enough for one strudel pastry
for 4-6*

1 Mix the flour and salt together in a bowl. Add the oil and water and mix to a soft dough.

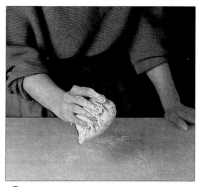

2 Knead thoroughly. This is best done by picking up the dough and slapping it down on the work surface. Do this until the dough becomes elastic in texture.

3 Brush the dough with oil to retain this elasticity and prevent a skin from forming on the resting dough.

4 Cover with a warm dish and leave for 10-15 minutes.

5 Brush with oil again then place on a clean, floured cloth. Flatten as much as possible, using your knuckles.

6 Using the back of your hands, stretch the dough out gently until almost transparent.

HOT WATER •CRUST PASTRY•

Despite being the pastry used for raised meat pies, hot water crust is ideal for vegetarian dishes, both sweet and savoury. The fat and water are boiled together then mixed with the flour to produce a soft dough which is extremely pliable when hot. It therefore has to be moulded into the tin when warm so you should always have the filling for the pie made in advance. Once a pie is made, however, it doesn't matter if it stands for a few hours before being cooked. Put the pie into a hot oven, then reduce the oven temperature so that it finishes cooking (I find a spring mould the best to use, but the pastry can be cooked in ordinary cake and loaf tins. If it doesn't turn out, it generally means the pastry isn't quite cooked.)

INGREDIENTS
350 g (12 oz) wholewheat flour
pinch of salt
150 g (5 oz) solid vegetable fat
100 ml (4 fl oz) water
Makes enough for a 23-25 cm (9-10 in) flan case

1 Put the flour and salt into a bowl. Chop the cooled fat into small pieces.

2 Put the water in a saucepan, add the fat and bring the mixture to a steady boil

3 Immediately pour the liquid on to the flour and stir in thoroughly with a wooden spoon.

4 As soon as the mixture is cool enough to handle, draw into a dough. If it seems dry and crumbly, add as much boiling water as needed.

• PASTRY TIPS •

☐ To prevent the base of pastries becoming soggy (especially when used with moist fruit fillings), bake the pastry blind first. To do this, roll out the pastry thinly and line a flan tin with it. Press the base and sides down firmly. Prick the base thoroughly all over with a fork. Bake for 5 minutes at gas mark 6 200°C (400°F), then put in the required filling and bake as instructed.

☐ Another way to prevent soggy pastry is to put the flan tin on a pre-heated baking sheet in the oven. This conducts the heat more efficiently and cooks the base more quickly.

☐ If your hands tend to be warm, use a pastry-blender to mix the fat into the flour.

☐ Always use lightly chilled fats in pastry-making. They rub into breadcrumbs without becoming soft and greasy.

☐ Always let pastry rest before rolling it out. This allows the gluten in the flour to lose its elasticity. If not allowed for, the pastry will shrink badly once rolled out, and during the baking process.

• MAKING SAUCES •

There are three basic sauces used in wholefood cookery which can be adapted to serve with a variety of grain, pulse and vegetable dishes.

•WHITE SAUCE•

When made with wholewheat flour, white sauce always has a nuttier flavour than with refined flour, and a fuller texture. It is best to infuse the milk to improve the flavour, especially if you are cutting down on seasoning. Use half an onion, peppercorns, a bay leaf, mace or nutmeg, or a small sprig of thyme or parsley. When using oil for the base of a roux, you must not overheat it before adding the flour, otherwise the flour fries and cannot absorb the oil properly.

INGREDIENTS
300 ml (½ pint) skimmed milk
30 ml (2 tbsp) sunflower oil
20 g (¾ oz) wholewheat flour
white pepper
For the infusion:
½ onion
6 peppercorns
1 bay leaf
1 blade mace
Makes 300 ml (½ pint) sauce

1 Heat the milk with the infusion ingredients. Bring to the boil, remove from the heat, cover and stand for 10 minutes.

2 Strain the milk into a jug or into a bowl.

3 Gently heat the oil. When just hot add the flour, stirring all the time. Cook for a few minutes.

4 Add the milk gradually, stirring well until completely smooth. Bring to boiling point stirring continuously, and simmer for 3-5 minutes. Season with pepper.

LOW-FAT •WHITE SAUCE•

If you are really concerned about your fat intake, try this sauce. Rice flour is used as the thickening agent, and no oil is added.

INGREDIENTS
15 ml (1 tbsp) rice flour
300 ml (½ pint) skimmed milk, infused as above
white pepper
Makes 300 ml (½ pint) sauce

1 Put the rice flour in a saucepan and mix to a paste with a little of the milk.

2 Stir in the remainder of the milk, bring to the boil and simmer for 5-7 minutes. Season with pepper.

• TOMATO • SAUCE

This is a good example of a sauce made with vegetables and their own juices. Variations on this idea could be made with celery or broccoli.

INGREDIENTS
10 ml (2 tsp) olive oil
1 small onion, finely chopped
1-2 cloves garlic, crushed
450 g (1 lb) tomatoes, skinned and roughly chopped
15-30 (1-2 tbsp) tomato purée
5 ml (1 tsp) miso, dissolved in a little water
5 ml (1 tsp) oregano or 10 ml (2 tsp) fresh basil
black pepper
Makes 300 ml (½ pint) sauce

1 Heat the oil and cook the onion and garlic over a very low heat for 10-15 mintues—they should not colour. Add the remaining ingredients. Cover and simmer for 45 minutes.

2 If you want a smooth sauce, purée this mixture in a food processor or liquidizer. Season with pepper.

• BROWN • SAUCE

It is much healthier to avoid all highly salted gravy mixes— vegetarian and otherwise. The points about oil and the thorough cooking of the flour (see page 43) also apply to this recipe. I find stock from aduki beans or continental lentils provides a particularly good flavour.

INGREDIENTS
1 onion, chopped
50 g (2 oz) mushrooms, chopped
30 ml (2 tbsp) sunflower oil
20 g (¾ oz) wholewheat flour
300 ml (½ pint) dark vegetable or bean stock
1 bay leaf
1 sprig fresh thyme
2.5 ml (½ tsp) mustard powder
up to 5 ml (1 tsp) miso, dissolved in a little water
up to 5 ml (1 tsp) shoyu
black pepper
Makes 300 ml (½ pint) sauce

1 Heat the oil and fry the vegetables gently for 5 minutes.

2 Add the flour, stir and cook for 3 minutes.

3 Pour on the stock and bring to the boil, stirring constantly.

4 Add the herbs and mustard powder. Simmer for 7-10 minutes. Add miso, shoyu and pepper to taste.

RECONSTITUTING
· FRUIT & PULSES ·

Pulses, one of the main staples of a wholefood vegetarian diet, are sold dried, and of these the larger beans and peas need to be soaked before cooking. The same is true if many dried fruits.

· PULSES ·

Soaking pulses (which include peas, beans and lentils) before cooking speeds up cooking times. Before soaking, pick over the pulses carefully to remove any sticks or stones and then soak in plenty of water. Pulses do cause flatulence, but by changing the soaking water two or three times this problem can be reduced. When you boil the beans (step 3), flavour the water with vegetables (onions, carrots) and seasonings (caraway, fennel, aniseed or kombu sticks) to make a good bean stock. Pulses usually take 30-50 minutes to cook (they will be soft all the way through when ready); in a pressure cooker they cook in roughly a third of the time.

1 Put the pulses in a large bowl and cover by at least 5-7.5 cm (2-3 in) cold water. Leave overnight.

2 Drain away the soaking water. Rinse the pulses well.

3 Put in a saucepan, cover with water and bring to the boil. Add any flavourings except for salt as this toughens the skins. Boil for 10 minutes, removing any scum from the surface. Lower heat and cook until pulses are tender.

4 Drain the pulses, keeping the liquid for stock (see page 47). Use the pulses immediately, or store, covered, in a refrigerator for up to 4 days.

· FRUIT ·

Dried fruits are useful stand-bys for the store cupboard. They are high in vitamins and minerals and are delicious raw as snacks or in salads, or cooked for fruit salads and compôtes. Try spicing the soaking water with nutmeg, cinnamon or vanilla essence for extra flavour.

1 Put the fruit in a large bowl and cover with plenty of water. Leave overnight.

2 The fruit will double or treble in size. Cook it in its soaking liquid.

COOKING
• GRAINS •

*Once you have weighed out the
amount of grain required, pour it
into a measuring cup or jug to
establish how many cups it makes.
Follow the chart below to gauge the
amount of cooking water needed.
Put the grain in a sieve and rinse
before cooking; it will not need
soaking. Buckwheat and millet are
best lightly roasted before boiling.
Don't stir the rice more than twice
when cooking, it will break up.*

Amount of Grain	Cooking Water	Cooking Time
1 cup Rice	2 cups	short-grain 25-30 mins. long-grain 30-35 mins.
1 cup Buckwheat	2½ cups	20-25 mins.
1 cup Millet	3 cups	20-25 mins.
1 cup Wheat or Barley	4 cups	50-60 mins.

1 Weigh out the required amount of grain. Pour into a measuring cup to establish the number of cups.

2 Bring the correct amount of water to the boil and add the grain. Stir once.

3 Bring back to the boil, cover and simmer until all the water has been absorbed. Add more boiling water if necessary.

To roast grains: brush a thick-based pan lightly with oil. Heat, add the dry grains and cook until pale brown (about 4 minutes). Cook as normal.

MAKING
• STOCK •

*Any liquid from cooking beans or
grains can be used as stock. Dark
stocks are best made from red or
black beans; for pale stocks use chick
peas or white bean cooking liquid.*

INGREDIENTS
15 ml (1 tbsp) olive or sunflower oil
2 carrots, roughly chopped
1 large onion, roughly chopped
1 stick kombu
1 bay leaf
1 sprig thyme
1.5 litres (2½ pints) water
miso or shoyu
Makes 1.1 litres (2 pints)

1 Heat the oil and gently fry the vegetables. Add the water and simmer for 1-1½ hours.

2 Strain into a clean container and season to taste with miso or shoyu.

SPROUTING
• SEEDS •

Sprouts are not only useful if you want cheap, fresh salads and stir-fries all year round, they also have a very high vitamin and mineral content.

I think the smaller seeds look more attractive when sprouted than the larger varieties and I have found the following particularly easy to grow: mung beans, aduki beans, alfalfa, mustard cress, whole lentils.

1 Having removed any split seeds, put 30 ml (2 tbsp) into a large, water-filled jam jar.

2 Soak overnight then drain away the soaking water.

3 Cover the jar with a muslin cloth and secure it with an elastic band.

4 Good drainage is essential for good growth, so leave the jar tilted upside down at an angle in a warm, airy place.

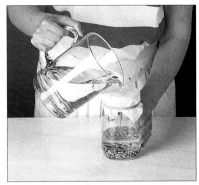

5 Rinse the seeds 2 or 3 times a day with lukewarm water. Shake the jar gently then drain well. After 2 or 3 days place in sunlight.

6 Sprouts have the best taste between 3 and 6 days later (when you choose to use them is a matter of taste). Tip them into a large bowl. Fill with water.

7 Remove any ungerminated seeds or husks which will float to the surface. Sprouted seeds will keep, covered in the refrigerator, for 4 days.

Using a salad sprouter: if you use a salad sprouter you can grow three varieties of seed simultaneously.

· STEAMING ·

Steaming is an excellent way of preserving most of the minerals and vitamins in vegetables. There are two basic types of steamer: specially designed metal ones which act as container for both the food and the boiling water, and expandible steel baskets which hold the food but have to be placed inside a saucepan containing boiling water. Whichever method you use, the layer of vegetables shouldn't be deeper than 1-5 cm (½-2 in).

1 Boil up a small amount of water in a pan and fit a steaming basket inside.

2 Add the chopped vegetables, cover and steam until just tender.

· STIR-FRYING ·

In this cooking technique the vegetables are cooked rapidly in the minimum amount of very hot oil so that they retain all their flavour and crisp texture. The traditional piece of equipment is a wok: a thin, round-bottomed, metal pan which conducts the heat well, allowing the food to cook quickly and evenly.

1 Chop the vegetables into evenly sized pieces.

2 Heat a wok over a high heat until smoke rises. Add 22.5 ml (1½ tbsp) oil and swirl it around.

3 Add the vegetables, putting in the ones requiring the longest cooking first.

4 Add the seasoning, then add the liquid to finish off cooking with a burst of steam.

·RECIPES·

•SOUPS•

• FENNEL SOUP •

This subtle-tasting, high-protein soup is low in saturated fats.

NUTRITIONAL PROFILE		per portion
Total calories		95
Protein	4g	√ √ √
Fibre	3g	√ √
Polyunsaturated fats	2g	√ √ √
Saturated fats	1g	√ √ √
Vitamins		Good source of:
		—
Minerals		Good source of:
		—

Illustrated opposite

INGREDIENTS

10 ml (2 tsp) sunflower oil
450 g (1 lb) fennel, trimmed and diced
40 g (1½ oz) cashew nut pieces
150 ml (¼ pint) skimmed milk
300 ml (½ pint) vegetable stock (see page 46)

1.25 ml (¼ tsp) anise seeds
5-10 ml (1-2 tsp) lemon juice
gomasio, or salt if preferred
black pepper
Serves 4

1 Heat the oil in a large saucepan and gently fry the fennel for 10-15 minutes or until soft.
2 Add the cashew nuts, milk and stock. Bring to the boil, cover and simmer for 15 minutes.
3 Cool slightly, then liquidize until smooth, adding the anise seeds and lemon juice to taste. Season with gomasio and pepper. Reheat before serving.

• PEASE POTTAGE •

Choose brightly coloured split peas for this nutritious, iron-rich soup.

NUTRITIONAL PROFILE		per portion
Total calories		140
Protein	7g	√ √ √
Fibre	6g	√ √ √
Polyunsaturated fats	1g	√ √ √
Saturated fats	0.5g	√ √ √
Vitamins		Good source of:
		A, B1, C, E
Minerals		Good source of:
		Fe

Illustrated opposite

INGREDIENTS

10 ml (2 tsp) sunflower oil
1 medium onion, chopped
1 medium carrot, chopped
1 medium parsnip, chopped
100 g (4 oz) green split peas
1 bay leaf

900 ml (1½ pints) vegetable stock (see page 46)
2.5 ml (½ tsp) mustard powder
10 ml (2 tsp) gomasio, or salt if preferred
black pepper
Serves 4-6

1 Heat the oil in a large saucepan and gently fry the onion for 4-5 minutes or until soft.
2 Add the carrot, parsnip and green split peas. Cook for 5 minutes, stirring frequently.
3 Stir in the stock, bay leaf and mustard powder. Bring to the boil, cover and simmer for 50 minutes.

Clockwise from the top: **All Saints' broth**; Pease pottage; Fennel soup

4 Cool slightly, then liquidize until smooth. Season with gomasio and pepper. Reheat gently before serving.

This soup is a perfect nutritional balance—high in protein and fibre, low in fat. It would be best served with dishes high in minerals and vitamins.

NUTRITIONAL PROFILE	*per portion*	
Total calories		120
Protein	8g	√ √ √
Fibre	10g	√ √ √
Polyunsaturated fats	2g	√ √ √
Saturated fats	0.5g	√ √ √
Vitamins	*Good source of:*	
		C
Minerals	*Good source of:*	
		—

Illustrated below

◆ ALL SAINTS' BROTH ◆

INGREDIENTS

50 g (2 oz) dried chestnuts, soaked over-night in 1.1 litres (2 pints) water, or 100 g (4 oz) fresh chestnuts
10 ml (2 tsp) sunflower oil
1 medium onion, finely grated
100 g (4 oz) aduki beans, soaked overnight

225 g (8 oz) celeriac, peeled and chopped
30 ml (2 tbsp) tomato purée
5 ml (1 tsp) dried thyme
15 ml (1 tbsp) shoyu
black pepper
Serves 4-6

1 Place the chestnuts and their soaking water in a saucepan. Bring to the boil, cover and simmer for 40-50 minutes or until soft. Leave to cool, then liquidize.
2 Heat the oil in a large saucepan and gently fry the onion for 4-5 minutes or until just brown. Drain the beans.
3 Add the beans and celeriac to the pan and cook for 3 minutes.
4 Pour in 900 ml (1½ pints) chestnut stock. Stir in the tomato purée and thyme. Bring to the boil and boil fast for 10 minutes. Reduce the heat, cover and simmer for 40-50 minutes or until the beans are well cooked. Season with shoyu and pepper. Serve hot.

Although coconut cream is high in saturated fats, the quantity used here is small enough to be allowable, and just sufficient to add a delicate velvety texture to the soup.

NUTRITIONAL PROFILE	*per portion*	
Total calories		170
Protein	7g	√√√
Fibre	7g	√√√
Polyunsaturated fats	2g	√√
Saturated fats	2g	√√
Vitamins		*Good source of:*
		A, B1, B6, C, FA
Minerals		*Good source of:*
		Fe

Illustrated opposite

· CAULIFLOWER ·
& CORIANDER SOUP

INGREDIENTS

50 g (2 oz) pot barley
50 g (2 oz) yellow split peas
10 ml (2 tsp) sunflower oil
1 medium onion, finely chopped
1 clove garlic, crushed
5 ml (1 tsp) fresh root ginger, grated
2.5 ml (½ tsp) turmeric
2.5 ml (½ tsp) coriander seeds, crushed
2.5 ml (½ tsp) cumin seeds
1 medium cooking apple, cored and chopped
1 medium carrot

1 fresh green chilli, deseeded and finely chopped
900 ml (1½ pints) vegetable stock (see page 46)
1 cauliflower, divided into florets
30 ml (2 tbsp) finely chopped fresh coriander leaves
gomasio, or salt if preferred
black pepper
25 g (1 oz) grated cream coconut
Serves 6-8

1 Place the barley and yellow split peas in a bowl. Cover with hot water and leave to soak for 1 hour. Drain.
2 Heat the oil in a large saucepan and gently fry the onion and garlic for 4-5 minutes or until soft. Add the ginger, turmeric, coriander and cumin and cook for 3-4 minutes.
3 Add the apple, carrot, chilli, barley and yellow split peas and fry for 2-3 minutes.
4 Pour over the stock, bring to the boil, cover and simmer for 1 hour.
5 Add the cauliflower and chopped coriander to the soup and cook for a further 10 minutes or until the cauliflower is just tender. Season with gomasio and pepper.
6 Place the creamed coconut in a bowl. Pour over 150 ml (¼ pint) boiling water and stir to dissolve. Mix the coconut liquid into the soup, and allow to heat through before serving.

A good source of vitamins A, C and E, and high in minerals, protein and fibre, this soup uses a spiced fruit stock to add another dimension to the spinach flavour.

NUTRITIONAL PROFILE	*per portion*	
Total calories		110
Protein	7g	√√√
Fibre	6g	√√√
Polyunsaturated fats	0.5g	√√
Saturated fats	1g	√√√
Vitamins		*Good source of:*
		A, C, E
Minerals		*Good source of:*
		Ca, Cu, Fe, Mg

Illustrated opposite

· SPINACH SOUP ·

INGREDIENTS

10 ml (2 tsp) olive oil
1 medium onion, chopped
1 clove garlic, crushed
350 g (12 oz) spinach, washed and shredded
450 ml (¾ pint) mixed apple and orange juice

2.25 cm (½ in) fresh root ginger, grated
5 ml (1 tsp) ground coriander
150 ml (¼ pint) yogurt or soured cream
gomasio, or salt if preferred
black pepper
Serves 4

1 Heat the oil in a large saucepan and gently fry the onion and garlic for 4-5 minutes or until the onion is soft.
2 Add the spinach and stir-fry for 2-3 minutes over a high heat until it becomes limp.
3 Pour over the fruit juices, ginger and coriander. Bring to the boil, cover and simmer for 20 minutes.
4 Cool slightly, then liquidize until smooth. Stir in the yogurt or cream. Season with gomasio and pepper. Reheat gently before serving.

Top left: **Spinach soup**; Top right: **Cauliflower and coriander soup**; Bottom: **Sweet red pepper soup** *(see page 54)*

This soup derives its richness from the tofu—a good way of providing a creamy texture while keeping fats low and protein high.

NUTRITIONAL PROFILE	*per portion*	
Total calories		100
Protein	7g	√√√
Fibre	2g	√
Polyunsaturated fats	2g	√√√
Saturated fats	1g	√√√
Vitamins	*Good source of:*	
	A, B1, B2, C, FA, N	
Minerals	*Good source of:*	
	Ca, Cu, Fe	

Illustrated on page 53

SWEET
◆ RED PEPPER SOUP ◆

INGREDIENTS

2 medium red peppers, halved and deseeded
10 ml (2 tsp) olive oil
1 medium onion, finely chopped
1 clove garlic, crushed
225 g (8 oz) tomatoes, skinned and chopped
30 ml (2 tbsp) tomato purée
300 ml (½ pint) vegetable stock (see page 46)
5 ml (1 tsp) dried marjoram
275 g (10 oz) silken tofu
gomasio, or salt if preferred
black pepper
Serves 4

1 Preheat the oven to gas mark 4, 180°C (350°F). Place the peppers in an overproof dish and bake for 15-20 minutes, turning them over occasionally so that the skin chars. Cool, then peel off the skin and dice the flesh finely.
2 Heat the oil in a large saucepan and gently fry the onion and garlic for 4-5 minutes or until soft. ▶

Left: **Mushroom kasha soup**; Right: **Artichoke soup**

3 Add the red pepper, tomatoes, purée, stock and marjoram. Bring to the boil, cover and simmer for 30 minutes.

4 Cut the tofu into pieces and liquidize until smooth. Pour into the soup and stir well. Season with gomasio and pepper. Heat through gently and serve hot.

✦ ARTICHOKE ✦
SOUP

INGREDIENTS

10 ml (2 tsp) sunflower oil
1 medium onion, finely chopped
450 g (1 lb) Jerusalem artichokes, peeled and diced
1 small potato, peeled and diced

300 ml (½ pint) skimmed milk
300 ml (½ pint) vegetable stock (see page 46)
gomasio, or salt if preferred
white pepper
Serves 4-6

1 Heat the oil in a large saucepan and gently fry the onion for 4-5 minutes or until soft.

2 Add the artichokes and potato and cook lightly for about 5 minutes but do not allow to colour.

3 Pour on the milk and stock. Bring to the boil, cover and simmer for 25-30 minutes.

4 Cool slightly, then liquidize until smooth. Season with gomasio and pepper and reheat before serving.

Artichokes are high in protein and are used here to produce a delicious creamy soup that is low in saturated fat.

NUTRITIONAL PROFILE	*per portion*	
Total calories		95
Protein	5g	√√√
Fibre	1g	√
Polyunsaturated fats	1g	√√√
Saturated fats	0g	√√√
Vitamins	*Good source of:*	C
Minerals	*Good source of:*	Ca

Illustrated opposite

✦ MUSHROOM KASHA ✦
SOUP

INGREDIENTS

10 ml (2 tsp) sunflower oil
1 medium onion, finely chopped
350 g (12 oz) mushrooms, sliced
25 g (1 oz) buckwheat
600 ml (1 pint) dark stock (see page 46)

15 ml (1 tbsp) shoyu
2.5 ml (½ tsp) paprika
black pepper
Garnish
mushrooms 30-45 ml (2-3 tbsp) or smetana
Serves 4-6

1 Heat the oil in a large saucepan and gently fry the onion for 4-5 minutes or until soft.

2 Add the mushrooms and buckwheat, cover and cook for 10 minutes.

3 Pour on the stock, bring to the boil, cover and simmer for 20 minutes.

4 Cool slightly, then liquidize until smooth, adding the shoyu and paprika.

5 Season with pepper and reheat before serving. Garnish with sliced, sautéed mushrooms or smetana.

One of the main ingredients of this highly nutritious soup is buckwheat (kasha in Russian), a grain high in riboflavin which is essential for both blood circulation and the control of blood pressure.

NUTRITIONAL PROFILE	*per portion*	
Total calories		60
Protein	2g	√√√
Fibre	3g	√√
Polyunsaturated fats	2g	√√√
Saturated fats	0.5g	√√√
Vitamins	*Good source of:*	C, E, N
Minerals	*Good source of:*	—

Illustrated opposite

Don't be put off by the amount of garlic in this recipe—the cloves add a wonderfully subtle flavour to the stock. Serve with a high-protein, high-fibre dish for balance.

NUTRITIONAL PROFILE	per portion	
Total calories	75	
Protein	2g	√
Fibre	2g	√
Polyunsaturated fats	1g	√√√
Saturated fats	0g	√√√
Vitamins	Good source of:	
	C	
Minerals	Good source of:	
	—	

Illustrated opposite

· CREAM OF POTATO ·
SOUP WITH GARLIC

INGREDIENTS

For the stock	For the soup
10 ml (2 tsp) sunflower oil	10 ml (2 tsp) sunflower oil
2 medium onions, quartered	1 medium onion, finely chopped
12 cloves garlic	2 cloves garlic, crushed
2 medium carrots, cut into chunks	225 g (8 oz) potatoes, diced
1 bay leaf	15 ml (1 tbsp) shoyu
sprig of thyme	10 ml (2 tsp) miso, dissolved in a little water
900 ml (1½ pints) water	*Serves 4*

1 For the stock: heat the oil in a large saucepan and gently fry the onion, whole cloves of garlic and carrot for 15-20 minutes.
2 Add the bay leaf, thyme and water. Bring to the boil, cover and simmer for 1-1½ hours. Strain, and reserve the stock.
3 For the soup: heat the oil in a large saucepan and fry the onion and garlic for 4-5 minutes until browned, stirring frequently.
4 Add the potato and fry for a further 5-8 minutes until browned.
5 Pour over the garlic stock. Bring to the boil, cover and simmer for 20 minutes.
6 Cool slightly, then liquidize until smooth, adding the shoyu and miso. Reheat gently before serving.

It is important to use well-flavoured stock with a good colour for this traditional Chinese soup which, although high in protein and fibre, and low in fat, may otherwise taste insipid.

NUTRITIONAL PROFILE	per portion	
Total calories	55	
Protein	3g	√√√
Fibre	2g	√
Polyunsaturated fats	0.5g	√√√
Saturated fats	0.5g	√√√
Vitamins	Good source of:	
	A, C	
Minerals	Good source of:	
	—	

Illustrated opposite

· EGG FLOWER ·
SOUP

INGREDIENTS

5 ml (1 tsp) sesame oil	15 cm (6 in) stick kombu
2 shallots, finely chopped	15 g (½ oz) dried Chinese mushrooms
4 sticks celery, diagonally sliced	pinch of cayenne
50 g (2 oz) Chinese leaves, shredded	5 ml (1 tsp) miso, dissolved in a little water
1 medium carrot, sliced	5-10 ml (1-2 tsp) shoyu
600 ml (1 pint) dark bean stock (see page 46)	5 ml (1 tsp) cornflour
	1 egg, beaten
	Serves 4

1 Heat the oil in a large saucepan and stir-fry the shallots, celery, Chinese leaves and carrot over a high heat for 3 minutes.
2 Add all the stock, kombu and dried mushrooms. Bring to the boil, cover and simmer for 15-20 minutes.
3 Season the soup with the cayenne, miso and shoyu.
4 Blend the cornflour with a little water. Mix some of the hot soup into this then pour into the soup. Bring to the boil, stirring, and simmer for 3 minutes.
5 Beat the egg into the soup and stir for 1-2 minutes until cooked. Serve immediately.

Clockwise from the top: **Minestrone alla Genovese** *(see page 58)*; **Egg flower soup**; **Cream of potato soup with garlic**; **Summer soup** *(see page 58)*

There is a fine distinction between a hearty soup and a casserole, and although this highly nutritious soup comes into the former category, it needs only wholewheat bread to make it a complete and satisfying meal.

NUTRITIONAL PROFILE	*per portion*	
Total calories	190	
Protein	11g	✓✓✓
Fibre	10g	✓✓✓
Polyunsaturated fats	1g	✓
Saturated fats	0.5g	✓✓✓
Vitamins	*Good source of:*	
	A, B₁, C, E, FA	
Minerals	*Good source of:*	
	Ca, Cu, Fe, Mg	

Illustrated on page 57

• MINESTRONE •
ALLA GENOVESE

INGREDIENTS

100 g (4 oz) cannellini or haricot beans, soaked overnight
10 ml (2 tsp) olive oil
1 medium onion, chopped
3 cloves garlic, crushed
100 g (4 oz) cabbage, shredded
100 g (4 oz) mushrooms, sliced
225 g (8 oz) courgettes, diced
1 small aubergine, diced
350 g (12 oz) tomatoes, skinned and chopped
30 ml (2 tbsp) tomato purée
10 ml (2 tsp) dried oregano
900 ml (1½ pints) bean stock (see page 46)
50 g (2 oz) wholewheat pasta
45-60 ml (3-4 tbsp) finely chopped fresh parsley
15-30 ml (1-2 tbsp) shoyu
black pepper
Serves 6-8

1 Drain the beans. Cover with plenty of fresh water, bring, uncovered, to the boil and boil fast for 10 minutes. Reduce the heat, skim, cover and simmer for 45-50 minutes or until soft. Drain and reserve the cooking water for stock. Make up to 900 ml (1½ pints) if necessary.
2 Heat the oil in a large saucepan and gently fry the onion and garlic for 4-5 minutes or until the onion is soft. Add the cabbage, mushrooms, courgettes, aubergine and tomatoes and cook for 5 minutes.
3 Stir in the tomato purée, oregano, beans and the reserved bean stock. Bring to the boil, cover and simmer for 45-50 minutes. Add more stock if necessary.
4 Add the pasta and parsley and cook for a further 10 minutes.
5 Season with shoyu and pepper. Serve hot.

Large portions of soup can be daunting so I prefer to serve just enough to whet the appetite. This chilled soup is high in protein and low in fat.

NUTRITIONAL PROFILE	*per portion*	
Total calories	50	
Protein	3g	✓✓✓
Fibre	1g	✓
Polyunsaturated fats	1g	✓✓✓
Saturated fats	0g	✓✓✓
Vitamins	*Good source of:*	
	A, C, E	
Minerals	*Good source of:*	
	Ca, Mg	

Illustrated on page 57

• SUMMER SOUP •

INGREDIENTS

10 ml (2 tsp) sunflower oil
3 spring onions, chopped
1 round lettuce, shredded
100 g (4 oz) Chinese leaves, shredded
150 ml (¼ pint) skimmed milk
300 ml (½ pint) yogurt
8 cardamom seeds, crushed
a little lemon juice
gomasio, or salt if preferred
black pepper
Serves 4

1 Heat the oil in a large saucepan and gently fry the spring onions for about 3 minutes.
2 Add the lettuce and Chinese leaves, cover and cook for 5-8 minutes.
3 Transfer the lettuce mixture to a liquidizer and add the milk and yogurt. Liquidize until smooth.
4 Mix in the cardamom seeds and lemon juice. Season with gomasio and pepper.
5 Chill thoroughly before serving.

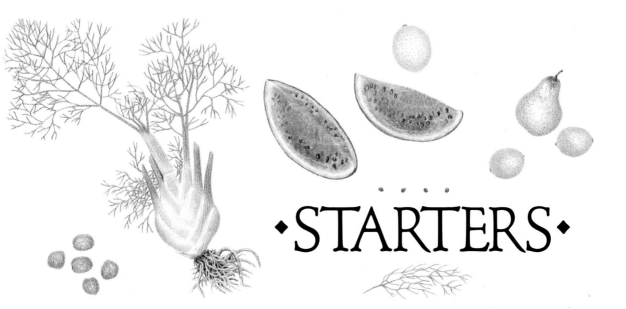

· STARTERS ·

High in both protein and fibre, and relatively low in fat, this is an impressive dish to start a meal with. It is very important, however, to make sure that the terrine is cold and well set before slicing it with a sharp knife or the effect of the layers will be lost.

NUTRITIONAL PROFILE	*per portion*	
Total calories		205
Protein	14g	√√√
Fibre	3g	√√√
Polyunsaturated fats	4g	√√√
Saturated fats	3g	√√√
Vitamins	*Good source of:*	
	A, B1, B12, C	
Minerals	*Good source of:*	
	Ca	

Illustrated on page 61

· VEGETABLE TERRINE ·

INGREDIENTS

8 large spinach leaves, washed	herb salt, or salt if preferred
300 ml (½ pint) skimmed milk	grated nutmeg
½ medium onion	black pepper
1 bay leaf	175 g (6 oz) quark
6 peppercorns	1 large egg
blade of mace	100 g (4 oz) peas
30 ml (2 tbsp) sunflower oil	100 g (4 oz) carrot, diced
25 g (1 oz) wholewheat flour	100 g (4 oz) asparagus

Serves 4-6

1 Pour boiling water over spinach; drain after 1 minute.
2 Place the milk in a saucepan with the onion, bay leaf, peppercorns and blade of mace. Bring almost to the boil, cover and leave to infuse for 10 minutes. Strain the milk and set aside.
3 Gently heat the oil in a saucepan. Stir in the flour to make a roux. Gradually add the flavoured milk and bring to the boil, stirring constantly. Season with herb salt, nutmeg and pepper.
4 Cool slightly, then stir in the quark and egg.
5 Lightly steam the peas, carrots and asparagus in separate pans or compartments of a steamer for 6-8 minutes. Preheat the oven to gas mark 3, 170°C (325°F).
6 Line a 450 g (1 lb) loaf tin with the spinach leaves, reserving one for the top.
7 Put in a layer of sauce, then a layer of carrot. Repeat with layers of sauce, peas, sauce, asparagus and finally sauce.
8 Fold over the leaves and place one on the top to cover the mixture completely. Place the tin in a *bain marie* or a roasting tin filled with about 2.5 cm (1 in) hot water.
9 Bake for 1 hour. Cool completely before turning out on to a serving plate. When cold, slice before serving.

Choose firm field mushrooms for this high-protein starter as they have a stronger flavour than button mushrooms and are much easier to fill.

NUTRITIONAL PROFILE	*per portion*	
Total calories		165
Protein	8g	√√√
Fibre	3g	√√
Polyunsaturated fats	5g	√√√
Saturated fats	2g	√√
Vitamins	*Good source of:*	
		C
Minerals	*Good source of:*	
		Fe, Mg, Zn

Illustrated opposite

HOT STUFFED
· MUSHROOMS ·

INGREDIENTS

4 large flat field mushrooms
10 ml (2 tsp) olive oil
50 g (2 oz) button mushrooms, diced
1 small green pepper, deseeded and diced
10 ml (2 tsp) capers
2 cloves garlic, crushed
40g (1½ oz) fresh wholewheat breadcrumbs
5 ml (1 tsp) dried thyme
15 ml (1 tbsp) lemon juice

15 ml (1 tbsp) sesame seeds
gomasio, or salt if preferred
black pepper
pinch of cayenne
For the dressing
200 ml (⅓ pint) yogurt
15 ml (1 tbsp) lemon juice
15 ml (1 tbsp) tahini
1 clove garlic, crushed
Serves 4

1 Cut the stalks out of the large mushrooms. Lightly steam the caps for 3-4 minutes until just softened. Place in a shallow heatproof dish, rounded sides down.
2 Preheat the oven to gas mark 4, 180°C (350°F), if using.
3 Heat the oil in a pan and gently fry the diced mushrooms, green pepper, capers and garlic for 3-4 minutes or until soft.
4 Remove from the heat, mix in the breadcrumbs, thyme, lemon juice and sesame seeds. Season with gomasio, pepper and cayenne.
5 Pile the mixture into the mushroom caps. Either place under a preheated moderate grill for 4-5 minutes or bake for 10-15 minutes.
6 Mix the dressing ingredients together thoroughly. Serve with the hot stuffed mushrooms.

In summer months, the aubergine in this Middle Eastern dip could be barbequed to produce a more smoky flavour. Serve with raw vegetables or wholewheat pitta bread to improve the overall fibre content.

NUTRITIONAL PROFILE	*per portion*	
Total calories		90
Protein	4g	√√√
Fibre	1g	√
Polyunsaturated fats	3g	√√√
Saturated fats	1g	√√√
Vitamins	*Good source of:*	
		—
Minerals	*Good source of:*	
		—

Illustrated opposite

· AUBERGINE DIP ·

INGREDIENTS

1 large aubergine
60 ml (4 tbsp) yogurt
15-30 ml (1-2 tbsp) lemon juice
45 ml (3 tbsp) tahini
60 ml (4 tbsp) finely chopped fresh parsley

2 cloves garlic, crushed
gomasio, or salt if preferred
black pepper
For serving
vegetable crudités or pitta bread
Serves 4-6

1 Preheat the oven to gas mark 4, 180°C (350°F).
2 Remove the aubergine stalk and prick the flesh 2-3 times. Place in an ovenproof dish and bake for about 20 minutes or until soft.
3 Peel off the skin and chop the flesh.
4 Put the aubergine flesh, yogurt, lemon juice, tahini, parsley and garlic into a liquidizer or food processor and blend until smooth. Season with gomasio and pepper.
5 Serve with crudités of carrot, cauliflower, radishes, corn and mange tout, or warm pitta bread.

Clockwise from top: **Vegetable terrine** *(see page 59)*; **Aubergine dip**; **Hot stuffed mushrooms**

◆ BALANCED MEAL 1 ◆

This meal is an excellent source of both protein and fibre. It is possible to include dishes like *Beetroot salad* and *Golden salad* which are low in protein because they are balanced by high-protein, high-fibre dishes like *Celebration roast* and *Spinach soup*.

◆ **Baked parsnips in orange**
For recipe, see page 136

After steaming, baking is the best way to preserve nutrients in cooked vegetables. The natural sweetness of the parsnips is well complemented here by the orange.

◆ **Hazel's potatoes**
For recipe, see page 136

Roast potatoes need not become a forbidden food once you've turned to a healthy regime of eating, as this dish proves. The potatoes here, baked lightly with a minimum amount of olive oil, are low in saturated fats.

◆ Celebration roast
For recipe, see page 74

This high-protein, high-fibre dish contrasts a creamy nut mixture with a dark, moist layer of mushrooms and walnuts.

◆ Tomato sauce
For recipe, see page 44

The tomato sauce is served here to enhance the flavour of the celebration roast, not to moisten it.

◆ Wine
A glass of dry white wine will add 75 calories to the profile of this meal.

◆ Golden salad
For recipe, see page 155

Using such exotic fruits as mango, passion fruit, pomegranate and dates, this fruit salad is an ideal way to end a meal—light, naturally sweet and fat-free.

◆ Beetroot salad
For recipe, see page 131

Raw beetroot has a far better flavour than bought, pre-cooked varieties which have often had preservatives and sugar added to them. It is mixed here with celeriac and turnip to produce a clean-tasting salad to follow the main course.

◆ Spinach soup
For recipe, see page 53

This nutritious, high-protein, high-fibre, low-fat soup is based on a spiced fruit stock made up from fruit juices, coriander and ginger. The last two ingredients provide just the right amount of tang to the soup.

NUTRITIONAL PROFILE	*per portion*	
Total calories	1350	
Protein	37g	✓ ✓ ✓
Fibre	39g	✓ ✓ ✓
Polyunsaturated fats	32g	✓ ✓ ✓
Saturated fats	11g	✓ ✓ ✓
Vitamins	*Good source of:*	
	A, B1, B2, C, E, N, FA	
Minerals	*Good source of:*	
	Ca, Fe, Cu, Mg	

Based on a classic Middle Eastern hors d'oeuvre, this low-fat dish uses fruit and nuts for substance along with bulgar wheat.

NUTRITIONAL PROFILE	*per portion*	
Total calories		160
Protein	5g	√√
Fibre	3g	√√
Polyunsaturated fats	5g	√√√
Saturated fats	1g	√√√
Vitamins	*Good source of:*	A, C
Minerals	*Good source of:*	Ca, Cu, Fe

Illustrated opposite

MIDDLE EASTERN
·STUFFED VINE LEAVES·

INGREDIENTS

50 g (2 oz) bulgar wheat
150 ml (¼ pint) vegetable stock
20 vine leaves, about 1 packet
10 ml (2 tsp) olive oil
1 medium onion, finely chopped
1 clove garlic, crushed

25 g (1 oz) dried apricots, diced
50 g (2 oz) walnuts, chopped
10 ml (2 tsp) crushed coriander seeds
5 ml (1 tsp) shoyu
gomasio, or salt if preferred
black pepper
Serves 4-6

1 Soak the bulgar wheat in the stock for 15 minutes. Drain and squeeze out excess moisture. Spread on a clean tea-towel to dry out slightly.
2 Rinse the vine leaves and set aside.
3 Heat the oil in a saucepan and fry the onion and garlic for 4-5 minutes or until the onion is soft.
4 Add the apricots, walnuts, soaked bulgar wheat and coriander to the pan and mix well. Cook for 10 minutes, adding a little more stock if the mixture begins to look dry. Season with shoyu, gomasio and pepper.
5 Preheat the oven to gas mark 4, 180°C (350°F).
6 Take a vine leaf and place with the stalk nearest you. Put about 15 ml (1 tbsp) of the mixture into the centre of each vine leaf. Fold in both sides to the centre, then roll the leaf up from the bottom. Place the vine leaves in a lightly oiled ovenproof dish. Cover with foil. Bake for 10-15 minutes. Serve hot or warm.

Meaning green in Russian, this high-fibre, low-fat starter is a refreshing combination of pear and fennel, in an unusual almond and cucumber dressing.

NUTRITIONAL PROFILE	*per portion*	
Total calories		150
Protein	4g	√
Fibre	6g	√√√
Polyunsaturated fats	4g	√√√
Saturated fats	1g	√√√
Vitamins	*Good source of:*	C, E
Minerals	*Good source of:*	–

Illustrated opposite

· ZYLEONE ·

INGREDIENTS

50 g (2 oz) ground almonds
15 ml (1 tbsp) white wine vinegar
75 g (3 oz) cucumber, peeled and roughly chopped
15 ml (1 tbsp) sunflower oil
225 g (8 oz) fennel, diced

225-275 g (8-10 oz) pear, 1 large or 2 small ones
Garnish
15 g (½ oz) toasted flaked almonds
fennel fronds
Serves 4

1 Put the almonds, vinegar and cucumber in a grinder, liquidizer or food processor and blend thoroughly.
2 Add the oil drop by drop as if making mayonnaise. The mixture will thicken slightly.
3 Chop the pear into bite-sized pieces. Mix with the fennel.
4 Stir the pear and fennel into the dressing until well coated.
5 Pile into individual dishes, garnish with toasted almonds and fennel fronds. Serve chilled.

Clockwise from the top: **Paw paw & lime salad with mint** *(see page 67)*; **Middle Eastern stuffed vine leaves; Zyleone**

This is a colourful way to serve leek vinaigrette, with the buttery taste and smooth texture of the leeks contrasting well with the sharp dressing. Thin slices of wholewheat bread, rolled up with cottage or curd cheese, could be served with this starter.

NUTRITIONAL PROFILE	*per portion*	
Total calories		85
Protein	3g	√√
Fibre	5g	√√
Polyunsaturated fats	0.5g	√√
Saturated fats	0.5g	√√√
Vitamins		*Good source of:*
		A, B1, B2, B6, C, E, FA, N
Minerals		*Good source of:*
		Ca, Cu, Fe, Mg, Zn

Illustrated on page 66

· LEEK AND TOMATO ·
TERRINE

INGREDIENTS

550 g (1¼ lb) leeks
15 ml (1 tbsp) olive oil
15 ml (1 tbsp) white wine vinegar
10 ml (2 tsp) concentrated apple juice
2.5 ml (½ tsp) whole grain mustard
1 clove garlic, crushed
gomasio, or salt if preferred

black pepper
225 g (8 oz) tomatoes, skimmed and sliced
2.5 ml (½ tsp) green peppercorns, lightly crushed
For serving
radicchio, lamb's lettuce, endive, whole-wheatbread (see page 31)

Serves 4-6

1 Clean the leeks and chop them in 2.5 cm (1 in) pieces. Steam for 5-8 minutes until soft. Drain well.
2 Mix the olive oil, vinegar, apple juice, mustard and garlic together. Season with gomasio and pepper.
3 Add the dressing to the warm leeks and toss.
4 Put a layer of half the leeks in the base of a lightly oiled 450 g (1 lb) loaf tin. Cover with a layer of tomatoes, sprinkle over the peppercorns, then top with the remaining leeks. Weight the mixture down well. Leave to cool.
5 When cold, turn out on to a bed of salad leaves. Serve in slices accompanied by wholewheat bread.

Also known as Papaya, this tropical fruit contains the digestive enzyme pepain.

NUTRITIONAL PROFILE	per portion	
Total calories		50
Protein	0.5g	√
Fibre	0g	—
Polyunsaturated fats	0g	√ √ √
Saturated fats	0g	√ √ √
Vitamins	Good source of:	
		—
Minerals	Good source of:	
		—

Illustrated on page 65

• PAW PAW & LIME •
SALAD WITH MINT

INGREDIENTS

2 paw paw *Garnish*
1 lime sprig fresh mint
  Serves 4

1 Cut the paw paw in half lengthways and discard the seeds.
2 Squeeze the juice of half the lime over the paw paw flesh. Use the remaining half as garnish, cut into very thin slices, together with the sprig of mint.
3 Arrange the paw paw halves on a bed of Chinese leaves and watercress sprigs.

These delicious savouries provide a high-protein start to a light meal.

NUTRITIONAL PROFILE	per portion	
Total calories		155
Protein	11g	√ √ √
Fibre	1g	√
Polyunsaturated fats	0.5g	√
Saturated fats	6g	√
Vitamins	Good source of:	
	A, B12, E	
Minerals	Good source of:	
		—

Illustrated opposite

• CHEESE DEVILS •

INGREDIENTS

175 g (6 oz) quark   pinch of cayenne
40 g (1½ oz) margarine   black pepper
1 (large) egg   175 g (6 oz) asparagus
5 ml (1 tsp) prepared English mustard   *Serves 4*

1 Cream the quark with the margarine in a bowl until smooth.
2 Beat in the egg and seasonings.
3 Steam the asparagus for 6-8 minutes until just tender. Cut into small pieces.
4 Meanwhile, preheat the oven to gas mark 3, 170°C (325°F).
5 Lightly oil four ramekin dishes and divide the asparagus pieces between them. Pour over the cheese mixture.
6 Bake for 30-40 minutes or until just set. Serve hot.

This refreshing low-fat starter should be served with a high-protein, high-fibre main course.

NUTRITIONAL PROFILE	per portion	
Total calories		150
Protein	2g	√
Fibre	1.5g	√
Polyunsaturated fats	3g	√ √
Saturated fats	1g	√ √ √
Vitamins	Good source of:	
	A, C, FA	
Minerals	Good source of:	
	Ca, Mg	

Illustrated on page 69

• COCKTAIL KEBABS •

INGREDIENTS

6 finger avocados, peeled and chopped   4 kumquats, halved
100 g (4 oz) cucumber, peeled and cut into   *For the dressing*
half-moons   30 ml (2 tbsp) orange juice
½ pink melon, watermelon or section   10 ml (2 tsp) lemon juice
of canteloupe, scooped into balls   15 ml (1 tbsp) sunflower oil
100 g (4 oz) grapes   fresh mint
  Serves 4

1 Place prepared fruit in a bowl. Put the dressing ingredients together in a screw-top jar and mix by shaking well. Pour over fruit and marinate for 2 hours.
2 Thread the cucumber, melon and kumquats alternately on to kebab skewers, ending with the avocado.

Top: **Leek and tomato terrine** *(see page 65)*; Bottom: **Cheese devils**

Tofu is a prime source of protein and in the form of this pâté can be used as a stuffing or served as a dip.

NUTRITIONAL PROFILE	*per portion*	
Total calories		330
Protein	12g	√√
Fibre	4g	√√
Polyunsaturated fats	9g	√√
Saturated fats	6g	√
Vitamins	*Good source of:*	
		A, E
Minerals	*Good source of:*	
		Ca

Illustrated opposite

• GOLDEN TOFU PÂTÉ •

INGREDIENTS

100 g (4 oz) sunflower seeds
275 g (10 oz) silken tofu
15 ml (1 tbsp) olive oil
45 ml (3 tbsp) wheatgerm
100 g (4 oz) carrot, finely grated
2.5 ml (½ tsp) dill weed

2.5 ml (½ tsp) paprika
gomasio, or salt if preferred
black pepper
For serving
4-6 large tomatoes or vegetable crudités
Serves 4-6

1 Grind 50 g (2 oz) sunfl[...] liquidizer or food processo[...]
2 Add the tofu, olive oil a[...] Transfer to a serving dish [...]
3 Stir in the grated carrot [...] paprika and season with g[...]
4 Cut the tops off the tom[...] stuff with the tofu mixtur[...]

Beans make excellent bases for vegetarian pâtés because they are high in protein and fibre but low in fat. They do, however, need to be well flavoured with spices or herbs. I also think the taste improves if the pâté is kept covered in the refrigerator for a few days before serving.

NUTRITIONAL PROFILE	*per portion*	
Total calories		190
Protein	9g	√√√
Fibre	8g	√√√
Polyunsaturated fats	4g	√√√
Saturated fats	1g	√√√
Vitamins	*Good source of:*	
		B1, C, N
Minerals	*Good source of:*	
		Ca, Fe, Mg

Illustrated opposite

• SPICED [...]

100 g (4 oz) Dutch brown bea[...]
medames, soaked over[...]
5 ml (1 tsp) coriand[...]
2.5 ml (½ tsp) cum[...]
5 ml (1 tsp) black musta[...]
30 ml (2 tbsp) sunfl[...]
1 medium onion, finely [...]
1 clove garlic, [...]
1 fresh green chilli, deseeded a[...]
1 cm (½ in) fresh root ginger [...]
and g[...]

1 Drain the beans. Cove[...] uncovered to the boil a[...] the heat, skim, cover and [...] soft. Drain.
2 Dry roast the coriander, [...] pan for about 3-4 minutes, u[...]
3 Add the oil to the pan an[...] minutes until soft. Stir in the chilli, ginger, garam masala and turmeric and cook for 3-4 minutes. Add the cooked beans and stir well.
4 Liquidize the mixture until smooth, adding the tomato purée and lemon juice. Season with gomasio and pepper. Leave overnight for the flavours to blend.
5 To make the banana raita, mix the banana, yogurt and cumin seeds together.
6 Serve with the pâté.

Clockwise from the top: **Cocktail kebabs** *(see page 67)*; **Golden tofu pâté**; **Spiced bean pâté**

BAKED
•SAVOURIES•

A root vegetable bake, covered
with a nutty sauce and sprinkled
with a crunchy topping. This dish is
high in fibre, low in saturated fat.

NUTRITIONAL PROFILE	per portion	
Total calories	380	
Protein	10g	√√
Fibre	8g	√√√
Polyunsaturated fats	7g	√√√
Saturated fats	3g	√√√
Vitamins	Good source of:	
	A, B1, B6, C, E, FA, N	
Minerals	Good source of:	
	Ca, Cu, Mg	

Illustrated opposite

• VEGETABLE BAKE •

INGREDIENTS

For the topping
50 g (2 oz) porridge oats
25 g (1 oz) brown rice flour
50 g (2 oz) cashew nuts, finely chopped
30 ml (2 tbsp) sunflower oil
5 ml (1 tsp) dried rosemary
For the filling
1 kg (2 lb) root vegetables (carrots,
parsnips, swede, turnip)

For the sauce
10 ml (2 tsp) sunflower oil
1 medium onion, finely chopped
25 g (1 oz) cashew nuts
30 ml (2 tbsp) brown rice flour
150 ml (¼ pint) skimmed milk
300 ml (½ pint) vegetable stock
5 ml (1 tsp) dried rosemary
gomasio, or salt if preferred
black pepper
Serves 4

1 For the topping: put the oats, rice flour and cashew nuts into a bowl. Mix in the oil and rosemary with the fingertips to form a light crumble.
2 For the filling: scrub or peel the vegetables and cut into bite-sized pieces. Steam for 10-12 minutes until just tender. Reserve the steaming water for stock.
3 Preheat the oven to gas mark 5, 190°C (375°F).
4 Heat the oil in a large saucepan and gently fry the onion for 4-5 minutes or until soft. Add the cashew nuts and lightly brown for 3-4 minutes.
5 Mix the rice flour to a smooth paste with a little of the milk.
6 Pour the milk and reserved stock into the pan and add the rice flour paste and rosemary. Bring to the boil and simmer until thickened, stirring constantly. Season with gomasio and pepper.
7 Cool slightly, then liquidize the sauce until smooth.
8 Put the steamed vegetables into a lightly oiled ovenproof dish. Pour over the sauce, then cover with the topping. Bake for 30 minutes and serve hot.

Many meatless meals are associated with the fasting period of Lent. The filling of this dish, which is high in most minerals and vitamins, as well as protein and fibre, can be adapted as a sauce for lasagne or a filling for stuffed peppers.

NUTRITIONAL PROFILE	*per portion*	
Total calories		330
Protein	19g	√√√
Fibre	13g	√√√
Polyunsaturated fats	2g	√√
Saturated fats	0.5g	√√√
Vitamins		*Good source of:*
		A, B1, B6, C, FA
Minerals		*Good source of:*
		Ca, Cu, Fe, Mg, Zn

Illustrated above

◆ LENTEN BAKE ◆

INGREDIENTS

225 g (8 oz) red lentils, cleaned
10 ml (2 tsp) sunflower oil
1 medium onion, finely chopped
175 g (6 oz) carrots, chopped
175 g (6 oz) swede, peeled and chopped
300 g (10 oz) cauliflower florets
10 ml (2 tsp) paprika
5 ml (1 tsp) dried thyme
2 bay leaves
15 ml (1 tbsp) miso
30 ml (2 tbsp) tomato purée
300 ml (½ pint) vegetable stock
15 ml (1 tbsp) shoyu
450 g (1 lb) potatoes, peeled
gomasio, or salt if preferred
black pepper
Serves 4

1 Place the lentils in a saucepan with 300 ml (½ pint) water. Bring, uncovered, to the boil, skim, cover and simmer for 10-15 minutes or until just soft. Drain.
2 Heat the oil in a large saucepan and gently fry the onion for 4-5 minutes or until soft.
3 Add the carrot, swede, cauliflower, paprika, thyme and bay leaves. Cook for 10 minutes over a gentle heat, stirring well. Add lentils.
4 Dissolve the miso and tomato purée in the stock, mix in the shoyu and pour over the lentil and vegetable mixture. Cook for 15 minutes.
5 Meanwhile, place the potatoes in a saucepan of water. Cook until tender. Drain and mash. Season with gomasio and pepper.
6 Preheat the oven to gas mark 4, 180°C (350°F).
7 Season the lentil mixture, remove the bay leaves then spoon into a lightly oiled ovenproof dish. Cover with the mashed potato.
8 Bake for 20 minutes. Serve hot.

Buckwheat, with its strong flavour, can be an acquired taste, so try boiling and tasting the grain separately first. For balance, serve this meal with a high-fibre starter or side dish.

NUTRITIONAL PROFILE	*per portion*	
Total calories	220	
Protein	9g	√ √ √
Fibre	2g	√
Polyunsaturated fats	2g	√ √ √
Saturated fats	0.5g	√ √ √
Vitamins	*Good source of:*	
	E	
Minerals	*Good source of:*	
	—	

Illustrated on page 71

· BUCKWHEAT ROAST ·

INGREDIENTS

15 ml (3 tsp) sunflower oil
150 g (5 oz) buckwheat
450 ml (¾ pint) boiling water
1 medium onion, finely chopped
10 ml (2 tsp) paprika
5 ml (1 tsp) ground ginger
5 ml (1 tsp) garam masala
pinch of cayenne

225 g (8 oz) red cabbage, shredded
25 g (1 oz) arame, soaked in warm water
 for 15 minutes
45 ml (3 tbsp) wheatgerm
shoyu, or salt if preferred
black pepper
For serving
Sharp mushroom sauce (see page 146)
Serves 4

1 Brown the buckwheat (see page 46). Pour over the boiling water, bring back to the boil, cover and simmer until tender. Drain.
2 Preheat the oven to gas mark 5, 190°C (375°F).
3 Heat the remaining oil in a large saucepan and gently fry the onion for 4-5 minutes or until just soft. Add the spices and cook for a few minutes.
4 Stir in the red cabbage, drained arame and cooked buckwheat. Cook over a gentle heat for 10 minutes, stirring frequently. Add the wheatgerm and season with shoyu and pepper.
5 Pack the mixture into a lightly oiled 450 g (1 lb) loaf tin. Bake for 45-50 minutes.
6 Cool in the tin for 10 minutes, then turn out. Serve hot with *Sharp mushroom sauce.*

In this dish, which is an excellent source of fibre, iron, calcium and vitamins, it is important to cook the vegetables slowly so that they have a chance to blend well. The seeds add a contrast in texture.

NUTRITIONAL PROFILE	*per portion*	
Total calories	260	
Protein	9g	√ √
Fibre	8g	√ √ √
Polyunsaturated fats	6g	√ √ √
Saturated fats	2g	√ √ √
Vitamins	*Good source of:*	
	A, B6, C, E, FA	
Minerals	*Good source of:*	
	Ca, Fe	

Illustrated opposite

· STUFFED MARROW ·

INGREDIENTS

1 marrow, weighing about 1 kg (2 lb)
10 ml (2 tsp) sunflower oil
350 g (12 oz) leeks, cleaned and finely
 sliced
3 sticks celery, chopped
350 g (12 oz) carrots, chopped
50 g (2 oz) porridge oats
25 g (1 oz) sunflower seeds

25 g (1 oz) pumpkin seeds
15 ml (1 tbsp) tahini
5 ml (1 tsp) miso, dissolved in a little water
gomasio, or salt if preferred
black pepper
For serving
Tomato sauce (see page 44)
Serves 6

1 Cut the marrow in half lengthways. Scoop out and discard the seeds. Take out approximately 450 g (1 lb) flesh and chop finely.
2 Heat the oil in a pan and fry the leeks very gently for 10 minutes.
3 Add the celery, carrot and marrow flesh. Cover and cook for 20 minutes or until the vegetables are soft, stirring frequently.
4 Preheat the oven to gas mark 4, 180°C (350°F).
5 Remove the pan from the heat and add the remaining ingredients. Mix well and season with gomasio and pepper.
6 Fill the marrow halves, cover and bake for 45-55 minutes or until cooked.
7 Serve hot, accompanied by *Tomato sauce.*

Top: **Celebration roast** *(see page 74)*; Bottom: **Stuffed marrow**

Successful nut roasts should be moist. They should include plenty of vegetables otherwise the nut and breadcrumb mix becomes too reminiscent of stuffing. This attractive dish, made with a creamy nut "meat" filled with a contrasting layer of mushrooms and walnuts, provides a near perfect nutritional balance.

NUTRITIONAL PROFILE	*per portion*	
Total calories		775
Protein	41g	√√
Fibre	15g	√√√
Polyunsaturated fats	7g	√√√
Saturated fats	2.5g	√√√
Vitamins		*Good source of:*
B1, B2, B6, B12, C, D, E, FA, N		
Minerals		*Good source of:*
Ca, Cu, Fe, Mg, Zn		

Illustrated on page 73

◆ CELEBRATION ROAST ◆

INGREDIENTS

30 ml (2 tbsp) sunflower oil
1 medium onion, finely chopped
5 sticks celery, finely chopped
15 ml (1 tbsp) wholewheat flour
300 ml (½ pint) white wine or stock
200 g (7 oz) almonds, ground
50 g (2 oz) wholewheat breadcrumbs
50 g (2 oz) porridge oats
1 apple, grated
2 eggs

juice of ½ lemon
gomasio, or salt if preferred
black pepper
Dark filling
10 ml (2 tsp) sunflower oil
1 medium onion, finely chopped
350 g (12 oz) mushrooms, diced
1 clove garlic, crushed
150 g (5 oz) walnuts, chopped
Serves 6-8

1 Heat the oil in a large saucepan and gently fry the onion for 4-5 minutes or until soft. Add the celery and fry for 5 minutes.
2 Sprinkle over the flour. Cook for 1-2 minutes, stirring, then pour over the wine or stock. Cook and stir for 1-2 minutes.
3 Mix the almonds, breadcrumbs, oats, grated apple and eggs together in a large bowl. Add the sauce and lemon juice. Season.
4 Preheat the oven to gas mark 5, 190°C (375°F).
5 For the filling: heat the oil in a saucepan and gently fry the onion until soft. Add other ingredients and cook for 10 minutes, stirring.
6 Lightly oil and line a 1 litre (2-2½ pint) savarin or ring mould with greaseproof paper. Spoon in a third of the creamy nut mixture, add the dark filling, the cover with remaining nut mixture.
7 Bake for 50-55 minutes. Cool in the tin for 10 minutes.

These attractive parcels are an excellent source of fibre and iron. Serve with Tomato and apricot relish (see page 145).

NUTRITIONAL PROFILE	*per portion*	
Total calories		270
Protein	9 g	✓✓
Fibre	10 g	✓✓✓
Polyunsaturated fats	4 g	✓✓✓
Saturated fats	2 g	✓✓✓
Vitamins	*Good source of:*	
	A, B6, C, E, FA	
Minerals	*Good source of:*	
	Ca, Fe, Mg, Zn	

Illustrated opposite

· LEAFY GREEN ·
PARCELS

INGREDIENTS

8 large spinach leaves
8 spring cabbage leaves
For the filling
225 g (8 oz) spinach, washed
10 ml (2 tsp) sunflower oil
1 medium onion, finely chopped
175 g (6 oz) hazelnuts, ground

50 g (2 oz) wholewheat breadcrumbs
30 ml (2 tbsp) finely chopped fresh coriander leaves
30 ml (2 tbsp) finely chopped fresh parsley
1 egg
15 ml (1 tbsp) shoyu
black pepper
Serves 4

1 Wash then blanch the spinach and cabbage leaves for 2 minutes in a little boiling water. Drain.
2 For the filling: shred the spinach. Place in a saucepan, cover and cook, with only the water still adhering to the leaves, for 6 minutes.
3 Heat the oil in a saucepan and gently fry the onion for 4-5 minutes or until soft. Add the hazelnuts and breadcrumbs and cook for 2 minutes.
4 Remove from the heat, add the herbs, cooked spinach, egg and shoyu. Season with pepper.
5 Preheat the oven to gas mark 4, 180°C (350°F).
6 Take one cabbage and one spinach leaf. Place 30-45 ml (2-3 tbsp) of the filling on each. Fold in the sides to the centre and roll up into a parcel. Continue using cabbage and spinach leaves alternately.
7 Place in a lightly oiled ovenproof dish. Add 30-45 ml (2-3 tbsp) water. Cover and bake for 30 minutes.

Only a small amount of pine nuts is needed to flavour this high-fibre, low-fat dish.

NUTRITIONAL PROFILE	*per portion*	
Total calories		425
Protein	10 g	✓✓
Fibre	7 g	✓✓✓
Polyunsaturated fats	7 g	✓✓✓
Saturated fats	3 g	✓✓✓
Vitamins	*Good source of:*	
	C, E, N	
Minerals	*Good source of:*	
	Fe, Mg	

Illustrated opposite

· PINE KERNEL ROAST ·

INGREDIENTS

175 g (6 oz) long-grain brown rice
10 ml (2 tsp) olive oil
1 medium onion, finely chopped
175 g (6 oz) courgettes, sliced
1 small aubergine, diced
75 g (3 oz) pine kernels
225 g (8 oz) tomatoes, skinned and chopped

75 g (3 oz) mixed nuts (cashews and almonds), ground
10 ml (2 tsp) ground cinnamon
6 cloves or 1.25 ml (¼ tsp) ground cloves
gomasio, or salt if preferred
black pepper
Serves 4

1 Weigh out rice and cook according to instructions, page 46.
2 Preheat the oven to gas mark 4, 180°C (350°F).
3 Heat the oil in a large saucepan and gently fry the onion for 4-5 minutes or until soft. Add the courgettes, aubergine and pine kernels and cook for 10 minutes.
4 Remove from the heat and mix in the remaining ingredients and cooked rice. Season with gomasio and pepper.
5 Put the mixture in a lightly oiled 450 g (1 lb) loaf tin, pressing it down firmly. Bake for 50 minutes.

Left: **Pine kernel roast**; **Leafy green parcels**

This healthy, highly nutritious version of the ever-popular fast-food dish is an excellent choice for children's meals. Aduki beans are particularly well suited for burgers, as both their colour and texture are good.

NUTRITIONAL PROFILE	*per portion*	
Total calories	530	
Protein	25g	√√√
Fibre	20g	√√√
Polyunsaturated fats	12g	√√√
Saturated fats	3g	√√√
Vitamins	*Good source of:*	
	A, B6, C, E, FA	
Minerals	*Good source of:*	
	Cu, Fe, Mg, Zn	

Illustrated opposite

· BEAN BURGERS ·

INGREDIENTS

225 g (8 oz) aduki beans, soaked overnight
10 ml (2 tsp) sunflower oil
1 medium onion, finely chopped
2 medium carrots, grated
100 g (4 oz) hazelnuts and walnuts, ground
100 g (4 oz) porridge oats
30 ml (2 tbsp) shoyu

30 ml (2 tbsp) tomato purée
1 egg, beaten
5 ml (1 tsp) dried thyme
cayenne pepper
To coat
1 egg white, beaten
100 g (4 oz) porridge oats
Serves 4-6

1 Drain the beans. Cover with plenty of fresh water, bring uncovered to the boil and boil fast for 10 minutes. Reduce the heat, skim, cover and simmer for 30-40 minutes or until soft. Drain and purée.
2 Preheat the oven to gas mark 4, 180°C (350°F).
3 Heat the oil in a saucepan and gently fry the onion for 4-5 minutes or until soft. Add the carrot and nuts and cook for 2-3 minutes.
4 Remove from the heat, mix in the beans and remaining ingredients.
5 Shape into 8-12 burgers. Dip into egg, coat with oats.
6 Place on a lightly oiled baking sheet and bake for 10 minutes, turn them over and bake for another 10 minutes. Serve hot.

The bean filling provides the major sauce of protein and fibre in this dish, which is complemented by a tomato and avocado sauce. For a lower fat content, omit the mozzarella topping.

NUTRITIONAL PROFILE	*per portion*	
Total calories	225	
Protein	11g	√√√
Fibre	10g	√√√
Polyunsaturated fats	1g	√√
Saturated fats	3g	√√
Vitamins	*Good source of:*	
	A, B1, B6, C, E, FA	
Minerals	*Good source of:*	
	Ca, Fe, Mg, Zn	

Illustrated opposite

· STUFFED TOMATOES ·

INGREDIENTS

100 g (4 oz) flageolet or cannellini beans, soaked overnight
10 ml (2 tsp) olive oil
3 spring onions, very finely chopped
2 cloves garlic, crushed
225 g (8 oz) tomatoes, skinned and chopped
30 ml (2 tbsp) tomato purée
12 stuffed green olives, sliced

10 ml (2 tsp) dried oregano
30 ml (2 tbsp) dried chervil
5 ml (1 tsp) miso, dissolved in a little water
½ avocado, peeled, stoned and cubed
black pepper
4 large tomatoes
50 g (2 oz) mozzarella cheese (optional)
Serves 4

1 Drain the beans. Cover with plenty of fresh water, bring, uncovered, to the boil and boil fast for 10 minutes. Reduce the heat, skim, cover and simmer for 20-25 minutes or until soft. Drain.
2 Heat the oil in a large saucepan and gently fry the spring onions and garlic for 2-3 minutes.
3 Add the tomatoes, purée, olives, oregano, chervil and miso. Cover and cook for 25 minutes.
4 Stir in the cooked beans and avocado. Season with pepper.
5 Preheat the oven to gas mark 4, 180°C (350°F).
6 To prepare the tomatoes, slice off the base and scoop out the seeds and flesh. Season the tomato shells with pepper.
7 Fill the tomato shells with the mixture. Cover with slices of mozzarella, or simply replace the tomato "lids".
8 Place in an ovenproof dish with 30-45 ml (2-3 tbsp) bean stock or water. Cover and bake for 30-35 minutes.

Top: **Stuffed tomatoes; Bean burgers**

This dish is an adaptation of the South African spiced fruit casserole. It is perfect for tofu, which absorbs the flavouring and colouring of the vegetables and spices, while providing a good source of low-fat, low-calorie protein.

NUTRITIONAL PROFILE	*per portion*	
Total calories		265
Protein	16g	√ √ √
Fibre	6g	√ √ √
Polyunsaturated fats	3g	√ √ √
Saturated fats	2g	√ √ √
Vitamins		*Good source of:*
		A, B1, B2, B6, C, E, FA
Minerals		*Good source of:*
		Ca, Cu, Fe, Mg, Zn

Illustrated below

· TOFU BOBOTIE ·

INGREDIENTS

10 ml (2 tsp) peanut oil
1 medium onion, finely chopped
450 g (1 lb) firm tofu, cut in chunks
5 ml (1 tsp) ground allspice
5 ml (1 tsp) ground cumin
2.5 ml (½ tsp) ground ginger
2.5 ml (½ tsp) turmeric
pinch of cayenne
6 curry leaves
450 g (1 lb) tomatoes, skinned and chopped
1 medium red pepper, deseeded and cut into strips
1 medium green pepper, deseeded and cut into strips
1 large aubergine, chopped
100 g (4 oz) sultanas
shoyu, or salt if preferred
black pepper
For the topping
2.5 ml (½ tsp) cumin seeds
300 ml (½ pint) yogurt
1 egg
juice of ½ lemon
Serves 4

1 Heat the oil in a saucepan and gently fry the onion for 4-5 minutes or until soft. Add the tofu and spices and fry for 5 minutes.
2 Stir in the remaining ingredients, cover and cook for 30 minutes. Season with shoyu and pepper.
3 Preheat the oven to gas mark 4, 180°C (350°F).
4 Spoon the mixture into a lightly oiled ovenproof dish.
5 Dry roast the cumin seeds in a heavy-based pan (see page 46) for 3-4 minutes or until lightly browned. Mix the topping ingredients together and pour over the bobotie.
6 Bake for 30 minutes. Serve hot.

· CASSEROLES ·

Always be careful when adding barley to a casserole or soup as a little goes a long way. It is a chewy grain which absorbs flavours well and therefore benefits from standing overnight. Serve with a cooked, dried pulse, or fresh green peas or mange tout, and a low-fat pudding for a balanced meal.

NUTRITIONAL PROFILE	*per portion*	
Total calories	230	
Protein	9g	✓ ✓ ✓
Fibre	11g	✓ ✓ ✓
Polyunsaturated fats	2g	✓ ✓ ✓
Saturated fats	0.5g	✓ ✓
Vitamins	*Good source of:*	
	A, B1, B2, B6, C, E, FA, N	
Minerals	*Good source of:*	
	Ca, Cu, Fe, Zn	

Illustrated on page 81

BARLEY
· BOURGIGNON ·

INGREDIENTS

100 g (4 oz) pot barley
10 ml (2 tsp) sunflower oil
175 g (6 oz) leeks, finely chopped
350 g (12 oz) button mushrooms, quartered
225 g (8 oz) parsnips, chopped
5 ml (1 tsp) dried thyme
5 ml (1 tsp) dried sage
1 bay leaf
150 ml (¼ pint) red wine
450 g (1 lb) tomatoes, skinned and chopped
30 ml (2 tbsp) tomato purée
shoyu, or salt if preferred
black pepper
225 g (8 oz) broccoli florets
Serves 4

1 Dry roast the barley for 2-3 minutes in a heavy-based pan. Add enough boiling water to cover by 2.5 cm (1 in) and cook for 40-45 minutes. Drain, reserving the cooking liquid.
2 Heat the oil in a large saucepan and gently fry the leeks for about 5 minutes until soft.
3 Add the mushrooms, parsnip, herbs and cooked barley. Stir in well and cook for 2-3 minutes.
4 Add the wine, tomatoes, purée and up to 150 ml (¼ pint) reserved stock. Bring to the boil, cover and cook gently for 35 minutes. Add a little reserved stock if the mixture begins to look dry. Season with shoyu and pepper.
5 Add the broccoli florets and cook for a further 8-10 minutes or until tender. Remove the bay leaf.

Illustrated opposite: **Tofu bobotie**

The seasonings of caraway and mustard complement the flavours of the Chinese leaves and celery well, and the smetana provides the traditional creaminess of this dish without all the fat.

NUTRITIONAL PROFILE	*per portion*	
Total calories	430	
Protein	21g	√√√
Fibre	7g	√√√
Polyunsaturated fats	10g	√√√
Saturated fats	6g	√√
Vitamins	*Good source of:*	
	A, B1, B2, B6, C, E, FA, N	
Minerals	*Good source of:*	
	Ca, Cu, Fe, Mg, Zn	

Illustrated opposite

PEANUT
· STROGANOV ·

INGREDIENTS

10 ml (2 tsp) sunflower oil
1 medium onion, finely chopped
350 g (12 oz) Chinese leaves, shredded
6 sticks celery, finely chopped
350 g (12 oz) button mushrooms
225 g (8 oz) roasted unsalted peanuts
2.5 ml (½ tsp) caraway seeds

5 ml (1 tsp) German mustard
150 ml (¼ pint) red wine
shoyu, or salt if preferred
black pepper
150 ml (¼ pint) smetana
For serving
wholewheat noodles
Serves 4

1 Heat the oil in a saucepan and gently fry the onion for 4-5 minutes or until soft.
2 Add the Chinese leaves, celery, mushrooms and peanuts and cook for 5 minutes, stirring frequently. Stir in the caraway seeds, mustard and red wine.
3 Cover and cook for 10 minutes.
4 Remove from the heat and season with shoyu and pepper. Cool slightly, then stir in the smetana. Serve immediately with boiled wholewheat noodles.

A quickly made, colourful vegetable stew inspired by Romanian cuisine. Extra protein and flavour are provided by the inclusion of corn and walnuts.

NUTRITIONAL PROFILE	*per portion*	
Total calories	315	
Protein	9g	√√
Fibre	8g	√√√
Polyunsaturated fats	12g	√√√
Saturated fats	2g	√√√
Vitamins	*Good source of:*	
	B1, B6, C, E, FA	
Minerals	*Good source of:*	
	Fe, Mg, Zn	

Illustrated opposite

· GHIUVETCH ·

INGREDIENTS

10 ml (2 tsp) sunflower oil
1 medium onion, finely chopped
4 sticks celery, diagonally sliced
15 ml (3 tsp) grated horseradish
15 ml (1 tbsp) paprika
450 g (1 lb) frozen sweetcorn kernels
100 g (4 oz) walnuts, roughly chopped
30 ml (2 tbsp) finely chopped fresh parsley
5 ml (1 tsp) dill weed

150 ml (¼ pint) vegetable stock
225 g (8 oz) red cabbage, shredded
shoyu, or salt if preferred
black pepper
Garnish
smetana or yogurt (optional)
For serving
Baked potatoes or Potatoes Florentine
  (see pages 138)
Serves 4-6

1 Heat the oil in a large saucepan and gently fry the onion for 4-5 minutes or until soft.
2 Add the celery, horseradish and paprika and cook for 2-3 minutes.
3 Stir in the sweetcorn, walnuts, herbs and stock. Cover and simmer for 10 minutes.
4 Add the red cabbage and cook for a further 10-15 minutes. Season with shoyu and pepper.
5 Serve hot, accompanied by *Baked potatoes* or *Potatoes Florentine*. Garnish with smetana or yogurt.

Clockwise from the top: **Ghiuvetch**; **Barley bourgignon** *(see page 79)*; **Peanut stroganov**

• BALANCED MEAL 2 •

This meal, with its creamy soup, moist main course and aubergine side dish, gives the impression of being rich but it is in fact low in saturated fats. The *Lentil pourgouri* and *Sweet red pepper soup* are the major sources of protein, with mangetout being served to improve the overall balance of fibre.

• **Sweet red pepper soup**
For recipe, see page 54

A rich soup, deriving its creaminess from high-protein, low-fat tofu.

• **Red & white salad**
For recipe, see page 160

A light way to end a substantial meal, this salad contrasts the smoothness of the lychees with the granular bite of the strawberries.

NUTRITIONAL PROFILE	*per portion*	
Total calories		620
Protein	27g	√ √ √
Fibre	24g	√ √ √
Polyunsaturated fats	5g	√ √ √
Saturated fats	3g	√ √ √
Vitamins		*Good source of:*
		C, FA, B1
Minerals		*Good source of:*
		Fe, Ca

◆ Wine

Healthy living need not preclude alcohol in moderation, and many white wines such as hock and Riesling have a low alcohol content—look for those around 9° to 10° proof. Remember, a glass of wine will add 75 calories to the meal.

◆ Lentil pourgouri
For recipe, see page 117

This simple, fragrant-tasting Middle Eastern dish is a combination of bulgar wheat, lentils and courgettes. It is served with yogurt which adds moisture to the dish.

◆ Aubergine bake
For recipe, see page 141

This dish is low in saturated fats, largely because the aubergine is baked and not fried. The dwarf sweetcorn provides an appealing, crunchy texture. The moistness of the dish ensures that the intrinsic dryness of the bulgar wheat doesn't overpower the whole meal.

◆ Steamed mangetout

These sweet-tasting pea pods should be so tender when raw that they need only the briefest steaming before serving.

High in protein because of the beans, this rich, dark casserole with its tangy sauce contains whole tiny vegetables for a contrast in texture.

NUTRITIONAL PROFILE	*per portion*
Total calories	210
Protein	14g ✓✓✓
Fibre	18g ✓✓✓
Polyunsaturated fats	2g ✓✓
Saturated fats	0.5g ✓✓✓
Vitamins	*Good source of:*
	A, B1, B6, C, E, FA
Minerals	*Good source of:*
	Ca, Fe

Illustrated opposite

◆ GEORGIA CASSEROLE ◆

INGREDIENTS

175 g (6 oz) black kidney beans, soaked overnight
10 ml (2 tsp) sunflower oil
225 g (8 oz) pickling onions or shallots, peeled
2.5 ml (½ tsp) ground allspice
2.5 ml (½ tsp) ground cinnamon
2.5 ml (½ tsp) dried thyme
100 g (4 oz) button mushrooms
100 g (4 oz) prunes
225 g (8 oz) tomatoes, skinned and chopped
150 ml (¼ pint) tomato juice
juice and rind of 1 orange
15 ml (1 tbsp) red wine vinegar
shoyu, or salt if preferred
black pepper
For serving
buckwheat or brown rice
Serves 4

1 Drain the beans. Cover with plenty of fresh water, bring to the boil and boil fast, uncovered, for 10 minutes. Reduce the heat, skim, cover and simmer for 35-40 minutes or until soft. Drain.

2 Heat the oil in a large saucepan and gently fry the onions for 4-5 minutes or until just brown. Add the spices and thyme and cook for 2-3 minutes.

3 Stir in the remaining ingredients, including the beans, cover, and cook for 40 minutes. Season with shoyu and pepper. Serve with boiled buckwheat or brown rice.

The red beans used here provide most of the protein and fibre in this tasty stew.

NUTRITIONAL PROFILE	*per portion*
Total calories	205
Protein	13g ✓✓✓
Fibre	14g ✓✓✓
Polyunsaturated fats	1g ✓✓
Saturated fats	0.5g ✓✓✓
Vitamins	*Good source of:*
	B1, B2, B6, C, FA, N
Minerals	*Good source of:*
	Ca, Cu, Fe, Mg, Zn

Illustrated opposite

SPICY ◆ BEAN GOULASH ◆

INGREDIENTS

175 g (6 oz) red kidney beans, soaked overnight
1 medium onion, finely chopped
15 ml (1 tbsp) olive oil
1 clove garlic, crushed
1 small red chilli, finely chopped
3 large red peppers, chopped
225 g (8 oz) mushrooms, chopped
1 medium potato, diced
10-15 ml (2-3 tsp) paprika
5 ml (1 tsp) thyme
30 ml (2 tbsp) tomato purée
5 ml (1 tsp) miso, dissolved in a little water
gomasio, or salt if preferred
black pepper
Serves 4

1 Drain the beans, cover with plenty of fresh water, bring uncovered to the boil and boil fast for 10 minutes. Reduce the heat, cover and simmer for 40 minutes or until soft. Drain, reserving the stock.

2 Heat the oil in a large saucepan and gently fry the onion in the oil for 4-5 minutes or until soft.

3 Add the garlic, chilli, peppers and mushrooms and cook for 5 minutes. Cover and cook for 15-20 minutes over a very gentle heat.

4 Add the cooked beans, potato, paprika, thyme, tomato purée and miso.

5 Simmer gently for 30 minutes, adding a little bean stock if necessary. Season with gomasio and pepper and serve hot with brown rice or wholewheat noodles.

A far cry from plain baked beans, the protein-and-fibre-rich haricot beans used here are served in a deliciously spicy mixture. Serve with a crisp green salad for a contrast in taste and texture.

NUTRITIONAL PROFILE	*per portion*	
Total calories		220
Protein	17g	√ √ √
Fibre	16g	√ √ √
Polyunsaturated fats	2g	√ √ √
Saturated fats	0.5g	√ √ √
Vitamins	*Good source of:*	
	B1, B6, C, E	
Minerals	*Good source of:*	
	Ca, Cu, Fe, Mg, Zn	

Illustrated on page 85

CHILLI
⋅ BAKED BEANS ⋅

INGREDIENTS

225 g (8 oz) haricot beans, soaked overnight
15 ml (3 tsp) sunflower oil
1 dried red chilli
2 medium onions, sliced into rings
3 cloves garlic
10 ml (2 tsp) dried oregano
5 ml (1 tsp) ground cumin
1 small green chilli, deseeded and very finely chopped
pinch of cayenne, or to taste

1 cm (½ in) fresh root ginger, grated
225 g (8 oz) tomatoes, skinned and chopped
30 ml (2 tbsp) tomato purée
10 ml (2 tsp) molasses
juice of ½ lemon
shoyu, or salt if preferred
black pepper
For serving
rye or wholewheat bread (see page 31)
Serves 4-6

1 Drain the beans. Cover with plenty of fresh water, bring uncovered to the boil and boil fast for 10 minutes. Reduce the heat, cover and simmer for a further 20-25 minutes or until soft. Drain, reserving the cooking liquid.
2 Heat the oil in a large saucepan and fry the red chilli for 2-3 minutes. Remove from the pan. ▶

Pisto Andalucia; Boiled brown rice *(see page 46)*

3 Add the onion and garlic to the pan and cook for 2-3 minutes. Stir in the cooked beans, oregano, cumin, green chilli, cayenne and ginger. Cook for 2-3 minutes.

4 Add the tomatoes, purée and molasses, cover and cook for 40-45 minutes, adding a little bean stock if the mixture begins to look dry. Flavour with the lemon juice and season with shoyu and pepper.

5 Serve on rye or wholewheat bread.

Spain, renowned for its Rioja wine, sherry and olives, provides the inspiration for this high-fibre, low-fat stew. Red, green or yellow peppers, broad beans, button mushrooms and young marrows could all be added for variation.

NUTRITIONAL PROFILE	*per portion*	
Total calories		140
Protein	4g	√√
Fibre	6g	√√√
Polyunsaturated fats	0.5g	√√
Saturated fats	1g	√√√
Vitamins	*Good source of:*	
	A, C, E, FA	
Minerals	*Good source of:*	
	Fe, Mg	

Illustrated opposite

PISTO
·ANDALUCIA·

INGREDIENTS

10 ml (2 tsp) olive oil
1 medium onion, finely chopped
2 cloves garlic, crushed
225 g (8 oz) courgettes, sliced
1 medium aubergine, diced
225 g (8 oz) green beans, chopped in half
1 fresh red chilli, deseeded and very finely chopped
450 g (1 lb) tomatoes, skinned and chopped
30 ml (2 tbsp) tomato purée

1 dessert apple, sliced into sections
2.5 ml (½ tsp) ground cinnamon
150 ml (¼ pint) red wine
30 ml (2 tbsp) dry sherry
75 g (3 oz) black olives, stoned
miso, or salt if preferred
black pepper
For serving
wholewheat noodles or brown rice
Serves 4

1 Heat the oil in a saucepan and gently fry the onion and garlic for 4-5 minutes or until the onion is soft.

2 Add the courgettes, aubergine, beans and chilli and cook for 10 minutes, stirring frequently.

3 Add the remaining ingredients, cover and simmer for 35-45 minutes. Season with miso and pepper. Serve with boiled wholewheat noodles or brown rice.

High in protein and fibre and low in fat, the creamy bean sauce of this dish is enhanced with the aromatic spices.

NUTRITIONAL PROFILE	*per portion*	
Total calories		325
Protein	21g	√√√
Fibre	6g	√√√
Polyunsaturated fats	4g	√√√
Saturated fats	1g	√√√
Vitamins	*Good source of:*	
	A, B1, B2, C, E, FA, N	
Minerals	*Good source of:*	
	Ca, Fe, Mg	

Illustrated on page 89

·SPINACH & BLACK-EYE·
BEAN FRICASSÉ

INGREDIENTS

225 g (8 oz) black-eye beans, soaked overnight
30 ml (2 tbsp) sunflower oil
1 medium onion, finely chopped
2 sticks celery, trimmed and finely chopped
15 ml (1 tbsp) wholewheat flour
300 ml (½ pint) skimmed milk
2.5 ml (½ tsp) grated nutmeg

12 juniper berries, crushed
1 bay leaf
350 g (12 oz) leaf spinach, washed and shredded
gomasio, or salt if preferred
black pepper
For serving
millet or wheat
Serves 4

1 Drain the beans. Cover with plenty of fresh water. Bring, uncovered, to the boil and boil fast for 10 minutes. Reduce the heat, skim, cover and simmer for 20-25 minutes or until soft. Drain. ▶

2 Heat the oil in a saucepan and gently fry the onion and celery for 6-8 minutes or until soft. Add the flour and cook for 3 minutes, stirring.
3 Stir in the milk, spices and bay leaf. Bring the sauce slowly to the boil, stirring constantly.
4 Add the cooked beans and simmer for 10 minutes.
5 Heat a large heavy-based pan. When hot, add handfuls of shredded spinach, stir briskly for about 2 minutes until limp.
6 When all the spinach is cooked, mix into the bean sauce. Season with gomasio and pepper. Remove the bay leaf. Serve with boiled millet or wheat.

Tofu, with its high protein content, provides a smooth contrast in texture to the crisply stir-fried vegetables. Serve with a salad like Avocado and tomato (see page 124) to enhance the overall vitamin content of the meal.

NUTRITIONAL PROFILE	*per portion*	
Total calories	260	
Protein	11g	√√√
Fibre	4g	√√
Polyunsaturated fats	3g	√√√
Saturated fats	1g	√√√
Vitamins	*Good source of:*	
	C, FA	
Minerals	*Good source of:*	
	Ca, Cu, Fe, Mg	

Illustrated opposite

• MARINATED TOFU •
WITH CRISP GREEN STIR-FRY

INGREDIENTS

350 g (12 oz) firm tofu, cut in slices
For the marinade
5 ml (1 tsp) sesame oil
2.5 ml (½ tsp) crushed fennel seeds
2.5 ml (½ tsp) crushed cloves
1 cm (½ in) fresh root ginger, finely chopped
10 ml (2 tsp) shoyu
15 ml (1 tbsp) tomato purée
30 ml (2 tbsp) concentrated apple juice
10 ml (2 tsp) arrowroot

10 ml (2 tsp) red wine vinegar
300 ml (½ pint) water
For the stir-fry
10 ml (2 tsp) sesame oil
3 spring onions, diced
4 sticks celery, chopped
225 g (8 oz) French beans, sliced
225 g (8 oz) courgettes, sliced
For serving
brown rice or millet
Serves 4

1 For the marinade: heat the oil in a saucepan and lightly roast the spices for 2-3 minutes. Add the remaining marinade ingredients and whisk together.
2 Gradually bring to the boil and stir until the sauce thickens and clears.
3 Add the slices of tofu and simmer for 20-25 minutes.
4 For the stir-fry: heat the oil in a wok or large frying pan. When hot, stir-fry the spring onions, celery, beans and courgettes for 2-3 minutes over a high heat, stirring constantly. Add a little of the marinade at the end of cooking to create some steam to soften the vegetables.
5 Place the vegetables on a bed of boiled brown rice or millet, pour over the tofu and sauce.

Top: **Marinated tofu with crisp green stir-fry**; Bottom: **Spinach and black-eye bean fricassé** *(see page 87)*

◆ BALANCED MEAL 3 ◆

This substantial meal provides an excellent source of both protein and fibre, while maintaining a low-fat profile. The relatively low protein levels of the strudel and salads are balanced out by the meal as a whole, which, apart from the nutritional element, is a happy blend of colour, texture and taste.

◆ **Crunchy green salad**
For recipe, see page 128

Despite a creamy mayonnaise dressing, this salad remains low in saturated fats. This is largely because yogurt and fruit juice have been used instead of oil. Chinese leaves were used to make up this salad, but white cabbage could have been chosen to provide an even crisper texture.

◆ **Fennel risotto**
For recipe, see page 116

High in fibre and low in fat, this tangy-tasting rice dish has all the creaminess of a classic risotto. The walnuts add a pleasing crunchiness to the overall texture of the dish.

90

NUTRITIONAL PROFILE		per portion
Total calories		1175
Protein	36g	✓✓✓
Fibre	27g	✓✓✓
Polyunsaturated fats	17g	✓✓✓
Saturated fats	7g	✓✓✓
Vitamins		Good source of:
		A, B1, B6, C, E, FA, N
Minerals		Good source of:
		Ca, Cu, Fe, Mg, Zn

◆ Spiced bean pâté and banana raita
For recipe, see page 68

Beans make excellent bases for vegetarian pâtés because they are high in protein and fibre but low in fat. The bean pâté shown here was well flavoured with coriander and cumin, and made slightly hot with the addition of ginger and chilli. The spiciness is complemented by a cooling raita, and the whole dish is served with a crisp crudité of yellow peppers, cucumber and celery.

◆ Fruit juice

Avoid artificially flavoured drinks and those with added preservatives. Choose fresh fruit juice or water instead. (A glass of orange juice contains about 65 calories.) For a long, refreshing drink add sparkling water to the juice.

◆ Radicchio salad
For recipe, see page 128

In a meal that already has ample sources of protein and fibre, this salad is used to provide additional variety of texture and colour. Radicchio was used here, but Chinese leaves or lamb's lettuce could have been used instead.

◆ Apple strudel
For recipe, see page 162

This light fruit pudding, based on the classic European pastry, is high in fibre and, for pastry, low in fat, especially when served with yogurt or smetana instead of cream.

PIES & FLANS

The light vegetable filling of this pie works well with the yeasted pastry to produce an ideal dish for a summer lunch or supper. It is notably high in protein, vitamins and minerals.

NUTRITIONAL PROFILE	per portion	
Total calories	430	
Protein	18g	√√√
Fibre	5g	√√
Polyunsaturated fats	5g	√√√
Saturated fats	6g	√√
Vitamins	Good source of:	
A, B1, B2, B6, B12, C, D, E, FA		
Minerals	Good source of:	
Ca, Cu, Fe, Mg, Zn		

Illustrated opposite

• SUMMER PIE •

INGREDIENTS

225 g (8 oz) new potatoes, scrubbed
175 g (6 oz) French beans, cut into 2.5 cm (1 in) lengths
225 g (8 oz) spinach, washed and shredded
30 ml (2 tbsp) sunflower oil
4 spring onions
15 ml (1 tbsp) wholewheat flour
300 ml (½ pint) skimmed milk
30 ml (2 tbsp) finely chopped fresh parsley
grated nutmeg
gomasio, or salt if preferred
black pepper
1 quantity of yeasted pastry (see page 40)
beaten egg for glazing
Serves 4

1 Boil the potatoes in a large saucepan of water for 20 minutes or until just tender. Drain and chop into bite-sized pieces.
2 Heat a heavy-based pan. Add the beans and spinach, cover and dry-fry for 6 minutes until barely cooked (the water remaining on the spinach will be enough to steam the beans lightly).
3 Heat the oil in a separate large saucepan and gently fry the spring onions for 3 minutes.
4 Sprinkle over the flour and cook for 2-3 minutes, stirring. Add the milk, stirring constantly. Bring the sauce to the boil and simmer for 5-7 minutes, stirring.
5 Add the potatoes, beans, spinach and parsley and season with nutmeg, gomasio and pepper.
6 Divide the pastry in two. Roll out one half and line a lightly oiled 18 x 18 cm (7 x 7 in) square tin. Fill with the vegetable sauce. Moisten the pastry edges. Roll out the remaining pastry to make the top. Seal and crimp the pastry edges. Prick well.
7 Preheat the oven to gas mark 6, 200°C (400°F).
8 Leave the pie to stand for 10 minutes, then brush with beaten egg to glaze. Bake for 20-25 minutes.

Illustrated opposite: **Summer pie**

Although this recipe is specifically designed to show you how best to use okara—a by-product of tofu-making (see page 36)—it could also be made with equivalent amounts of millet flakes, buckwheat or brown rice. Serve in combination with high-protein, low-fat dishes.

NUTRITIONAL PROFILE	*per portion*	
Total calories	360	
Protein	6g	√
Fibre	8g	√ √ √
Polyunsaturated fats	3g	√ √ √
Saturated fats	8g	√
Vitamins	*Good source of:*	
	A, B1, C, D, E	
Minerals	*Good source of:*	
	Cu, Fe, Mg, Zn	

Illustrated below

◆ OKARA PIE ◆

INGREDIENTS

10 ml (2 tsp) sunflower oil
1 medium onion, finely chopped
1 clove garlic, crushed
2 sticks celery, chopped
100 g (4 oz) carrot, sliced
30 ml (2 tbsp) tomato purée
15 ml (1 tbsp) miso
150 ml (¼ pint) vegetable stock or water
5 ml (1 tsp) dried sage

5 ml (1 tsp) dried thyme
175 g (6 oz) okara
225 g (8 oz) potatoes, boiled and chopped
225 g (8 oz) Brussels sprouts, quartered
shoyu, or salt if preferred
black pepper
hot water crust pastry (see page 42)
beaten egg for glazing (optional)
Serves 6

1 Heat the oil in a saucepan and gently fry the onion and garlic for 4-5 minutes. Add the celery and carrot and cook for 5 minutes.
2 Dissolve the tomato purée and miso in the stock, and add the herbs.
3 Mix the okara, potatoes, sprouts and stock mixture into the pan. Cook gently for 15 minutes. Season with shoyu and pepper.
4 Preheat the oven to gas mark 7, 220°C (425°F).
5 Use two-thirds of the dough to line the base and sides of a 18 cm (7 in) spring mould. Pack in the okara filling.
6 Roll out the remaining dough to make the lid. Seal and crimp the edges. Brush with beaten egg and prick well.
7 Bake for 20 minutes, then reduce the oven temperature to gas mark 5, 190°C (375°F) and bake for 35-40 minutes. Serve hot.

The combination of low-fat, high-fibre pastry and high-protein tofu, plus vegetables rich in vitamins and minerals, makes this an ideal dish for ensuring a balanced meal. Vary the vegetables you use according to season, but make sure you get a good mixture of colour, texture and flavour.

NUTRITIONAL PROFILE	*per portion*			
Total calories	225			
Protein	13g	√	√	√
Fibre	6g	√	√	√
Polyunsaturated fats	5g	√	√	√
Saturated fats	1g	√	√	√
Vitamins	*Good source of:*			
	A, B1, B2, C, E			
Minerals	*Good source of:*			
	Ca, Cu, Fe, Mg, Zn			

Illustrated opposite

• TOFU FLAN •

INGREDIENTS

1 quantity of low-fat or shortcrust pastry (see page 39)
10 ml (2 tsp) sunflower oil
1 medium onion, finely chopped
100 g (4 oz) button mushrooms, sliced
100 g (4 oz) carrots, sliced
100 g (4 oz) spring greens, shredded
100 g (4 oz) broccoli florets
2.5 ml (½ tsp) caraway seeds
5 ml (1 tsp) dried basil
2.5 ml (½ tsp) dill weed
15 ml (1 tbsp) wholewheat flour
15 ml (1 tbsp) cider vinegar
275 g (10 oz) silken tofu
gomasio, or salt if preferred
black pepper
Garnish
sunflower seeds
paprika
Serves 6-8

1 Preheat the oven to gas mark 6, 200°C (400°F).
2 Roll out the pastry and line a 20 cm (8 in) flan ring. Prick the base well and bake blind for 4 minutes.
3 Heat the oil in a saucepan and gently fry the onion for 3 minutes. Add the mushrooms, carrots, greens and broccoli. Cover and cook very gently over a low heat for 10-15 minutes, stirring frequently. Add a little water if the mixture begins to look dry.
4 Sprinkle over the caraway, herbs and flour, stir and cook for 2-3 minutes.
5 Remove from the heat and mix in the cider vinegar and tofu. Season with gomasio and pepper.
6 Fill the pastry case with the mixture and then garnish with sunflower seeds and paprika.
7 Bake for 30-35 minutes. Serve warm.

For a low-fat filling, omit the hard cheese and mix the parsnips with 50 g (2 oz) cottage cheese, then garnish with blue poppy seeds.

NUTRITIONAL PROFILE	*per portion*			
Total calories	345			
Protein	13g	√	√	√
Fibre	11g	√	√	√
Polyunsaturated fats	3g	√	√	√
Saturated fats	3g	√	√	√
Vitamins	*Good source of:*			
	C, E, FA, N			
Minerals	*Good source of:*			
	Ca, Cu, Mg, Zn			

Illustrated on page 97

• PARSNIP FLAN •

INGREDIENTS

1 quantity of low-fat or shortcrust pastry (see page 39)
10 ml (2 tsp) olive oil
450 g (1 lb) onions, sliced in rings
1-2 cloves garlic, crushed
450 g (1 lb) parsnips, scrubbed and diced
10 ml (2 tsp) dried rosemary
gomasio, or salt if preferred
black pepper
50 g (2 oz) Cheddar cheese, grated
Serves 4-6

1 Preheat the oven to gas mark 6, 200°C (400°F).
2 Roll out the pastry and line a 20 cm (8 in) flan ring. Prick the base well and bake blind for 4 minutes.
3 Heat the oil in a frying pan and gently fry the onion and garlic for 4-5 minutes or until soft. Then add a little water so that they can braise for about 10 minutes without burning.
4 Steam the parsnips for about 12-15 minutes until tender. Mash well, then mix in the rosemary and seasoning.
5 Fill the pastry case with the onion rings, cover with mashed parsnip and top with cheese.
6 Bake for 30-35 minutes. Serve warm.

I first tasted a version of these pasties in York, and thought the bean and vegetable combination delightful. The secret lies in the slow cooking of the vegetables and beans so that the flavours blend well. The filling combines with the pastry to produce a high-protein, high-fibre dish.

NUTRITIONAL PROFILE		per portion
Total calories		235
Protein	10g	√√√
Fibre	9g	√√√
Polyunsaturated fats	2g	√√
Saturated fats	3g	√√
Vitamins		Good source of:
		A, B1, B2, B6, C, E, FA, N
Minerals		Good source of:
		Ca, Fe, Mg, Zn

Illustrated opposite

· YORKSHIRE PASTIES ·

INGREDIENTS

For the filling
100 g (4 oz) mixed red kidney beans and black-eye beans, soaked overnight
10 ml (2 tsp) sunflower oil
100 g (4 oz) leeks, cleaned and sliced
100 g (4 oz) carrots, diced
100 g (4 oz) swede, peeled and diced
5 ml (1 tsp) dried sage
5 ml (1 tsp) dried rosemary

5 ml (1 tsp) dried thyme
15 ml (1 tbsp) tomato purée
2.5 ml (½ tsp) yeast extract
150 ml (¼ pint) bean stock
shoyu, or salt if preferred
black pepper
1 quantity of yeasted pastry (see page 40)
beaten egg
Makes 6 pasties

1 Drain the beans. Cover with plenty of fresh water, bring uncovered to the boil and boil fast for 10 minutes. Reduce the heat, skim, cover and simmer for 35-40 minutes or until soft. Drain, reserving the stock.
2 Heat the oil in a saucepan and gently fry the leeks, carrots and swede for 5 minutes.
3 Add the cooked beans, herbs, tomato purée and yeast extract dissolved in the bean stock.
4 Cover and gently simmer the mixture for 20-30 minutes so that all the flavours are well blended. Season with shoyu and pepper.
5 Preheat the oven to gas mark 6, 200°C (400°F).
6 Roll out the pastry and cut six 10 cm (4 in) rounds, using a small plate or saucer as a guide.
7 Put 30 ml (2 tbsp) of filling on each round and brush the edges with a little beaten egg. Fold over and seal, crimping the edges. Brush with beaten egg, then prick a small hole in either side of each pasty. Place on a baking sheet.
8 Bake for 15-20 minutes. Serve hot or cold.

Nut creams are a good alternative to dairy-based quiches—they are high in protein and are not generally high in saturated fats.

NUTRITIONAL PROFILE		per portion
Total calories		475
Protein	15g	√√
Fibre	1g	√
Polyunsaturated fats	7g	√√√
Saturated fats	6g	√√
Vitamins		Good source of:
		B1, B2, N
Minerals		Good source of:
		Cu, Fe, Mg

Illustrated opposite

CASHEW & · MUSHROOM FLAN ·

INGREDIENTS

1 quantity of low-fat or shortcrust pastry (see page 39)
10 ml (2 tsp) olive oil
175 g (6 oz) mushrooms, chopped
175 g (6 oz) cashew nut pieces
5 ml (1 tsp) dried marjoram

175 g (6 oz) mixed nuts (cashews, hazelnuts, unsalted peanuts), ground
up to 300 ml (½ pint) water
10 ml (2 tsp) shoyu
paprika
Serves 6

1 Preheat the oven to gas mark 6, 200°C (400°F).
2 Roll out the pastry and line a 20 cm (8 in) flan ring. Prick the base well and bake blind for 4 minutes.
3 Heat the oil in a frying pan and gently fry the mushrooms for 5 minutes or until soft. Add most of the cashew nut pieces, reserving a few for the topping, and toast for about 3 minutes until lightly browned, stirring frequently. ▶

4 Mix the ground nuts and marjoram in a bowl, add the shoyu then stir in sufficient water to produce the consistency of double cream.
5 Stir in the toasted cashew and mushroom mixture.
6 Fill the pastry case with the mixture and garnish with the remaining cashew pieces. Sprinkle with paprika.
7 Bake for 30-35 minutes. Serve warm or cold.

The low protein content of the pastry in this pie is successfully balanced by the high protein level of the aduki bean filling.

NUTRITIONAL PROFILE	*per portion*	
Total calories	735	
Protein	27g	√√√
Fibre	11g	√√√
Polyunsaturated fats	6g	√
Saturated fats	10g	√
Vitamins	*Good source of:*	
	B1, B2, B6, C, E, FA, N	
Minerals	*Good source of:*	
	Ca, Cu, Fe, Mg, Zn	

Illustrated on page 99

⬩ HUNGARIAN PIE ⬩

INGREDIENTS

175 g (6 oz) aduki beans, soaked overnight
10 ml (2 tsp) sunflower oil
1 medium onion, finely chopped
225 g (8 oz) courgettes, finely chopped
175 g (6 oz) red cabbage, shredded
100 g (4 oz) mushrooms, chopped
5 ml (1 tsp) caraway seeds
5 ml (1 tsp) dill weed
30 ml (2 tbsp) tomato purée

30 ml (2 tbsp) porridge oats
15 ml (1 tbsp) shoyu
black pepper
1 quantity of hot water crust pastry
 (see page 42)
beaten egg for glazing
For serving
Sharp mushroom sauce (see page 146)
Serves 4-6

1 Drain the beans. Cover with plenty of fresh water, bring uncovered to the boil and boil fast for 10 minutes. Reduce the heat, skim, cover and simmer for 40-45 minutes or until soft. Drain, reserving the stock.
2 Heat the oil in a saucepan and gently fry the onion for 4-5 minutes until soft. Add the courgettes, cabbage, mushrooms, caraway and dill weed, stir and cook for 5 minutes. ▸

3 Stir in the cooked beans, tomato purée, oats and shoyu. Add a little reserved stock if the mixture begins to look dry. Cook for 5-10 minutes. Season with pepper.

4 Preheat the oven to gas mark 7, 220°C (425°F).

5 Use two-thirds of the dough to line an 18 cm (7 in) cake tin or spring mould. Pack in the aduki bean filling. Moisten the dough edges with water.

6 Roll out the remaining dough to make a lid. Seal and crimp the dough edges. Brush with beaten egg and prick well.

7 Bake for 20 minutes, then reduce the oven temperature to gas mark 5, 190°C (375°F) and bake for 35-40 minutes.

8 Serve hot, with *Sharp mushroom sauce*.

Flans and quiches are often synonymous with rich cheese fillings and are therefore rather high in fat. I prefer to use simple vegetable combinations which, when bound together with a well-flavoured sauce, produce delicious, light and low-fat results.

NUTRITIONAL PROFILE	*per portion*	
Total calories		360
Protein	13g	√ √ √
Fibre	2g	√
Polyunsaturated fats	7g	√ √ √
Saturated fats	3g	√ √ √
Vitamins		*Good source of:*
	B2, B6, B12, C, E, FA, N	
Minerals		*Good source of:*
	Ca, Cu, Fe, Mg, Zn	

Illustrated opposite

CELERY &
• GREEN PEPPER FLAN •

INGREDIENTS

1 quantity of low-fat or shortcrust pastry (see page 39)
425 ml (¾ pint) skimmed milk
½ onion
four peppercorns
blade of mace
30 ml (2 tbsp) sunflower oil
6 sticks celery, chopped
1 large green pepper, deseeded and diced

2.5 ml (½ tsp) celery seeds
25 g (1 oz) wholewheat flour
2 eggs
15 ml (1 tbsp) grated horseradish
2.5 ml (½ tsp) paprika
gomasio, or salt if preferred
black pepper
Garnish
2.5 ml (½ tsp) paprika
Serves 6

1 Preheat the oven to gas mark 6, 200°C (400°F).

2 Roll out the pastry and line a 20 cm (8 in) flan ring. Prick the base well and bake blind for 4 minutes.

3 Meanwhile, place the milk in a saucepan with the onion, peppercorns and mace. Bring almost to the boil, remove from the heat and leave to infuse for 10 minutes. Strain and reserve the milk.

4 Heat the oil in a large saucepan and cook the celery, green pepper and celery seeds very slowly for 10-15 minutes.

5 Add the flour and cook for 3 minutes, stirring well.

6 Pour over the flavoured milk and mix well. Bring the sauce to the boil and simmer for 5 minutes, stirring. Cool slightly.

7 Beat in the eggs, then add the horseradish, paprika, gomasio and the pepper.

8 Pour the filling into the pastry case and dust with paprika.

9 Bake for 30-35 minutes. Serve warm.

Left: **Celery & green pepper flan**; Top: **Hungarian pie** *(see page 97)*

Yellow and green split peas and lentils make excellent high-protein puréed bases for flan fillings. They combine particularly well with broccoli, tomatoes and leeks, but should always be well spiced and flavoured.

NUTRITIONAL PROFILE	per portion	
Total calories	340	
Protein	17g	√√√
Fibre	11g	√√√
Polyunsaturated fats	4g	√√
Saturated fats	1g	√√√
Vitamins	Good source of:	
	B1, B3, B6, C, E, FA	
Minerals	Good source of:	
	Cu, Fe, Mg, Zn	

Illustrated on page 100

◆ GOLDEN FLAN ◆

INGREDIENTS

175 g (6 oz) yellow split peas
1 quantity of low-fat or shortcrust pastry (see page 39)
1 medium onion, finely chopped
5 ml (1 tsp) garam masala
2.5 ml (½ tsp) turmeric
5 ml (1 tsp) paprika
5 ml (1 tsp) ground cumin seeds
pinch of cayenne
10 ml (2 tsp) sunflower oil
½ cauliflower, divided into florets
5-10 ml (1-2 tsp) miso, dissolved in a little water
black pepper
Garnish
sesame seeds
Serves 6

1 Steep the split peas in boiling water for 1 hour.
2 Drain the split peas, cover with fresh water, bring, uncovered, to the boil, cover and simmer for about 40-45 minutes until soft. Drain.
3 Preheat the oven to gas mark 6, 200°C (400°F).
4 Roll out the pastry and line a 20 cm (8 in) flan ring. Prick the base well and bake blind for 4 minutes.
5 Liquidize the onion and spices to a paste in 30 ml (2 tbsp) water.
6 Heat the oil in a large saucepan and fry the spicy paste for 3 minutes. Add the cooked peas and continue frying for 3 minutes.
7 Meanwhile, lightly steam the cauliflower for 6-8 minutes.
8 Mix with the split peas. Stir in the miso, then season with pepper.
9 Fill the pastry case with the mixture and garnish with sesame seeds.
10 Bake for 30-35 minutes. Serve warm or cold.

A relatively low-fat, smooth pastry is used here instead of the traditional Greek filo dough. Breadcrumbs and sesame seeds absorb the juices of the cooked vegetables, keeping the pastry drier; they also add texture to the pie.

NUTRITIONAL PROFILE	*per portion*	
Total calories		290
Protein	9g	√ √
Fibre	3g	√ √
Polyunsaturated fats	4g	√ √ √
Saturated fats	2g	√ √ √
Vitamins	*Good source of:*	
	A, B1, C, E, FA	
Minerals	*Good source of:*	
	Ca, Cu, Fe, Mg	

Illustrated below

⬥ KOLOKITHOPITA ⬥

INGREDIENTS

10 ml (2 tsp) olive oil
1 medium onion, finely chopped
2 cloves garlic, crushed
700 g (1½ lb) courgettes, thinly sliced
350 g (12 oz) tomatoes, skinned and diced
15 ml (1 tbsp) tomato purée
10 ml (2 tsp) cumin seeds
20 ml (4 tsp) dried basil

gomasio, or salt if preferred
black pepper
1 quantity of strudel pastry (see page 41)
50 g (2 oz) fresh wholewheat breadcrumbs
15-30 ml (1-2 tbsp) toasted sesame seeds
olive oil
For serving
Tomato sauce (see page 44)
Serves 4-6

1 Heat the oil in a large saucepan and gently fry the onion and garlic for 4-5 minutes or until soft.
2 Add the courgettes, tomatoes, purée, cumin and basil, cover and stew very gently for 25-30 minutes. Season with gomasio and pepper. Leave to cool.
3 Preheat the oven to gas mark 6, 200°C (400°F).
4 Stretch out the strudel dough to a thin rectangle. Mix the breadcrumbs and sesame seeds together. Cover the dough with the breadcrumb mixture. Spread over the courgette filling, almost to the edges. Brush the edges with olive oil.
5 Fold in the longer side edges to meet in the middle. Roll up the dough like a Swiss roll. Transfer to a lightly oiled baking sheet. Brush with olive oil.
6 Bake for 45-55 minutes. Serve hot, accompanied with *Tomato sauce*.

·PASTA·
PIZZA &
·PANCAKES·

In this lasagne, which is high in protein and fibre but low in saturated fats, a tangy yogurt sauce is used to flavour the layers of pasta. For a less sharp version, use more milk and less yogurt.

NUTRITIONAL PROFILE	*per portion*	
Total calories		385
Protein	20g	✓✓✓
Fibre	6g	✓✓✓
Polyunsaturated fats	3g	✓✓
Saturated fats	3g	✓✓✓
Vitamins	*Good source of:*	
	A, B1, B2, C, FA	
Minerals	*Good source of:*	
	Ca, Cu, Fe, Mg, Zn	

Illustrated on page 103

·MUSHROOM LASAGNE·

INGREDIENTS

10 ml (2 tsp) olive oil
1 medium onion, finely chopped
2 cloves garlic, crushed
1 bay leaf
2.5 ml (½ tsp) dried thyme
225 g (8 oz) mushrooms, sliced
30 ml (2 tbsp) cornflour
300 ml (½ pint) skimmed milk
300 ml (½ pint) yogurt

350 g (12 oz) broccoli florets
100 g (4 oz) carrots, diced
25 g (1 oz) pine kernels
gomasio, or salt if preferred
black pepper
9 pieces wholewheat lasagne
10 ml (2 tsp) cornflour
30 ml (2 tbsp) freshly grated Parmesan
Serves 4

1 Heat the oil in a saucepan and gently fry the onion and garlic for 4-5 minutes or until the onion is soft.
2 Add the bay leaf, thyme and mushrooms and cook over a gentle heat for 10 minutes. Dissolve the cornflour in a little of the milk.
3 Pour the remaining milk over the mushrooms. When heated through, stir in the cornflour. Cook for 5 minutes until thickened, stirring all the time. Remove the bay leaf. Remove pan from the heat and stir in 150 ml (¼ pint) of the yogurt. Season with the gomasio and pepper.
4 Steam the broccoli and carrot until fairly soft. Place in a bowl, then mix in the pine kernels and season with gomasio and pepper.
5 Preheat the oven to gas mark 4, 180°C (350°F).
6 Meanwhile, cook the lasagne in a large saucepan of boiling salted water for 8-10 minutes or until *al dente.*
7 Put a layer of mushroom sauce in the bottom of a lightly oiled oblong ovenproof dish. Cover with a layer of lasagne, then the broccoli mixture, then the sauce. Repeat, ending with lasagne.
8 Mix the 10 ml (2 tsp) cornflour with the remaining 150 ml (¼ pint) yogurt. Pour this over the lasagne. Sprinkle with Parmesan cheese.
9 Bake for 25-30 minutes. Serve hot.

This meal manages to reach a nutritious ideal — it is high in protein and fibre, low in saturated fats and is an excellent source of all the essential vitamins and minerals. Buy good-quality walnuts for this dish and store in an airtight container — otherwise the taste will be bitter.

NUTRITIONAL PROFILE	*per portion*	
Total calories		595
Protein	25g	√√√
Fibre	16g	√√√
Polyunsaturated fats	17g	√√√
Saturated fats	4g	√√√
Vitamins	*Good source of:*	
A, B1, B2, B6, B12, C, D, E, FA, N		
Minerals	*Good source of:*	
Ca, Cu, Fe, Mg, Zn		

Illustrated opposite

· WALNUT RAVIOLI ·

INGREDIENTS

For the dough	175 g (6 oz) walnuts, very finely chopped
350 g (12 oz) wholewheat flour	30 ml (2 tbsp) finely chopped fresh basil
pinch of salt	45 ml (3 tbsp) finely chopped fresh parsley
2 eggs	3 cloves garlic, crushed
225 g (8 oz) spinach, cooked and puréed	30 ml (2 tbsp) tomato purée
For the filling	shoyu, or salt if preferred
1 medium onion, finely chopped or minced	black pepper
4 sticks celery, finely chopped or minced	beaten egg for sealing
	Serves 4 as a main course or 6 as a starter

1 For the pasta dough: mix the flour and salt together in a large bowl or on a work surface. Make a well in the centre and add the eggs and spinach. Using your fingers, or a fork, gradually draw the flour into the centre to make a dough. Knead thoroughly until the dough is no longer sticky. Cover and leave to rest for half an hour.
2 Mix the filling ingredients together in a large bowl. Season with shoyu and pepper.
3 Roll out the pasta dough very thinly to a rectangle. Mark half into 2.5-5 cm (1-2 in) squares. Dot a teaspoon of filling on each square. Brush the edges and in between the rows of filling with beaten egg. Cover with the remaining dough. Press firmly along the edges and between the rows to seal. Use a pastry wheel to cut out the ravioli squares. Leave to dry for 30 minutes.
4 Cook the ravioli in a large saucepan of boiling salted water for 8-10 minutes or until *al dente*. Drain. Serve hot with *Tomato* or *Mushroom sauce* (see page 44 or 146).

Blending quark with skimmed milk, as here, produces a light cream, lower in fat than single cream.

NUTRITIONAL PROFILE	*per portion*	
Total calories		125
Protein	11g	√√√
Fibre	3g	√√
Polyunsaturated fats	0.5g	√
Saturated fats	0.5g	√√√
Vitamins	*Good source of:*	
B1, B12		
Minerals	*Good source of:*	
—		

Illustrated on page 104

· TAGLIATELLE ·

INGREDIENTS

10 ml (2 tsp) olive oil	175 g (6 oz) quark
3 spring onions, chopped	150 ml (¼ pint) skimmed milk
1 small red pepper, deseeded and chopped	gomasio, or salt if preferred
4 canned or cooked artichoke hearts,	black pepper
quartered	225 g (8 oz) fresh wholewheat tagliatelle
175 g (6 oz) peas	*Serves 4*

1 Heat the oil in a saucepan and gently fry the spring onions for 4-5 minutes.
2 Add the red pepper, artichoke hearts and peas, cover and cook for 10 minutes, adding a little water if the mixture begins to look dry.
3 Liquidize the quark with the skimmed milk until a smooth cream. Pour this into the vegetables and heat through gently. Season with gomasio and pepper.
4 Cook the tagliatelle in a large saucepan of boiling salted water for 3-4 minutes or until *al dente*. Drain.
5 Toss the tagliatelle well with the sauce. Serve immediately.

Left: **Walnut ravioli**; Right: **Mushroom lasagne** *(see page 101)*

*Either continental or brown lentils
can be used for this recipe's sauce.
I think lentils make an excellent
introduction for a non-vegetarian to
the pulse family as they are high in
protein, easy to digest and, because
of their small size, do not overpower
the dish.*

NUTRITIONAL PROFILE	*per portion*	
Total calories		530
Protein	26g	✓ ✓ ✓
Fibre	9g	✓ ✓ ✓
Polyunsaturated fats	1g	✓
Saturated fats	2g	✓ ✓ ✓
Vitamins		*Good source of:*
	A, B1, B2, B6, C, E, FA, N	
Minerals		*Good source of:*
	Ca, Cu, Fe, Mg, Zn	

Illustrated opposite

· SPAGHETTI ·
WITH LENTIL BOLOGNAISE

INGREDIENTS

175 g (6 oz) brown or continental lentils
15 ml (1 tbsp) olive oil
1 medium onion, finely chopped
2 cloves garlic, crushed
350 g (12 oz) mushrooms, diced
5 ml (1 tsp) dried marjoram
1 bay leaf

450 g (1 lb) tomatoes, skinned and chopped
30 ml (2 tbsp) tomato purée
shoyu, or salt if preferred
black pepper
For serving
350 g (12 oz) wholewheat spaghetti
15-30 ml (1-2 tbsp) grated Parmesan
Serves 4

1 Place the lentils in a large saucepan of water. Bring, uncovered, to the boil, skim, cover and simmer for about 40 minutes or until soft. Drain.
2 Heat the oil in a large saucepan and fry the onion and garlic for 4-5 minutes or until the onion is soft.
3 Add the mushrooms, cooked lentils, marjoram and bay leaf and cook for 10 minutes.
4 Stir in the tomatoes and purée. Cover and cook for 20-25 minutes. Remove the bay leaf. Season with shoyu and pepper.
5 Cook the spaghetti in a large saucepan of boiling salted water for about 8-10 minutes until just tender. Drain.
6 Pile the Bolognaise sauce over the cooked spaghetti.

*Use a plain bread dough for this
pizza or, for a lighter but richer
version, yeasted pastry (see page
40). For a lower fat version omit the
mozzarella.*

NUTRITIONAL PROFILE	*per portion*	
Total calories		420
Protein	25g	✓ ✓ ✓
Fibre	16g	✓ ✓ ✓
Polyunsaturated fats	2g	✓ ✓
Saturated fats	4g	✓ ✓ ✓
Vitamins		*Good source of:*
	A, B1, B2, B6, C, D, E, N	
Minerals		*Good source of:*
	Ca, Cu, Fe, Mg, Zn	

Illustrated on page 106

· PIZZA CALZONE ·

INGREDIENTS

350 g (12 oz) leaf spinach, washed
10 ml (2 tsp) olive oil
1 medium onion, finely chopped
2 cloves garlic, crushed
225 g (8 oz) mushrooms, sliced
15 ml (1 tbsp) tomato purée

shoyu, or salt if preferred
grated nutmeg
black pepper
100 g (4 oz) mozzarella cheese, diced
350 g (12 oz) wholewheat bread dough or
    yeasted pastry (see page 40)
Serves 4

1 Finely shred the spinach. Stir-fry in a wok or large, heavy-based pan for 6 minutes over a high heat until soft.
2 Heat the oil in a saucepan and gently fry the onion and garlic for 4-5 minutes until the onion is soft.
3 Add the mushrooms and cook for 8-10 minutes.
4 Preheat the oven to gas mark 6, 200°C (400°F).
5 Mix the cooked spinach and tomato purée into the mushrooms. Season with shoyu, nutmeg and pepper. Add the cheese.
6 Divide the dough into 4 pieces. Roll each one into an 18 cm (7 in) round. Divide the filling between the circles. Brush the edges with water, then fold them over and pinch edges together. Place on lightly oiled baking sheet. Bake for 5-8 minutes or until base is cooked.

Top: **Tagliatelle** *(see page 102)*; Bottom: **Spaghetti with lentil bolognaise**

Pizzas can be made with a variety of toppings and when made with wholewheat flour are guaranteed to be a good source of fibre in any meal.

NUTRITIONAL PROFILE	*per portion*	
Total calories	350	
Protein	15g	√√√
Fibre	11g	√√√
Polyunsaturated fats	2g	√√
Saturated fats	1g	√√√
Vitamins	Good source of:	
	A, B1, B6, C, FA, N	
Minerals	Good source of:	
	Fe, Cu, Mg, Zn	

Illustrated below

·AMERICAN HOT·
PIZZA

INGREDIENTS

350 g (12 oz) wholewheat bread dough (see page 31)
For the topping
15 ml (1 tbsp) olive oil
225 g (8 oz) onions, finely chopped
2 cloves garlic, crushed
450 g (1 lb) tomatoes, skinned and chopped
30 ml (2 tbsp) tomato purée
5 ml (1 tsp) dried oregano

1 small green chilli, deseeded and diced
5 ml (1 tsp) green peppercorns
gomasio, or salt if preferred
black pepper
Garnish
50-100 g (2-4 oz) mozzarella cheese, cubed
green pepper rings
black olives
Serves 4

1 Preheat the oven to gas mark 6, 200°C (400°F).
2 Roll out the dough and line a Swiss roll tin. Prick and leave to prove for 10 minutes. Bake for 4-5 minutes.
3 Heat the oil in a saucepan and cook the onion and garlic very gently for 10-15 minutes, adding a little water if necessary.
4 Add the tomatoes, tomato purée, oregano, chilli and peppercorns. Cook the mixture for 15-20 minutes until the sauce is thick. Season with gomasio and pepper.
5 Spread the sauce over the prepared base. Sprinkle the cheese over the top. Arrange the pepper rings and olives on top.
6 Bake for 20 minutes. Serve hot.

You don't have to rely on a cheese topping for either protein or interest in a pizza. Here, the protein comes from the dough, and the unusual combination of sweet and sharp flavours from the olives, basil, sultanas and pine kernels.

NUTRITIONAL PROFILE	*per portion*	
Total calories	385	
Protein	16g	√√√
Fibre	12g	√√√
Polyunsaturated fats	2g	√√
Saturated fats	1g	√√√
Vitamins	*Good source of:*	
	A, B1, B6, C, E, FA, N	
Minerals	*Good source of:*	
	Cu, Mg, Zn	

Illustrated opposite

• PIZZA BASILICA •

INGREDIENTS

350 g (12 oz) wholewheat bread dough (see page 31)
For the topping
15 ml (1 tbsp) olive oil
225 g (8 oz) onions, finely chopped
2 cloves garlic, crushed
450 g (1 lb) tomatoes, skinned and chopped
30 ml (2 tbsp) tomato purée
30 ml (2 tbsp) chopped fresh basil
30 ml (2 tbsp) chopped fresh parsley
gomasio, or salt if preferred
black pepper
2 canned or cooked artichoke hearts, halved
15 ml (1 tbsp) sultanas
15 g (½ oz) pine kernels
5 ml (1 tsp) sesame seeds
5 ml (1 tsp) capers
8 green olives
Serves 4

1 Preheat the oven to gas mark 6, 200°C (400°F).
2 Roll out the dough and line a Swiss roll tin. Prick and leave to prove for 10 minutes. Bake for 4-5 minutes.
3 Heat the oil in a saucepan and cook the onion and garlic very gently for 10-15 minutes, adding a little water if necessary to prevent sticking.
4 Add the tomatoes, tomato purée, basil and parsley. Cook the mixture for 15-20 minutes until the sauce is thick. Season with gomasio and pepper.
5 Spread the sauce over the prepared base.
6 Arrange the artichoke hearts at each corner, then sprinkle over the sultanas, pine kernels, sesame seeds, capers and olives.
7 Bake for 20 minutes. Serve hot.

If you make this batter without egg, you should increase the liquid: the mixture takes longer to cook and is slightly more difficult to turn over. Made with water or soya milk instead of milk, the batter is heavier and needs longer to cook.

NUTRITIONAL PROFILE	*per portion*	
Total calories	135	
Protein	6g	√√√
Fibre	3g	√√
Polyunsaturated fats	1g	√√
Saturated fats	1g	√√√
Vitamins	*Good source of:*	
	B12	
Minerals	*Good source of:*	
	Ca	

Illustrated on page 109

• PANCAKES •

INGREDIENTS

1 egg
300 ml (½ pint) skimmed milk
5 ml (1 tsp) sunflower oil (optional)
100 g (4 oz) wholewheat flour
small pinch of salt
Makes 8-10 pancakes

1 Liquidize the egg, milk and oil, if using. Add the flour and salt and liquidize for 30-40 seconds. (If you're not using a liquidizer, beat the egg and milk mixture into the flour until you have a smooth batter.)
2 Let the mixture stand for 30 minutes then liquidize or beat again.
3 Heat a non-stick or heavy-based pan and pour in 30-45 ml (2-3 tbsp) of the batter, quickly tipping the pan so the batter spreads out evenly into a circle. Cook for 2-3 minutes. Toss or flip over with a slice and cook the other side for a further 2-3 minutes.
4 To keep pancakes hot, stack them on a lightly oiled heatproof plate and keep warm in a moderate oven or under a low grill.

Variation: Buckwheat pancakes

These dark, speckled pancakes, with the distinctive flavour of buckwheat, make a change from wholewheat pancakes. Use 50 g (2 oz) buckwheat flour instead of 50 g (2 oz) wholewheat flour, then make in exactly the same way.

Left: **Pizza calzone** *(see page 105)*; Centre: **American hot pizza**; Right: **Pizza basilica**

A simple filling for either wholewheat or buckwheat pancakes. Cottage or curd cheese could be used as a low-fat alternative to ricotta.

NUTRITIONAL PROFILE	*per portion*	
Total calories		130
Protein	6g	✓✓✓
Fibre	0.5g	✓
Polyunsaturated fats	0.5g	✓✓
Saturated fats	5g	✓
Vitamins	*Good source of:*	
	A, B12, E	
Minerals	*Good source of:*	
	—	

Illustrated opposite

◆ RICOTTA, HAZELNUT ◆
& ASPARAGUS PANCAKES

INGREDIENTS

100 g (4 oz) asparagus	black pepper
50 g (2 oz) hazelnuts	8 pancakes
350 g (12 oz) ricotta	*For serving*
1 egg	Broccoli and sunflower sauce (see page 146)
gomasio, or salt if preferred	*Makes 8 pancakes*

1 Preheat the oven to gas mark 4, 180°C (350°F).
2 Lightly steam the asparagus for 6-8 minutes. Chop into small pieces.
3 Dry roast the hazelnuts for 3-5 minutes in a heavy-based frying pan. Chop coarsely.
4 Mix the asparagus, hazelnuts, ricotta and egg together. Season with gomasio and pepper.
5 Divide the filling between 8 pancakes and roll up. Arrange the stuffed pancakes in a lightly oiled ovenproof dish. Cover with foil and bake for 20 minutes.
6 Serve hot with *Broccoli and sunflower sauce.*

The creamy mixture of the beans and parsnips provides a high-protein, low-fat filling for these pancakes. Serve with a high-fibre side dish.

NUTRITIONAL PROFILE	*per portion*	
Total calories		83
Protein	4g	✓✓✓
Fibre	1g	✓
Polyunsaturated fats	2g	✓✓✓
Saturated fats	0.5g	✓✓✓
Vitamins	*Good source of:*	
	E, FA	
Minerals	*Good source of:*	
	Cu, Fe, Mg	

Illustrated opposite

BUTTER BEAN &
◆ PARSNIP PANCAKES ◆

INGREDIENTS

100 g (4 oz) butter beans, soaked overnight	black pepper
350 g (12 oz) parsnips, diced	8-10 pancakes
25 g (1 oz) sunflower seeds	*For serving*
5 ml (1 tsp) crushed rosemary	smetana, yogurt or Tomato sauce (see
5 ml (1 tsp) French mustard	page 44)
miso	*Makes 8-10 pancakes*

1 Drain the butter beans. Cover with plenty of fresh water, bring uncovered to the boil and boil fast for 10 minutes. Reduce the heat, skim, cover and simmer for 45-50 minutes or until soft. Drain, reserving a little cooking liquid to mix with the miso.
2 Lightly steam the parsnips for 8-10 minutes until soft.
3 Preheat the oven to gas mark 4, 180°C (350°F).
4 Toast the sunflower seeds in a heavy-based pan or under a pre-heated grill for 3-4 minutes until just brown.
5 Mash together the butter beans and parsnip. Mix in the sunflower seeds, rosemary, mustard and season with miso and pepper. (It's easier to add the miso if it is dissolved in a little of the bean stock.)
6 Spoon 15-30 ml (1-2 tbsp) of the filling into each pancake, then roll up. Arrange the stuffed pancakes in a lightly oiled ovenproof dish. Cover with foil and bake for 15-20 minutes.
7 Serve hot with smetana, yogurt or tomato sauce.

Clockwise from the top: **Wholewheat blinis** *(see page 110)*; **Austrian pancakes** *(see page 110)*; **Butter bean and parsnip pancakes**; **Ricotta, hazelnut and asparagus pancakes**

BALANCED
• MEAL 4 •

The substantial main course in this meal is deliberately served with lighter dishes to prevent the meal from being too heavy. The meal also shows how the addition of whole-wheat noodles and courgettes can improve the overall fibre level.

• Paw paw & lime salad with mint
For recipe, see page 67

This light, easy-to-prepare starter uses paw paw (a tropical fruit containing the digestive enzyme pepain) at its simplest—just peeled and sprinkled with lime juice to offset its natural sweetness.

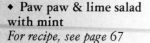

NUTRITIONAL PROFILE	*per portion*	
Total calories		875
Protein	34g	√√√
Fibre	17g	√√√
Polyunsaturated fats	12g	√√√
Saturated fats	9g	√√√
Vitamins	*Good source of:*	
	A, C, E, B1, B2, FA	
Minerals	*Good source of:*	
	Mg, Fe, Ca, Cu, Zn	

• Wholewheat noodles

Wholewheat noodles have been used here as an alternative to potatoes or rice. They are a good way of making up the fibre levels in a meal which may otherwise be too low.

• Tofu bobotie
For recipe, see page 78

This spicy fruit casserole is an adaptation of the traditional South African dish. This version makes excellent use of tofu, a high-protein soya bean product. Although tofu has little taste of its own when uncooked, it absorbs the flavours of what it is cooked with very well.

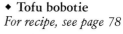

◆ **Iced cashew cream**
For recipe, see page 160

Containing no double
cream, this pudding owes
its richness to the
pulverized nuts and fruit.
The fat level in this dish
is desirably low.

◆ **Mineral water**

Mineral waters, whether
still or carbonated, are a
refreshing, calorie-free
accompaniment to meals.
Check the label for the
specific mineral content.

◆ **Steamed courgettes**

Steaming is one of the
best ways of preserving
the nutrients in
vegetables. Salt should
ideally not be added—
gomasio could be tried
instead. If you find
you cannot do without a
dab of butter on the
vegetables, try using a
margarine high in
polyunsaturates, or use
yogurt or chives, instead.

◆ **Sweetcorn salad with
beansprouts**
For recipe, see page 132

This crisp salad is a good
choice to make when
serving a substantial dish
like tofu bobotie because
its lightness and range of
ingredients make such a
pleasing contrast.

This tangy rice dish is high in fibre and low in fat, despite having all the creaminess of a classic risotto.

NUTRITIONAL PROFILE	*per portion*	
Total calories		320
Protein	7g	√
Fibre	7g	√ √ √
Polyunsaturated fats	6g	√ √ √
Saturated fats	1g	√ √ √
Vitamins	*Good source of:*	
	B6, C, E, FA	
Minerals	*Good source of:*	
	Cu	

Illustrated opposite

• FENNEL RISOTTO •

INGREDIENTS

10 ml (2 tsp) sunflower oil
1 medium onion, finely chopped
5 ml (1 tsp) grated lemon rind
450 g (1 lb) fennel, diced
225 g (8 oz) short-grain brown rice
black pepper

juice of ½ lemon
50 g (2 oz) walnuts, roughly chopped
350 g (12 oz) tomatoes, skinned and chopped
gomasio, or salt if preferred
Serves 4

1 Heat the oil in a large saucepan and gently fry the onion for 4-5 minutes or until soft.
2 Add the lemon rind and fennel and cook for 2-3 minutes.
3 Add the rice and one cup, about 250 ml (8 fl oz), boiling water. Stir, bring to the boil and cook covered, until all the water has been absorbed, stirring occasionally.
4 Add the tomatoes, lemon juice, walnuts and ½ cup, about 100 ml (4 fl oz), boiling water. Stir again and cook until all the liquid is absorbed. If the rice isn't yet cooked, add a little more boiling water if necessary.
5 Once cooked, the risotto should have a creamy consistency. Season with gomasio and pepper. Garnish with a fennel frond. Serve hot.

This dish, with its crispy stir-fried vegetables coated in a creamy peanut sauce, is a perfect combination of tastes and textures. It is also an excellent source of protein and fibre.

NUTRITIONAL PROFILE	*per portion*	
Total calories		590
Protein	23g	√ √ √
Fibre	9g	√ √ √
Polyunsaturated fats	8g	√ √ √
Saturated fats	5g	√ √ √
Vitamins	*Good source of:*	
	B1, B6, C, E, FA, N	
Minerals	*Good source of:*	
	Ca, Cu, Fe, Mg, Zn	

Illustrated opposite

• PEANUT PILAU •
WITH STIR-FRIED VEGETABLES

INGREDIENTS

225 g (8 oz) long-grain brown rice
For the sauce
15 ml (1 tbsp) peanut oil
1 medium onion, finely chopped
1 clove garlic, crushed
1 green chilli, deseeded and diced
1.5 cm (½ in) fresh root ginger, grated
275 g (10 oz) silken tofu plus 150 ml
(¼ pint) water or 300 ml (½ pint)
skimmed milk

100 g (4 oz) ground roasted peanuts
5 ml (1 tsp) shoyu
For the stir-fry
15 ml (1 tbsp) peanut oil
175 g (6 oz) white cabbage, shredded
175 g (6 oz) fresh green beans, sliced
175 g (6 oz) mung bean sprouts
½ cucumber, diced
50 g (2 oz) peanuts
5 ml (1 tsp) shoyu
Serves 4

1 Measure the rice and bring twice the volume of water, about 500 ml (18 fl oz), to the boil. Add the rice and stir once. Cover and simmer for about 25 minutes or until cooked. Add a little extra water at the end if necessary.
2 For the sauce, heat the oil in a saucepan and gently fry the onion and garlic for 4-5 minutes or until soft. Add the chilli and ginger and cook for 3 minutes.
3 Liquidize the onion mixture with the remaining sauce ingredients. Heat through gently.
4 For the stir-fry: heat the oil in a wok or large frying pan. When hot stir-fry the cabbage, beans, bean sprouts and cucumber over high ▶

Left: **Peanut pilau with stir-fried vegetables**; Right: **Fennel risotto**

heat for 3 minutes, stirring constantly. Stir in the peanuts and shoyu.
5 To serve, pile the rice on to a warm serving dish. Top with the stir-fry vegetables, pour over the sauce and garnish with tomato slices.

This simple, fragrant Middle Eastern dish is high in protein, low in saturated fats, and is a good source of iron.

NUTRITIONAL PROFILE	*per portion*	
Total calories		340
Protein	14g	√ √ √
Fibre	3g	√ √
Polyunsaturated fats	1g	√
Saturated fats	1g	√ √ √
Vitamins	*Good source of:*	
		C, FA
Minerals	*Good source of:*	
		Fe, Mg

Illustrated on page 118

◆ LENTIL POURGOURI ◆

INGREDIENTS

10 ml (2 tsp) olive oil
100 g (4 oz) green lentils, cleaned
5 ml (1 tsp) ground allspice
12 cardamom pods, cracked
225 g (8 oz) bulgar wheat
25 g (1 oz) currants

450 g (1 lb) courgettes, sliced
gomasio, or salt if preferred
black pepper
Garnish
30 ml (2 tbsp) sesame seeds
5 ml (1 tsp) coriander seeds
Serves 4

1 Heat the oil in a large saucepan and gently fry the lentils and spices for 3-4 minutes.
2 Add 600 ml (1 pint) cold water. Cover and simmer for 30 minutes.
3 Add the bulgar wheat and currants and a little extra water if the mixture begins to look dry. Cook for 10 minutes, stirring frequently.
4 Meanwhile, steam the courgettes for about 6 minutes. Mix the courgettes into the lentil mix. Season with gomasio and pepper.
5 For the garnish: dry roast the seeds in a heavy-based pan for 3-4 minutes. Crush them to a fine powder using a pestle and mortar.
6 Spoon the pourgouri on to a warm serving dish and sprinkle over the garnish. Serve with hung yogurt and salad.

The velvety texture of the rice in this Indonesian dish is achieved by first soaking and then cooking it in coconut milk.

NUTRITIONAL PROFILE	*per portion*	
Total calories		390
Protein	9g	√
Fibre	4g	√ √
Polyunsaturated fats	2g	√ √
Saturated fats	6g	√ √
Vitamins		*Good source of:*
		C
Minerals		*Good source of:*
		Fe

Illustrated above

· NASI KUNYIT ·

INGREDIENTS

50 g (2 oz) creamed coconut
425 ml (¾ pint) hot water
225 g (8 oz) long-grain brown rice
10 ml (2 tsp) turmeric
20 peppercorns, tied in muslin
For the stir-fry
15 ml (1 tbsp) peanut oil
225 g (8 oz) mange tout, trimmed and halved

6 sticks celery, diagonally sliced
1 paw paw, peeled, deseeded and chopped
12 radishes, sliced
50 g (2 oz) cashew nut pieces
gomasio, or salt if preferred
black pepper
For serving
Ankake sauce (see page 145)
Serves 4

1 Grate the coconut into the water to dissolve it.
2 Soak the rice in the coconut water for 30 minutes, adding the turmeric and peppercorns.
3 Bring the rice to the boil in the soaking water, cover and simmer for 30 minutes or until soft, adding a little boiling water if necessary. Remove the peppercorns.
4 Heat the oil in a wok or large frying pan. When hot, stir-fry the celery, mange tout, paw paw and radishes over a high heat for 4 minutes, stirring constantly. Stir in the nuts.
5 Season the rice with gomasio and pepper. Transfer to a warm serving platter. Top with the vegetable stir-fry and garnish with coriander. Serve hot, accompanied by *Ankake sauce*.

Clockwise from the top: **Lentil pourgouri** *(see page 117)*; **Chick pea couscous**; **Nasi kunyit**

By liquidizing the onion, garlic and ginger it is possible to make a spicy paste to which yogurt can be added without curdling. This produces a delicious creamy, sharp-flavoured sauce which is nevertheless low in saturated fat.

NUTRITIONAL PROFILE	*per portion*	
Total calories		295
Protein	16g	✓✓✓
Fibre	13g	✓✓✓
Polyunsaturated fats	2g	✓✓
Saturated fats	1g	✓✓✓
Vitamins	*Good source of:*	
	A, B1, B2, B6, C, E, FA, N	
Minerals	*Good source of:*	
	Ca, Cu, Fe, Mg, Zn	

Illustrated opposite

◆CHICK PEA COUSCOUS◆

INGREDIENTS

225 g (8 oz) chick peas, soaked overnight
1 medium onion, chopped
3 cloves garlic
2.5 cm (1 in) fresh root ginger, grated
10 ml (2 tsp) sunflower oil
2 bay leaves
15 ml (1 tbsp) garam masala
2.5 ml (½ tsp) ground cinnamon
175 g (6 oz) tomatoes, skinned and chopped

150 ml (¼ pint) yogurt
2.5 ml (½ tsp) turmeric
225 g (8 oz) okra, trimmed
225 g (8 oz) sweet potatoes, peeled and chopped
gomasio, or salt if preferred
black pepper
about 225 g (8 oz) couscous
Serves 4

1 Drain the peas. Cover with plenty of fresh water, bring uncovered to the boil and boil fast for 10 minutes. Reduce the heat, skim, cover and simmer for 25-30 minutes or until soft. Drain, reserving the cooking liquid.
2 Liquidize the onion, garlic and ginger with 45 ml (3 tbsp) water.
3 Heat the oil in a large saucepan and add the onion paste, bay leaves, garam masala and cinnamon. Cook for 2-3 minutes.
4 Add the tomatoes. Stir in the yogurt, 15 ml (1 tbsp) at a time.
5 Add 150 ml (¼ pint) of the pea stock, the turmeric, okra, sweet potato and cooked chick peas. Cover and simmer for 25-30 minutes.
6 Meanwhile, rinse the couscous in hot water. Place in a sieve lined with muslin or in a *couscousière*. Cover and position over the stew for the last 15 minutes' cooking time.
7 Transfer the couscous to a warm serving dish. Season the stew with gomasio and pepper, remove the bay leaf, and pour over the couscous. Garnish with coriander.

This dish is low in saturated fats, and is a good source of all minerals except calcium.

NUTRITIONAL PROFILE	*per portion*	
Total calories		355
Protein	12g	✓✓
Fibre	4g	✓✓
Polyunsaturated fats	6g	✓✓✓
Saturated fats	2g	✓✓✓
Vitamins	*Good source of:*	
	B1, E, N	
Minerals	*Good source of:*	
	Ca, Fe, Mg, Zn	

Illustrated on page 120

◆ BEETROOT KASHA ◆

INGREDIENTS

10 ml (2 tsp) sunflower oil
1 medium onion, finely chopped
4 sticks celery, chopped
225 g (8 oz) buckwheat
900 ml (1½ pints) hot water
15 ml (1 tbsp) shoyu
10-15 ml (2-3 tsp) grated horseradish
black pepper
450 g (1 lb) baby beetroots

For the sauce
200 ml (⅓ pint) skimmed milk
1 onion
1 bay leaf
4 peppercorns
30 ml (2 tbsp) sunflower oil
20 ml (1 heaped tbsp) wholewheat flour
60-75 ml (4-5 tbsp) yogurt or smetana
5-10 ml (1-2 tsp) grated horseradish
black pepper
Serves 4

1 Heat the oil in a large saucepan and gently fry the onion for 4-5 minutes or until soft.
2 Add the celery and cook for 2-3 minutes. Stir in the buckwheat and stir-fry for 3 minutes until lightly roasted.
3 Pour on the water, stir once, bring to the boil, cover and cook for 20-25 minutes. Add a little boiling water if mixture look dry. ▸

4 Stir in the shoyu and horseradish. Season with pepper.

5 Either bake the baby beetroots in a preheated oven, gas mark 4, 180°C (350°F) for about 45 minutes or steam for 20 minutes or until tender. Skin when cool enough to handle and set to one side.

6 For the sauce, place the milk, onion, bay leaf and peppercorns in a saucepan. Bring almost to the boil, remove from the heat and leave to infuse for 10 minutes. Strain.

7 Heat the oil in a saucepan and stir in the flour. Cook for 3 minutes, stirring.

8 Pour on the milk, stirring constantly. Bring the sauce to boiling point and simmer for 5 minutes, stirring. Cool slightly, then add the yogurt or smetana. Season with horseradish and pepper.

9 To serve, pile the kasha on to a warm serving plate. Slice or arrange the baby beetroots on top. Serve the sauce separately.

Beetroot kasha *(see page 119)*

•SALADS•

This recipe uses high-protein tofu to replace both the cheese and the mayonnaise dressing.

NUTRITIONAL PROFILE		*per portion*
Total calories		210
Protein	9g	✓✓✓
Fibre	4g	✓✓
Polyunsaturated fats	7g	✓✓✓
Saturated fats	2g	✓✓✓
Vitamins		*Good source of:*
		—
Minerals		*Good source of:*
		Ca, Cu, Mg

Illustrated on page 123

• SOHO SALAD •

INGREDIENTS

225 g (8 oz) firm tofu, diced   10 ml (2 tsp) sesame oil
2 red apples, chopped   juice of ½ lemon
10 sticks celery, diagonally sliced   1 clove garlic, crushed
50 g (2 oz) raisins   5-10 ml (1-2 tsp) gomasio
50.g (2 oz) walnuts (optional)   black pepper
For the dressing   *Serves 4*
150 g (5 oz) silken tofu

1 Liquidize the silken tofu with the other dressing ingredients.
2 Place the salad ingredients in a bowl and mix in the dressing.
3 Serve on a bed of crisp lettuce.

This salad should be served with a high-protein bean dish for proper nutritional balance.

NUTRITIONAL PROFILE		*per portion*
Total calories		110
Protein	2g	✓
Fibre	3g	✓✓✓
Polyunsaturated fats	2g	✓✓✓
Saturated fats	0.5g	✓✓✓
Vitamins		*Good source of:*
		A, C, E
Minerals		*Good source of:*
		—

Illustrated on page 123

•WILD RICE SALAD •

INGREDIENTS

75 g (3 oz) wild rice   rind and juice of ½ orange
100 g (4 oz) carrot, grated   5 ml (1 tsp) concentrated apple juice
1 large bunch watercress   1 cm (½ in) fresh root ginger, grated
For the dressing   shoyu, or salt if preferred
15 ml (1 tbsp) sunflower oil   black pepper
Serves 4

1 Measure the rice. Bring twice the volume of water, about 225-300 ml (8-10 fl oz), to the boil. Add the rice, cover and simmer for 35-40 minutes or until just tender. Drain.
2 Put the dressing ingredients together in a screw-top jar and mix by shaking well. Pour over the rice while it is still warm and mix together. Allow to cool completely.
3 Mix in the carrot and watercress.

High in vitamin E, endive is combined here with buckwheat. This is sprinkled through the salad to provide substance without overwhelming the delicate taste of the endive.

NUTRITIONAL PROFILE	*per portion*	
Total calories		110
Protein	4g	✓✓
Fibre	2g	✓
Polyunsaturated fats	2g	✓✓✓
Saturated fats	0.5g	✓✓✓
Vitamins	*Good source of:*	
		E
Minerals	*Good source of:*	
		—

Illustrated opposite

• BUCKWHEAT SALAD •
WITH ENDIVE

INGREDIENTS

75 g (3 oz) buckwheat	1 clove garlic, crushed
1 endive	15 ml (3 tsp) snipped chives
1 red onion, cut into rings	15 ml (1 tbsp) sunflower oil
½ punnet salad cress	5 ml (1 tsp) white wine vinegar
For the dressing	herb salt, or salt if preferred
juice of ½ lemon	black pepper
5 ml (1 tsp) lemon rind	*Serves 4-6*

1 Dry roast the buckwheat in a heavy-based saucepan for 3 minutes. Cover with 350 ml (12 fl oz) water. Bring uncovered to the boil, cover and simmer for 20 minutes or until soft. Drain if necessary. Cool.
2 Put the dressing ingredients together in a screw-top jar and mix by shaking well.
3 Mix the buckwheat with the endive, onion and salad cress in a bowl.
4 Pour the dressing over the salad and toss.

The secret of this salad's low-fat filling is quark, which provides a creamy texture without the calories.

NUTRITIONAL PROFILE	*per portion*	
Total calories		280
Protein	14g	✓✓✓
Fibre	2g	✓
Polyunsaturated fats	1g	✓
Saturated fats	2g	✓✓✓
Vitamins	*Good source of:*	
		B12, C, D, E
Minerals	*Good source of:*	
		Zn

Illustrated opposite

• STUFFED EGG •
SALAD

INGREDIENTS

4-6 hard-boiled eggs	5 ml (1 tsp) dill weed
175 g (6 oz) long-grain brown rice	10 ml (2 tsp) finely chopped fresh parsley
8 asparagus spears, lightly steamed	gomasio, or salt if preferred
4 tomatoes, quartered	black pepper
8 black olives	*For filling (2)*
10 ml (2 tsp) capers	12 black olives, stoned and finely chopped
10 ml (2 tsp) chopped fresh parsley	50 g (2 oz) quark
For filling (1)	10 ml (2 tsp) red wine vinegar
100 g (4 oz) asparagus, lightly steamed	pinch of dried thyme
and chopped	pinch of cayenne
50 g (2 oz) quark	black pepper
	Serves 4-6

1 Shell the eggs, slice in half and remove the yolks.
2 Blend 2 egg yolks with all the ingredients in filling 1. Season with gomasio and pepper.
3 Blend the remaining 2 egg yolks with all the ingredients in filling 2. Season with the peppers.
4 Measure the rice and bring twice the volume of water, about 475 ml (16 fl oz), to the boil. Add the rice, cover and simmer for about 25 minutes or until tender. Cool. Season well.
5 Mix the remaining salad ingredients with the rice.
6 Spoon the asparagus mixture into half the egg whites, the olive mixture into the remainder.

Clockwise from the top: **Stuffed egg salad**; **Soho salad** *(see page 121)*; **Buckwheat salad with endive**; **Wild rice salad** *(see page 121)*

This classic Greek salad derives its protein from the feta cheese.

NUTRITIONAL PROFILE	per portion	
Total calories	145	
Protein	7g	√√√
Fibre	1g	√
Polyunsaturated fats	1g	√√
Saturated fats	4g	√√√
Vitamins	Good source of:	
	A, B12, C	
Minerals	Good source of:	
	Ca	

Illustrated opposite

• HORIATIKI •

INGREDIENTS

225 g (8 oz) tomatoes
7.5 cm (3 in) piece of cucumber
100-225 g (4-8 oz) feta cheese
12 green or black olives
For the dressing
15 ml (1 tbsp) olive oil

15 ml (1 tbsp) lemon juice
30 ml (2 tbsp) chopped fresh parsley
1 clove garlic, crushed
15 ml (1 tbsp) chopped fresh basil
black pepper
Serves 4

1 Chop the tomatoes, cucumber and feta cheese into bite-sized pieces.
2 Mix together with the olives in a bowl.
3 Put the dressing ingredients together in a screw-top jar and mix by shaking well.
4 Pour the dressing over the salad and toss.

This substantial peasant dish from Syria is a rich source of protein and fibre.

NUTRITIONAL PROFILE	per portion	
Total calories	235	
Protein	11g	√√√
Fibre	6g	√√√
Polyunsaturated fats	2g	√√√
Saturated fats	3g	√√
Vitamins	Good source of:	
	A, B1, B2, B12, C, D, E, FA	
Minerals	Good source of:	
	Fe, Mg, Zn	

Illustrated opposite

• FATTOUSH •

INGREDIENTS

1 cos or iceberg lettuce
1 medium red pepper, deseeded and diced
4 hard-boiled eggs
4 tomatoes, sliced
10 ml (2 tsp) capers
16 black olives
4 thinly cut slices wholewheat bread
2 cloves garlic
15 ml (1 tbsp) walnut or olive oil

For the dressing
15 ml (1 tbsp) walnut or olive oil
10 ml (2 tsp) white wine vinegar
15 ml (1 tbsp) finely chopped fresh parsley
5 ml (1 tsp) dried tarragon
gomasio, or salt if preferred
black pepper
Serves 4

1 Prepare all the salad ingredients and place in a bowl.
2 Toast the wholewheat bread and rub with the cut cloves of garlic. Lightly sprinkle with oil. Break into small pieces.
3 Put the dressing ingredients together in a screw-top jar and mix by shaking well.
4 Toss the garlic toast and dressing into the salad.

This salad is high in protein and iron, and low in saturated fat.

NUTRITIONAL PROFILE	per portion	
Total calories	155	
Protein	7g	√√√
Fibre	4g	√√
Polyunsaturated fats	1g	√√
Saturated fats	2g	√√√
Vitamins	Good source of:	
	A, B6, C, E, FA	
Minerals	Good source of:	
	Ca, Fe	

Illustrated opposite

•TOMATO SALAD •

INGREDIENTS

12 cherry tomatoes
1 avocado, halved, stoned and peeled
100 g (4 oz) quark
juice of 1 lemon
1 clove garlic, crushed
15 ml (1 tbsp) finely chopped fresh basil

gomasio, or salt if preferred
black pepper
1 bunch watercress, divided into sprigs
lamb's lettuce
6 spring onions, sliced lengthways
juice of ½ lemon
Serves 4

1 Cut a lid off the base of each tomato. Spoon out the seeds and the flesh.
2 Liquidize the avocado, quark, lemon juice, garlic and basil. Season, then fill the tomatoes.
3 Toss salad ingredients in lemon juice. Arrange tomatoes on top.

Clockwise from the top: **Tomato salad**; **Horiatiki**; **Fattoush**; **Fiesta salad**

The saturated fat level of the dressing is kept low by using only 10 ml (2 tsp) sesame oil.

NUTRITIONAL PROFILE	*per portion*	
Total calories		115
Protein	4g	✓ ✓
Fibre	4g	✓ ✓
Polyunsaturated fats	0.5g	✓ ✓
Saturated fats	0g	✓ ✓ ✓
Vitamins	*Good source of:*	
		A, C
Minerals	*Good source of:*	
		—

Illustrated below

♦ FIESTA SALAD ♦

INGREDIENTS

175 g (6 oz) long-grain brown rice
1 paw paw
1 mango
¼ cucumber, sliced
100 g (4 oz) peas, lightly steamed
gomasio
black pepper
For the dressing
10 ml (2 tsp) sesame oil

juice of ½ lime
juice of ½ orange or 30 ml (2 tbsp) mango juice
2.5 ml (½ tsp) ground cinnamon
15 ml (1 tbsp) finely chopped fresh mint
Garnish
sprigs of mint or sweet cicely
Serves 4

1 Measure the rice and bring twice the volume of water, about 475 ml (16 fl oz), to the boil. Add the rice, cover and simmer for about 25 minutes or until tender.

2 Put the dressing ingredients together in a screw-top jar and mix by shaking well.

3 Pour over the rice while it is still warm, and combine together. Allow to cool completely.

4 To prepare the paw paw: cut in half lengthways. Remove the seeds and skin. Slice the flesh. To prepare the mango, cut the flesh away from the stone, then peel.

5 Mix the fruit and vegetables into the rice.

6 Season with gomasio and pepper. Garnish with mint or sweet cicely.

Potato salads are often coated in heavy, high-fat, creamy dressings. Here I mixed the mayonnaise with yogurt, but you could use all yogurt.

NUTRITIONAL PROFILE	*per portion*	
Total calories		260
Protein	5g	√
Fibre	3g	√ √
Polyunsaturated fats	6g	√ √ √
Saturated fats	2g	√ √ √
Vitamins	*Good source of:*	
	B6, C, E	
Minerals	*Good source of:*	
	—	

Illustrated opposite

• POTATO SALAD •

INGREDIENTS

450 g (1 lb) potatoes
½ cucumber, diced
3 artichoke hearts, sliced
3 spring onions, diced
30 ml (2 tbsp) finely chopped fresh parsley
15 ml (1 tbsp) sunflower seeds
5 ml (1 tsp) dill weed

For the dressing
60 ml (4 tbsp) mayonnaise
60 ml (4 tbsp) yogurt
5 ml (1 tsp) lemon juice
5 ml (1 tsp) wholegrain mustard
herb salt, or salt if preferred
Serves 4

1 Scrub and cube the potatoes. Bring a large saucepan of water to the boil. Add the potatoes, cover and simmer for 15-20 minutes until tender. Drain and place in a bowl.
2 Mix the dressing ingredients together. Spoon over the potatoes while they are still warm and toss together. Leave to cool completely.
3 When cold, mix in the remaining salad ingredients.

With pulses as major ingredients, this salad is an ideal source of both protein and fibre.

NUTRITIONAL PROFILE	*per portion*	
Total calories		215
Protein	13g	√ √ √
Fibre	12g	√ √ √
Polyunsaturated fats	3g	√ √ √
Saturated fats	1g	√ √ √
Vitamins	*Good source of:*	
	B1, B2, C, E, FA, N	
Minerals	*Good source of*	
	Ca, Cu, Fe, Mg, Zn	

Illustrated opposite

• BEAN SALAD •

INGREDIENTS

225 g (8 oz) cooked red kidney beans
225 g (8 oz) cooked chick peas
225 g (8 oz) fresh peas, lightly steamed
6 spring onions, diced
gomasio
black pepper
For the dressing
60 ml (4 tbsp) orange juice

30 ml (2 tbsp) lemon juice
15 ml (1 tbsp) sunflower oil
1 clove garlic, crushed
10 ml (2 tsp) shoyu
5 ml (1 tsp) concentrated apple juice
5 ml (1 tsp) dried thyme
5 ml (1 tsp) dried oregano
100 g (4 oz) mushrooms, thinly sliced
Serves 6-8

1 Mix the cooked beans and peas together with the spring onions.
2 Mix all the dressing ingredients together, except the mushrooms, then stir in the mushrooms. Leave to stand for 30 minutes.
3 Pour the dressing over the bean salad and toss. Season.

Unusual for a salad, this is substantially high in protein.

NUTRITIONAL PROFILE	*per portion*	
Total calories		260
Protein	11g	√ √ √
Fibre	5g	√
Polyunsaturated fats	1g	√ √
Saturated fats	1g	√ √ √
Vitamins	*Good source of:*	
	A, C, E	
Minerals	*Good source of:*	
	Fe, Mg	

Illustrated opposite

•PASTA & LENTIL SALAD•

INGREDIENTS

100 g (4 oz) continental lentils, cleaned
100 g (4 oz) wholewheat pasta shells
450 g (1 lb) tomatoes, quartered
For the dressing
30 ml (2 tbsp) white wine vinegar
30 ml (2 tbsp) olive oil

60 ml (4 tbsp) finely chopped fresh parsley
4 spring onions, very finely chopped
15 ml (1 tbsp) capers, chopped
2 gherkins, chopped
herb salt, or salt if preferred
black pepper
Serves 4-6

1 Bring the lentils to the boil in a saucepan of water. Cover and simmer for 30-40 minutes. Drain. Cook pasta in boiling water for 8-10 minutes. Drain. Mix with lentils and tomatoes.
2 Put the dressing ingredients together in a screw-top jar and mix by shaking well. Pour over salad and toss. Serve on top of lettuce.

Clockwise from the top: **Potato salad**; **Bean salad**; **Pasta & lentil salad**

• SPINACH SALAD •

INGREDIENTS

50 g (2 oz) spinach leaves
100 g (4 oz) mushrooms, diced
8-10 radishes, sliced
25 g (1 oz) alfalfa sprouts, rinsed
For the dressing
15 ml (1 tbsp) olive or walnut oil

15 ml (1 tbsp) red wine vinegar
15 ml (1 tbsp) lemon juice
1 cm (½ in) finely chopped fresh root ginger
1 clove garlic, crushed
15 ml (1 tbsp) dry sherry
black pepper
Serves 4

1 Wash the spinach leaves thoroughly. Dry.
2 Combine the salad ingredients together in a bowl.
3 Put the dressing ingredients together in a screw-top jar and mix by shaking well.
4 Pour the dressing over the salad and toss. Serve chilled.

This deliciously crisp salad and is served with a piquant sherry-flavoured dressing.

NUTRITIONAL PROFILE	*per portion*	
Total calories		50
Protein	2g	√√
Fibre	1g	√
Polyunsaturated fats	0.5g	√√√
Saturated fats	0.5g	√√
Vitamins	*Good source of:*	
		—
Minerals	*Good source of:*	
		—

Illustrated opposite

• RADICCHIO SALAD •

INGREDIENTS

100 g (4 oz) radicchio, divided into leaves
100 g (4 oz) carrot, grated
50 g (2 oz) chicory, divided into leaves
½ punnet mustard and cress
1 avocado, halved, stoned, peeled and diced
3 spring onions, diced

For the dressing
15 ml (1 tbsp) olive oil
15 ml (1 tbsp) lemon juice
2.5 ml (½ tsp) ready-made mustard
black pepper
Serves 4

1 Prepare and mix together all the salad ingredients in a bowl.
2 Put the dressing ingredients together in a screw-top jar and mix by shaking well.
3 Pour the dressing over the salad and toss. Serve immediately.

Radicchio is used here, but Chinese leaves or lamb's lettuce could be used instead.

NUTRITIONAL PROFILE	*per portion*	
Total calories		155
Protein	3g	√
Fibre	2g	√
Polyunsaturated fats	2g	√√√
Saturated fats	2g	√√
Vitamins	*Good source of:*	
	A, B1, C, E, FA, N	
Minerals	*Good source of:*	
		—

Illustrated opposite

CRUNCHY • GREEN SALAD •

INGREDIENTS

225 g (8 oz) white cabbage or Chinese leaves, shredded
1 small green pepper, deseeded and diced
3 sticks celery, chopped
3 spring onions, diced
For the dressing
45 ml (3 tbsp) mayonnaise

30 ml (2 tbsp) yogurt
15 ml (1 tbsp) orange juice
5 ml (1 tsp) grated orange rind
herb salt, or salt if preferred
Garnish
½ bunch watercress
Serves 4

1 Prepare and mix the vegetables together in a large bowl.
2 Stir the dressing ingredients together to make a thin cream.
3 Pour the dressing over the salad and toss. Garnish with watercress. Serve chilled.

This is the ideal salad to serve with a rich grain or pulse dish.

NUTRITIONAL PROFILE	*per portion*	
Total calories		100
Protein	2g	√
Fibre	2g	√
Polyunsaturated fats	3g	√√√
Saturated fats	1g	√√√
Vitamins	*Good source of:*	
		C
Minerals	*Good source of:*	
		—

Illustrated opposite

Clockwise from the top: **Radicchio salad; Spinach salad; Crunchy green salad**

If you are watching your fat intake strictly, use plain not hung yogurt for the dressing.

NUTRITIONAL PROFILE		per portion
Total calories		160
Protein	5g	✓✓
Fibre	1g	✓
Polyunsaturated fats	6g	✓✓✓
Saturated fats	2g	✓✓
Vitamins		Good source of:
		A, C, E, FA
Minerals		Good source of:
		Ca, Fe, Mg

Illustrated below

⋅ CHINESE LEAF ⋅
& GRAPEFRUIT SALAD

INGREDIENTS

1 grapefruit
350 g (12 oz) Chinese leaves, shredded
For the dressing
1 egg yolk
45 ml (3 tbsp) sunflower oil

15 ml (1 tbsp) grapefruit juice
30 ml (2 tbsp) hung yogurt
Garnish
salad cress
Serves 4

1 Place the grapefruit on a board and cut downwards to remove the peel and pith. To separate each segment from its membrane, over a bowl cut on either side of the membrane to release skinless segments. Dice the segments. Reserve 15 ml (1 tbsp) grapefruit juice.
2 For the dressing, beat the egg yolk. Add the oil a drop at a time to make a mayonnaise. When 30 ml (2 tbsp) have been added, mix in the grapefruit juice.
3 Add the remaining oil, 5 ml (1 tsp) at a time, then stir in the yogurt.
4 Combine the Chinese leaves and grapefruit in a bowl.
5 Mix the mayonnaise dressing into the salad and toss.

Clockwise from the top: **Beansprout salad**; **Chinese leaf & grapefruit salad**; **Courgette & broad bean salad**; **Beetroot salad**

Raw beetroot has an excellent flavour; it is also a good source of vitamins C and E.

NUTRITIONAL PROFILE		per portion
Total calories		100
Protein	2g	√
Fibre	5g	√ √
Polyunsaturated fats	4g	√ √ √
Saturated fats	1g	√ √
Vitamins		Good source of:
		C, E
Minerals		Good source of:
		—

Illustrated opposite

◆ BEETROOT SALAD ◆

INGREDIENTS

225 g (8 oz) uncooked beetroot, peeled
175 g (6 oz) celeriac, peeled
175 g (6 oz) white turnip
For the dressing
30 ml (2 tbsp) sunflower oil

15 ml (1 tbsp) lemon juice
5 ml (1 tsp) French mustard
3 spring onions, very finely chopped
black pepper
Serves 4

1 Grate the beetroot, celeriac and turnip and mix together in a bowl.
2 Put the dressing ingredients together in a screw-top jar and mix by shaking well. Season with pepper.
3 Pour the dressing over the salad and toss.

The beans are responsible for the high protein content of this salad.

NUTRITIONAL PROFILE		per portion
Total calories		70
Protein	6g	√ √ √
Fibre	2g	√
Polyunsaturated fats	0.5g	√ √
Saturated fats	0.5g	√ √ √
Vitamins		Good source of:
		C
Minerals		Good source of:
		Ca, Fe

Illustrated opposite

◆ COURGETTE ◆
& BROAD BEAN SALAD

INGREDIENTS

350 g (12 oz) courgettes
225 g (8 oz) broad beans

2.5 ml (½ tsp) cumin seeds
150 ml (¼ pint) yogurt
Serves 4

1 Grate the courgettes finely. Place in a bowl with the broad beans.
2 Dry roast the cumin seeds in a heavy-based frying pan for about 3 minutes.
3 Mix the yogurt and cumin seeds into the vegetables. Serve chilled.

Beansprouts are a marvellous addition to any diet because of their vitamin and mineral content.

NUTRITIONAL PROFILE		per portion
Total calories		95
Protein	5g	√ √ √
Fibre	3g	√ √
Polyunsaturated fats	3g	√ √ √
Saturated fats	1g	√ √ √
Vitamins		Good source of:
		C, E
Minerals		Good source of:
		—

Illustrated opposite

◆ BEANSPROUT ◆
SALAD

INGREDIENTS

275 g (10 oz) beansprouts
1 medium red pepper, deseeded and diced
225 g (8 oz) cauliflower florets
100 g (4 oz) button mushrooms, sliced
For the dressing
15 ml (1 tbsp) sunflower oil

30 ml (2 tbsp) red wine vinegar
10 ml (2 tsp) sesame oil
5 ml (1 tsp) concentrated apple juice
5 ml (1 tsp) shoyu
1 cm (½ in) fresh root ginger, grated
Serves 4

1 Combine the salad ingredients in a bowl.
2 Put the dressing ingredients together in a screw-top jar and mix by shaking well.
3 Pour the dressing over the salad and toss.

The strong flavour of red cabbage goes very well with the sprouts in this high-fibre, low-fat salad.

NUTRITIONAL PROFILE	*per portion*	
Total calories	130	
Protein	5g	✓✓
Fibre	6g	✓✓✓
Polyunsaturated fats	1g	✓✓
Saturated fats	0.5g	✓✓✓
Vitamins	*Good source of:*	
	B6, C, E, FA	
Minerals	*Good source of:*	
	Ca	

Illustrated opposite

I like to eat French beans raw, but if you prefer them cooked, steam them to preserve their nutrients.

NUTRITIONAL PROFILE	*per portion*	
Total calories	80	
Protein	2g	✓
Fibre	3g	✓✓
Polyunsaturated fats	5g	✓✓✓
Saturated fats	1g	✓✓
Vitamins	*Good source of:*	
	C, E	
Minerals	*Good source of:*	
	—	

Illustrated opposite

This crisp and colourful salad is a good source of protein, fibre and iron.

NUTRITIONAL PROFILE	*per portion*	
Total calories	110	
Protein	5g	✓✓✓
Fibre	4g	✓✓
Polyunsaturated fats	2g	✓✓✓
Saturated fats	0.5g	✓✓✓
Vitamins	*Good source of:*	
	C, E	
Minerals	*Good source of:*	
	Fe	

Illustrated opposite

◆ WINTER SALAD ◆

INGREDIENTS

350 g (12 oz) red cabbage, shredded
175 g (6 oz) Brussels sprouts, finely chopped
3 clementines, peeled and segmented
25-50 g (1-2 oz) hazelnuts

For the dressing
20 ml (4 tsp) hazelnut oil
5 ml (1 tsp) lemon juice
black pepper
Serves 4-6

1 Combine the red cabbage, sprouts and clementines in a bowl.
2 Dry roast the hazelnuts in a heavy-based pan for 3-4 minutes. Cool and roughly chop. Sprinkle over the salad.
3 Put the dressing ingredients together in a screw-top jar and mix by shaking well.
4 Spoon the dressing over the salad and toss.

◆ GREEN BEAN ◆
JULIENNE

INGREDIENTS

225 g (8 oz) French beans
8 sticks celery
25 g (1 oz) sunflower seeds
For the dressing
juice of ½ lemon

15 ml (1 tbsp) sunflower oil
5 ml (1 tsp) concentrated apple juice
gomasio, or salt if preferred
black pepper
Serves 4

1 Slice the French beans into matchstick-sized lengths. Cut the celery into julienne strips. Place in a bowl and mix together.
2 Put the dressing ingredients together in a screw-top jar and mix by shaking well.
3 Pour dressing over the salad. Toss well and add the sunflower seeds.

◆ SWEETCORN SALAD ◆
WITH BEANSPOUTS

INGREDIENTS

225 g (8 oz) fresh or frozen sweetcorn kernels
225 g (8 oz) beansprouts (aduki or lentil)
100 g (4 oz) mouli, scrubbed and chopped
1 medium green pepper, deseeded and diced
12 radishes, sliced

For the dressing
15 ml (1 tbsp) sunflower oil
5 ml (1 tsp) white wine vinegar
5 ml (1 tsp) fennel seeds
2.5 ml (½ tsp) paprika
Serves 4

1 Cook the sweetcorn in a saucepan of boiling water for about 5 minutes or until lightly cooked.
2 Combine the salad ingredients together in a bowl.
3 Put the dressing ingredients together in a screw-top jar and mix by shaking well. Pour the dressing over the salad and toss.

Bulgar wheat is a useful ingredient for salads as it is quick to prepare and has a good, light texture. As with all grains, it absorbs flavours to give an integrated, nutritious result.

NUTRITIONAL PROFILE	*per portion*	
Total calories		325
Protein	9g	√√
Fibre	6g	√√√
Polyunsaturated fats	7g	√√√
Saturated fats	3g	√√√
Vitamins	*Good source of:*	
		A, E
Minerals	*Good source of:*	
		Mg

Illustrated below

·TURKISH WHEAT·
SALAD

INGREDIENTS

175 g (6 oz) bulgar wheat
10 ml (2 tsp) gomasio, or 2.5 ml (½ tsp) salt if preferred
75 g (3 oz) dried apricots
25 g (1 oz) pumpkin seeds
25 g (1 oz) sunflower seeds
45 ml (3 tbsp) finely chopped fresh parsley

For the dressing
juice of ½ lemon
30-45 m (2-3 tbsp) orange juice
30 ml (2 tbsp) sunflower oil
gomasio, or salt if preferred
For serving
8-10 leaves of radicchio
3-4 spring onions, sliced lengthways
Serves 4-6

1 Mix the bulgar wheat with the gomasio. Pour over 300 ml (½ pint) boiling water and leave to stand for 15-20 minutes.
2 Cut the dried apricots into tiny slivers.
3 Mix the apricots, seeds and parsley into the wheat.
4 Put the dressing ingredients together in a screw-top jar and mix by shaking well.
5 Pour the dressing over the salad and toss. Serve on a bed of radicchio, with spring onions on top.

Clockwise from the top: Green bean julienne; Turkish wheat salad; Sweetcorn salad with beansprouts; Winter salad

◆ BALANCED MEAL 5 ◆

This light but filling meal is an excellent balance of nutritional components—protein, fibre, polyunsaturated and, to a lesser extent, saturated fats. It also provides a subtle range of tastes—from the earthy *Artichoke soup* to the delicate mango pudding.

NUTRITIONAL PROFILE	*per portion*
Total calories	880
Protein	21g ✓✓✓
Fibre	30g ✓✓✓
Polyunsaturated fats	14g ✓✓✓
Saturated fats	5g ✓✓✓
Vitamins	*Good source of:* A, C, E, FA
Minerals	*Good source of:* Ca, Fe, Cu, Mg, Zn

◆ **Chinese leaf & grapefruit salad**
For recipe, see page 130

This salad combines the tangy taste of grapefruit with the crispness of the Chinese leaves, and it is offset by a yogurt dressing.

◆ **Artichoke soup**
For recipe, see page 55

Artichokes are high in protein, and they have been used in this dish to produce a thick, substantial soup which, although creamy in taste, is low in saturated fats.

◆ **Julienne of winter vegetables**
For recipe, see page 138

The carrots, parsnips and turnips used here have been baked, both to preserve as many nutrients as possible and to retain the vegetables' firm texture and shape.

♦ Grape juice

It is possible to buy non-alcoholic juices which nevertheless have a similar taste to light, white wines. These are ideal alternatives for those who choose not to drink. A glass will contain about 70 calories.

♦ Mango & orange sorbet
For recipe, see page 160

Sorbets provide a refreshing, low-fat end to a meal, and when including the fruits used here, will be high in vitamins A and C.

♦ Leafy green parcels
For recipe, see page 75

These spinach and cabbage leaf parcels, enclosing a tasty coriander-flavoured mixture of hazelnuts and spinach, are high in fibre and low in saturated fats. Their flavour is complemented by the apricot and tomato relish.

♦ Apricot and tomato relish
For recipe, see page 145

This tasty, high-fibre, low-fat fruit and vegetable relish is a versatile accompaniment to bakes, stir-fries and steamed vegetables.

•VEGETABLES•

These roast potatoes are low in saturated fats.

NUTRITIONAL PROFILE	*per portion*	
Total calories		165
Protein	3g	√
Fibre	2g	√
Polyunsaturated fats	1g	√√
Saturated fats	1g	√√
Vitamins	*Good source of:*	
		C
Minerals	*Good source of:*	
		—

Illustrated opposite

HAZEL'S
• POTATOES •

INGREDIENTS
450 g (1 lb) potatoes juice of ½ lemon
30-45 ml (2-3 tbsp) olive oil *Serves 4*

1 Preheat the oven to gas mark 6, 200°C (400°F).
2 Peel and cut the potatoes into pieces. Place in a saucepan of water, bring to the boil and parboil for 10-15 minutes until almost cooked. Drain.
3 Heat the oil in an ovenproof dish in the oven for a few minutes.
4 Put the potatoes in the dish and sprinkle with lemon juice. Bake for 20-25 minutes until well cooked and lightly browned.

After steaming, baking is the best way to preserve nutrients.

NUTRITIONAL PROFILE	*per portion*	
Total calories		80
Protein	2g	√√
Fibre	5g	√√
Polyunsaturated fats	1g	√√√
Saturated fats	0g	√√√
Vitamins	*Good source of:*	
		C, E, N
Minerals	*Good source of:*	
		—

Illustrated opposite

• BAKED PARSNIPS •
IN ORANGE

INGREDIENTS
450 g (1 lb) parsnips 30-45 ml (2-3 tbsp) water
juice of 1 orange 10 ml (2 tsp) sunflower oil
Serves 4

1 Preheat the oven to gas mark 6, 200°C (400°F).
2 Scrub or peel the parsnips and cut lengthways. Put in a lightly oiled ovenproof dish.
3 Mix together the orange juice, water and oil. Pour this over the parsnips.
4 Bake for 40-50 minutes, adding a little more water or orange juice during the cooking if the parsnips begin to look dry. Serve hot.

Clockwise from the top: **Julienne of winter vegetables** *(see page 138)*; **Baked parsnips in orange**; **Hazel's potatoes**

Serve with a high-protein, high-mineral dish for nutritional balance.

NUTRITIONAL PROFILE		per portion
Total calories		180
Protein	2g	✓
Fibre	4g	✓✓
Polyunsaturated fats	4g	✓✓✓
Saturated fats	1g	✓✓✓
Vitamins		Good source of:
		A, C, E
Minerals		Good source of:
		—

Illustrated on page 137

Potatoes are a good source of protein and fibre, and are not especially fattening except when filled with butter and hard, full-fat cheeses.

NUTRITIONAL PROFILE		per portion
Total calories		190
Protein	6g	✓✓
Fibre	4g	✓✓
Polyunsaturated fats	neg	✓
Saturated fats	neg	✓✓✓
Vitamins		Good source of:
		—
Minerals		Good source of:
		—

Illustrated opposite

These high-protein, high-fibre potatoes are also high in vitamins.

NUTRITIONAL PROFILE		per portion
Total calories		355
Protein	19g	✓✓✓
Fibre	8g	✓✓✓
Polyunsaturated fats	1g	✓
Saturated fats	6g	✓
Vitamins		Good source of:
		A, B1, B2, B6, B12, C, E, FA
Minerals		Good source of:
		Ca, Cu, Fe, Mg, Zn

Illustrated opposite

• JULIENNE •
OF WINTER VEGETABLES

INGREDIENTS
550 g (1¼ lb) mixed root vegetables, cut into matchstick-sized pieces
30 ml (2 tbsp) sunflower oil
10 ml (2 tsp) maple syrup
10 ml (2 tsp) whole grain mustard
gomasio, or salt if preferred
black pepper
Serves 4

1 Preheat the oven to gas mark 6, 200°C (400°F).
2 Heat oil in an ovenproof dish. Mix syrup and mustard together.
3 Put the vegetables in the dish and add the mustard mix. Toss well.
4 Cover and bake for 25-30 minutes. Add a little water if the vegetables begin to look dry. Season with gomasio and pepper. Serve hot.

• BAKED POTATOES •

INGREDIENTS
4 medium to large potatoes
100 ml (4 fl oz) smetana or yogurt
herb salt, or salt if preferred
15 ml (1 tbsp) chopped fresh parsley, chives or coriander
black pepper
Serves 4

1 Preheat the oven to gas mark 6, 200°C (400°F).
2 Scrub the potatoes thoroughly and pierce the skins.
3 Bake for 1-1½ hours or until soft.
4 Mix the smetana or yogurt with the herbs and season with herb salt and pepper.
5 Slit the cooked potatoes open and spoon the smetana mixture on top.

Variation: The potatoes can be served with a more elaborate filling, for example, one of the pancake fillings (see page 108), or sauces such as *Tomato* or *Sharp mushroom* (see page 44 or 146).

• POTATO FLORENTINE •

INGREDIENTS
4 large potatoes
225 g (8 oz) spinach or spring greens, washed and finely shredded
1 egg, beaten
200 g (7 oz) quark
25 g (1 oz) margarine
50 g (2 oz) Cheddar cheese, grated (optional)
15 ml (1 tbsp) finely chopped fresh parsley
5 ml (1 tsp) finely chopped fresh rosemary
gomasio, or salt if preferred
black pepper
Serves 4

1 Preheat the oven to gas mark 6, 200°C (400°F).
2 Scrub the potatoes and pierce the skins. Bake for 1-1½ hours.
3 Stir-fry the spinach in a large heavy-based pan for 6 minutes until soft, or steam for 3-4 minutes.
4 Cut each potato in half. Scoop out the flesh and mash. Mix with ▶

Clockwise from the top: **Baked potatoes with smetana and chives; Potato Florentine; Baked potatoes with chilli bean sauce**

spinach and remaining ingredients. Season and pile into the shells.
5 Reduce the oven temperature to gas mark 4, 180°C (350°F) and heat the potatoes through for 10-15 minutes.

With its high protein content, this is an extremely easy-to-prepare dish.

NUTRITIONAL PROFILE	*per portion*	
Total calories	130	
Protein	8g	√√√
Fibre	7g	√√√
Polyunsaturated fats	1g	√√
Saturated fats	1g	√√√
Vitamins	*Good source of:*	
	C	
Minerals	*Good source of:*	
	—	

Illustrated below

·BAKED POTATOES·
WITH CHILLI BEAN SAUCE

INGREDIENTS

4 large potatoes
For the sauce
100 g (4 oz) mixed red kidney beans and black-eye beans, soaked overnight
1 fresh red chilli, deseeded
15 ml (1 tbsp) olive oil
2 medium onions, finely chopped
1 fresh green chilli, deseeded and very finely chopped

1 cm (½ in) fresh root ginger, grated
2.5 ml (½ tsp) fennel seeds
30 ml (2 tbsp) tomato purée
shoyu, or salt if preferred
black pepper
Garnish
yogurt or smetana
Serves 4

1 Preheat the oven to gas mark 6, 200°C (400°F).
2 Scrub the potatoes thoroughly and pierce the skins several times with a skewer. Bake for 1-1½ hours or until soft.
3 Meanwhile, drain the beans. Cover with plenty of fresh water and add the red chilli. Bring uncovered to the boil and boil fast for 10▶

minutes. Reduce the heat, skim, cover and simmer for 35-40 minutes or until the beans are soft. Drain, reserve the cooking liquid and remove the chilli.

4 Heat the oil in a large saucepan and gently fry the onions, green chilli, ginger and fennel seeds for 4-5 minutes or until soft.

5 Add the cooked beans and tomato purée. Lightly mash everything together adding a little reserved stock if necessary. Season with shoyu and pepper.

6 Slit the cooked potatoes open, spoon in the sauce and top with yogurt or smetana.

This dish is high in vitamins C and E, and low in saturated fats.

NUTRITIONAL PROFILE	*per portion*	
Total calories		65
Protein	2g	√
Fibre	2g	√
Polyunsaturated fats	2g	√√√
Saturated fats	0.5g	√√√
Vitamins		*Good source of:*
		C, E
Minerals		*Good source of:*
		—

Illustrated opposite

• RUSSIAN RED CABBAGE •

INGREDIENTS

225 g (8 oz) red cabbage
225 g (8 oz) white turnip
15 ml (1 tbsp) sunflower oil
15 ml (1 tbsp) red wine vinegar
30 ml (2 tbsp) orange juice
5 ml (1 tsp) paprika
2.5 ml (½ tsp) cumin seeds
shoyu
black pepper
Serves 4

1 Shred the red cabbage.

2 Scrub the turnips and grate finely. Mix with the red cabbage.

3 Heat the oil in a large saucepan and gently fry the cabbage mixture for 2-3 minutes.

4 Add the remaining ingredients, cover and cook gently for 35-45 minutes, stirring occasionally. Serve hot or cold.

Because the aubergine in this recipe is baked and not fried, the fat content remains desirably low. Serve with baked savouries like Pine kernel roast (see page 75), or Lentil pourgouri (see page 117).

NUTRITIONAL PROFILE	*per portion*	
Total calories		75
Protein	2g	√√
Fibre	3g	√√
Polyunsaturated fats	2g	√√√
Saturated fats	0.5g	√√√
Vitamins		*Good source of:*
		C, E
Minerals		*Good source of:*
		—

Illustrated opposite

• AUBERGINE BAKE •

INGREDIENTS

1 medium aubergine
10 ml (2 tsp) sunflower oil
1 medium onion, finely chopped
2.5 ml (½ tsp) cumin seeds
2.5 ml (½ tsp) turmeric
5 ml (1 tsp) ground coriander
5 ml (1 tsp) garam masala
1 medium green pepper, deseeded and diced
100 g (4 oz) dwarf sweetcorn
15 ml (1 tbsp) tomato purée
150 ml (¼ pint) vegetable stock or water
10 ml (2 tsp) shoyu
black pepper
Serves 4

1 Preheat the oven to gas mark 6, 200°C (400°F).

2 Remove the aubergine stalk. Prick the skin 2-3 times. Bake for 15-20 minutes or until soft. Cool and chop into bite-sized pieces.

3 Heat the oil in a large saucepan and gently fry the onion for 4-5 minutes. Stir in the spices and fry for 3 minutes.

4 Add the baked aubergine pieces, green pepper and sweetcorn, mix in well.

5 Dissolve the tomato purée in the stock. Pour over the vegetables.

6 Transfer to an ovenproof dish. Reduce the oven temperature to gas mark 4, 180°C (350°F). Cover the dish and bake for 45 minutes. Season with shoyu and pepper. Serve hot.

Top: **Aubergine bake**; Russian red cabbage

High in vitamins C and E, these vegetables are low in saturated fats.

NUTRITIONAL PROFILE	per portion	
Total calories		35
Protein	1g	√√
Fibre	2g	√
Polyunsaturated fats	1g	√√√
Saturated fats	0g	√√√
Vitamins	Good source of:	
	C, E	
Minerals	Good source of:	
	—	

Illustrated opposite

• FENNEL & RED PEPPER •
STIR-FRY

INGREDIENTS

350 g (12 oz) fennel, about 1 large bulb   10 ml (2 tsp) sunflower oil
1 large red pepper, deseeded   black pepper
Serves 3-4

1 Trim the fennel and chop into matchstick-sized pieces.
2 Slice the pepper into thin strips.
3 Heat the oil in a wok or large frying pan. When hot, stir-fry the pepper and fennel for 4-5 minutes over a high heat, stirring constantly. Season with pepper. Serve immediately.

This high-protein dish is served with a tangy, sweet and sour sauce.

NUTRITIONAL PROFILE	per portion	
Total calories		205
Protein	10g	√√√
Fibre	3g	√√
Polyunsaturated fats	2g	√√√
Saturated fats	1g	√√√
Vitamins	Good source of:	
	A, C	
Minerals	Good source of:	
	Ca, Cu, Fe, Mg	

Illustrated opposite

• TOFU STIR-FRY •
WITH ANKAKE SAUCE

INGREDIENTS

1 quantity of Ankake sauce (see page 145)   6 spring onions
225 g (8 oz) carrots   350-450 g (12 oz-1 lb) firm tofu
225 g (8 oz) mouli   10 ml (2 tsp) sunflower oil
6 sticks celery   *Serves 3-4*

1 Cut the carrots, mouli, celery and spring onions into matchstick-sized pieces. Slice the tofu.
2 Heat the oil in a wok or large frying pan. When hot, stir-fry the vegetables for 3-4 minutes over a high heat, stirring constantly, until just soft. Add the tofu and cook for another 2 minutes.
3 Heat up the Ankake sauce and serve immediately with *Stir-fry*.

The liquid added at the end provides a burst of steam to finish off the cooking.

NUTRITIONAL PROFILE	per portion	
Total calories		145
Protein	9g	√√√
Fibre	7g	√√√
Polyunsaturated fats	2g	√√√
Saturated fats	1g	√√√
Vitamins	Good source of:	
	A, C, E, FA	
Minerals	Good source of:	
	Ca, Fe, Mg	

Illustrated opposite

• GREEN VEGETABLE •
& ALMOND STIR-FRY

INGREDIENTS

10 ml (2 tsp) sesame oil   350 g (12 oz) Chinese leaves, shredded
50 g (2 oz) blanched almonds, halved   15 ml (1 tbsp) dry sherry
1 dried red chilli   juice of 1 lemon
225 g (8 oz) green beans, sliced   15 ml (1 tbsp) water
350 g (12 oz) broccoli florets   gomasio, or salt if preferred
Serves 3-4

1 Heat the oil in a wok or large frying pan. When hot, toast the almonds and chilli for 2 minutes. Remove and discard chilli.
2 Add the vegetables and stir-fry for 3-4 minutes.
3 Mix the sherry, lemon juice and water together. Pour over the vegetables, then stir in the toasted almonds. Cook for 1 minute.
4 Serve immediately, sprinkled with gomasio.

If you cannot find fresh, use tinned oyster mushrooms for this dish.

NUTRITIONAL PROFILE	*per portion*	
Total calories		155
Protein	9g	✓✓✓
Fibre	3g	✓✓
Polyunsaturated fats	5g	✓✓✓
Saturated fats	1g	✓✓✓
Vitamins	*Good source of:*	
	C, FA, N	
Minerals	*Good source of:*	
	Fe, Mg, Zn	

Illustrated above

◆ BEANSPROUT ◆
& SESAME STIR-FRY

INGREDIENTS

For the sauce
45 ml (3 tbsp) tahini
30 ml (2 tbsp) water
15 ml (1 tbsp) shoyu
30 ml (2 tbsp) dry sherry
5 ml (1 tsp) concentrated apple juice
5 ml (1 tsp) red wine vinegar
30 ml (2 tbsp) chopped fresh coriander

For the stir-fry
225 g (8 oz) beansprouts, rinsed
225 g (8 oz) oyster mushrooms, sliced
1 cauliflower, divided into florets
1 medium red pepper, deseeded and diced
1 clove garlic, crushed
10 ml (2 tsp) sesame oil
Serves 4

1 Mix the sauce ingredients together. Leave to stand for 1 hour before making the stir-fry.
2 Meanwhile, prepare the beansprouts, mushrooms, cauliflower, pepper and garlic.
3 Heat the oil in a wok or large frying pan. When hot, stir-fry the vegetables for 3-4 minutes over a high heat, stirring constantly, until just soft.
4 Serve immediately, accompanied by the sauce.

From the left: Fennel and red pepper stir-fry; Beansprout and sesame stir-fry;
Tofu stir-fry with ankake sauce; Green vegetable & almond stir-fry

143

Despite being fried, this dish remains low in saturated fat.

NUTRITIONAL PROFILE	*per portion*	
Total calories	75	
Protein	2g	√
Fibre	1g	√
Polyunsaturated fats	2g	√√√
Saturated fats	0.5g	√√√
Vitamins	*Good source of:*	
	C, E	
Minerals	*Good source of:*	
	—	

Illustrated below

◆ SPICED COURGETTE ◆
& APPLE

INGREDIENTS

225 g (8 oz) courgettes
1 medium dessert apple
10 ml (2 tsp) sunflower oil
10 ml (2 tsp) lemon juice
15 ml (1 tbsp) concentrated apple juice

2.5 ml (½ tsp) ground cinnamon
2.5 ml (½ tsp) grated nutmeg
25 g (1 oz) hazelnuts, finely chopped
gomasio, or salt if preferred
black pepper
Serves 3-4

1 Chop the courgettes and apple into finger-sized pieces (chunky matchsticks).
2 Heat the oil in a large saucepan and fry the courgette and apple pieces for 3 minutes.
3 Mix in the other ingredients. Cover and cook for 10-15 minutes until the courgette and apple are just soft. Season with gomasio and black pepper.

Spiced courgette and apple

SAUCES
◆·&·SPREADS·◆

A tasty high-fibre fruit and vegetable relish to serve with stir-fries and steamed vegetables, or with baked savouries.

NUTRITIONAL PROFILE	per portion	
Total calories		250
Protein	9g	√√
Fibre	7g	√√√
Polyunsaturated fats	0g	√√√
Saturated fats	0g	√√√
Vitamins	Good source of:	
		A, C
Minerals	Good source of:	
		—

Illustrated on page 147

◆ APRICOT & TOMATO ◆
RELISH

INGREDIENTS

75 g (3 oz) dried apricots. sliced thinly
5 ml (1 tsp) coriander seeds
225 g (8 oz) tomatoes, skinned and chopped
1 small onion, diced
1 medium green pepper, deseeded and chopped
60 ml (4 tbsp) orange juice

juice of ½ lemon
15 ml (1 tbsp) tomato purée
15 ml (1 tbsp) white wine vinegar
15 ml (1 tbsp) concentrated apple juice
5 ml (1 tsp) shoyu, or salt if preferred
1.25 cm (½ in) fresh root ginger, grated
Makes about 300 ml (½ pint)

1 Place apricots in a saucepan with 300 ml (½ pint) water. Cook until soft. Drain, reserving juice.
2 Dry roast seeds (see page 46). Cool and crush. Mix with remaining ingredients and 60 ml (4 tbsp) of juice. Cover and simmer for 1-1½ hours.

This sweet and sour fruit sauce has a strong but pleasant flavour of miso.

NUTRITIONAL PROFILE	per portion	
Total calories		
Protein	3g	√
Fibre	—	—
Polyunsaturated fats	0.5g	√
Saturated fats	0.5g	√√√
Vitamins	Good source of:	
		C
Minerals	Good source of:	
		—

Illustrated on page 147

◆ ANKAKE ◆
SAUCE

INGREDIENTS

200 ml (⅓ pint) pineapple juice
5 ml (1 tsp) honey
5 ml (1 tsp) red wine vinegar

15 ml (1 tbsp) miso
5 ml (1 tsp) arrowroot
Makes about 300 ml (½ pint)

1 Mix all the ingredients together in a saucepan.
2 Bring to the boil and simmer for 2-3 minutes until the sauce thickens, stirring all the time.

A light, creamy sauce with a slightly nutty flavour. Serve with baked savouries or with pastry dishes.

NUTRITIONAL PROFILE	per portion	
Total calories	60	
Protein	4g	✓✓✓
Fibre	3g	✓✓
Polyunsaturated fats	4g	✓✓✓
Saturated fats	1g	✓✓
Vitamins	Good source of:	C, E
Minerals	Good source of:	—

Illustrated opposite

Low in saturated fats, this is a versatile sauce which can be served with both grain and pastry dishes.

NUTRITIONAL PROFILE	per portion	
Total calories	65	
Protein	2g	✓✓
Fibre	1g	✓
Polyunsaturated fats	0.5g	✓✓
Saturated fats	0.5g	✓✓✓
Vitamins	Good source of:	C
Minerals	Good source of:	—

Illustrated opposite

Relatively low in fats, this simple sauce is like a nut mayonnaise.

NUTRITIONAL PROFILE	per portion	
Total calories	125	
Protein	3g	✓✓
Fibre	1g	✓
Polyunsaturated fats	5g	✓✓✓
Saturated fats	2g	✓✓
Vitamins	Good source of:	—
Minerals	Good source of:	—

Illustrated opposite

· BROCCOLI ·
& SUNFLOWER SAUCE

INGREDIENTS
225 g (8 oz) broccoli florets
25 g (1 oz) sunflower seeds
60 ml (4 tbsp) smetana or silken tofu
10 ml (2 tsp) lemon juice
gomasio, or salt if preferred
black pepper
Makes about 450 ml (¾ pint)

1 Steam the broccoli florets for 8-10 minutes until tender.
2 Grind the sunflower seeds in a grinder, liquidizer or food processor.
3 Liquidize the broccoli with 300 ml (½ pint) of the steaming water. Add the smetana, lemon juice and sunflower seeds and liquidize again. Season to taste with gomasio and pepper.
4 Reheat very gently before serving.

· SHARP MUSHROOM ·
SAUCE

INGREDIENTS
10 ml (2 tsp) olive oil
225 g (8 oz) pickling onions
225 g (8 oz) button mushrooms
150 ml (¼ pint) tomato juice
150 ml (¼ pint) apple juice
15 ml (1 tbsp) red wine vinegar
5 ml (1 tsp) shoyu
pinch of dried thyme
shoyu, or salt if preferred
black pepper
Makes about 450 ml (¾ pint)

1 Heat the oil in a saucepan and gently fry the onions for about 5-6 minutes until just brown.
2 Stir the remaining ingredients into the pan, mixing well. Bring to the boil, cover and simmer for 20 minutes, stirring occasionally. Season with extra shoyu if necessary, and pepper.

PEANUT &
· SESAME SAUCE ·

INGREDIENTS
30 ml (2 tbsp) tahini
15 ml (1 tbsp) peanut butter
15 ml (1 tbsp) sesame oil
15 ml (1 tbsp) red wine vinegar
10 ml (2 tsp) concentrated apple juice
10 ml (2 tsp) shoyu, or salt if preferred
2.5 cm (1 in) fresh root ginger, grated
200 ml (7 fl oz) water
pinch of cayenne
black pepper
Makes about 300 ml (½ pint)

1 Liquidize ingredients, except the water and peppers.
2 Gradually add the water, liquidizing until the sauce is smooth.
3 Season with cayenne and black pepper.

Clockwise from the top: **Peanut & sesame sauce**; Carob sauce *(see page 148)*; **Sharp mushroom sauce**; **Ankake sauce** *(see page 145)*; **Broccoli & sunflower sauce**; Centre: **Apricot & tomato relish** *(see page 145)*

As you lose your taste for sugar you may find that custards need no flavouring other than vanilla. To start with, however, try this sauce sweetened with dates and carob.

NUTRITIONAL PROFILE	*per portion*	
Total calories		95
Protein	3g	√ √
Fibre	1g	√
Polyunsaturated fats	0g	√ √ √
Saturated fats	2g	√ √ √
Vitamins	*Good source of:*	
	—	
Minerals	*Good source of:*	
	—	

Illustrated on page 147

• CAROB •
SAUCE

INGREDIENTS

50 g (2 oz) dried stoned dates   5-10 ml (1-2 tsp) carob powder
15 ml (1 tbsp) rice flour   4-6 drops vanilla essence
300 ml (½ pint) milk   *Makes about 300 ml (½ pint)*

1 Gently stew the dates in a little water for about 10-15 minutes until soft. Beat to a stiff purée.
2 Combine the rice flour with a little of the milk to dissolve. Then stir in the remaining milk.
3 Bring to the boil and cook gently for 5 minutes, stirring. (The rice flour will thicken the milk on standing).
4 Liquidize the milk with the dates, carob and vanilla until quite smooth.
5 Reheat gently before serving.

Left: **Survival spread**; Centre: **Sweet Tahini spread**; Bottom right: **Better butter**

The addition of lecithin and skimmed milk gives this spread a creamier texture and nuttier flavour.

NUTRITIONAL PROFILE	*per portion*	
Total calories	1830	
Protein	0g	—
Fibre	0g	—
Polyunsaturated fats	62g	√√√
Saturated fats	65g	√
Vitamins	*Good source of:*	
	A, D, E	
Minerals	*Good source of:*	
	—	

Illustrated opposite

BETTER
• BUTTER •

INGREDIENTS
100 g (4 oz) butter   10 ml (2 tsp) lecithin granules
120 ml (8 tbsp) sunflower oil   30 ml (2 tbsp) skimmed milk
Makes 225 g (8 oz)

1 Liquidize the butter and oil together until well mixed.
2 Dissolve the lecithin in the milk. Add this to the butter mixture and combine well.
3 Leave in the refrigerator to firm up.

This high-fibre, low-fat spread has a slightly chocolaty flavour.

NUTRITIONAL PROFILE	*per portion*	
Total calories	680	
Protein	5g	√√
Fibre	9g	√√√
Polyunsaturated fats	4g	√√√
Saturated fats	1g	√√√
Vitamins	*Good source of:*	
	B1, N	
Minerals	*Good source of:*	
	Ca, Fe, Mg, Zn	

Illustrated opposite

SWEET
• TAHINI SPREAD •

INGREDIENTS
100 g (4 oz) dried stoned dates   5 ml (1 tsp) carob powder
60 ml (4 tbsp) tahini   *Makes about 175 g (6 oz)*

1 Gently stew the dates in a little water for about 10-15 minutes until soft. Beat to a smooth purée.
2 Liquidize the dates with the tahini and carob until completely smooth.
3 Use immediately or store for 3-4 days in a screw-top container.

You can alter the amount of Brewer's yeast, according to taste.

NUTRITIONAL PROFILE	*per portion*	
Total calories	105	
Protein	5g	√√√
Fibre	1g	√
Polyunsaturated fats	4g	√√√
Saturated fats	1g	√√
Vitamins	*Good source of:*	
	B1, N	
Minerals	*Good source of:*	
	Ca, Fe, Mg, Zn	

Illustrated opposite

• SURVIVAL •
SPREAD

INGREDIENTS
60 ml (4 tbsp) tahini   up to 10 ml (2 tsp) brewer's yeast
45 ml (3 tbsp) water   5 ml (1 tsp) miso
Makes about 110 g (4 oz)

1 Mix the tahini and water together in a bowl to make a smooth cream.
2 Add the yeast and miso and combine well.
3 Use immediately or store for up to a week in a screw-top jar.

◆ BALANCED MEAL 6 ◆

A wholesome meal that is surprisingly low in fats. The major source of
protein is the *Celery & green pepper flan,* with the *Wild rice salad,*
Fruit pie and the slice of bread being the major sources of fibre.

◆ Summer soup
For recipe, see page 58

Served chilled, this
high-protein soup, based on
lettuce and Chinese
leaves, is an ideal
starter for a summer meal.
The cardamom and yogurt
add to the delicate
flavour of the main
ingredients.

◆ Wholewheat bread
For recipe, see page 31

Wholewheat bread is one of
the best sources of fibre
in our diet. It is
important not to use
refined flours as most of
their nutrients and
roughage have been
removed in manufacture.

◆ Green bean julienne
For recipe, see page 132

Salads are often used to
provide a contrast in
texture, as well as taste,
and this is certainly true
of this dish where raw
green beans and fresh
celery have been used to
complement the soft
filling of the flan.

◆ Celery & green pepper flan
For recipe, see page 98

This high-protein, low-fat flan is a simple combination of vegetables in a well-flavoured, milky sauce. The horseradish and celery seeds add a special tang to the taste of the filling. The wholewheat pastry base is an excellent source of fibre, and, because it was rolled out thinly, is light and delicate in texture.

◆ Apple juice

High in vitamin C, apple juice is available both still and carbonated. Always choose natural juices, and make sure no preservatives or colourings have been added. A glass of apple juice contains about 50 calories.

NUTRITIONAL PROFILE	*per portion*	
Total calories		1095
Protein	37g	√√√
Fibre	23g	√√√
Polyunsaturated fats	17g	√√√
Saturated fats	9g	√√√
Vitamins	*Good source of:*	
	A, B1, B2, B6, B12, N, E, FA	
Minerals	*Good source of:*	
	Fe, Mg, Zn, Ca, Cu	

◆ Fresh fruit pie
For recipe, see page 157

Pies need not be unhealthy so long as you use the freshest ingredients, use a good wholewheat pastry and do not use sugar. In this pie, the fresh peaches and pears are sweetened with sultanas, and they are enclosed in a light yeasted pastry.

◆ Wild rice salad
For recipe, see page 121

This salad is an interesting combination of textures and tastes—the firmness of the rice is set off by the peppery taste of the watercress and the spiciness of the fresh root ginger.

◆PUDDINGS◆

It's quite possible to make this low-fat, seemingly rich pudding without sugar by using a well-flavoured, sugar-free jam.

NUTRITIONAL PROFILE	*per portion*	
Total calories		240
Protein	12g	√ √ √
Fibre	1g	√
Polyunsaturated fats	0.5g	√
Saturated fats	1g	√ √ √
Vitamins	*Good source of:*	
	B12, C, D	
Minerals	*Good source of:*	
	Ca	

Illustrated opposite

◆TROPICAL◆
TRIFLE

INGREDIENTS

For the sponge	300 ml (½ pint) fruit juice
2 eggs	1 paw paw
25 g (1 oz) concentrated pear and apple spread	2 bananas, sliced
	175 g (6 oz) quark
50 g (2 oz) wholewheat flour	90 ml (6 tbsp) skimmed milk
For the trifle	*Garnish*
45 ml (3 tbsp) sugar-free jam	toasted flaked almonds
30 ml (2 tbsp) medium dry sherry	*Serves 6*

1 Preheat the oven to gas mark 5, 190°C (375°F).
2 Whisk the eggs and fruit spread until very thick and creamy. Fold in half the flour, then fold in the remainder very carefully.
3 Butter and flour an 18 cm (7 in) sandwich tin. Spoon in the mixture evenly.
4 Bake for 20 minutes. Turn out of the tin and cool on a wire rack.
5 Cut the sponge in half, spread with jam and sandwich together again. Cut into 2.5 cm (1 in) cubes. Place in the bottom of a glass dish.
6 Sprinkle over the sherry. Pour over the fruit juice.
7 Cut the paw paw in half lengthways. Remove the seeds and skin. Slice the flesh.
8 Arrange the banana and paw paw slices in layers over the sponge.
9 Liquidize the quark with the milk and spread over the fruit.
10 Decorate with some toasted flaked almonds.

Top: **Tropical trifle; Baked tofu cheesecake** *(see page 154)*

Cheesecake is a slight misnomer as no cheese is used in this dish; protein-rich tofu is used instead. If you are trying tofu for the first time, you may wish to blend in a little cottage cheese or sweetening such as honey or maple syrup.

NUTRITIONAL PROFILE	*per portion*	
Total calories	180	
Protein	8g	√ √ √
Fibre	3g	√ √
Polyunsaturated fats	2g	√ √ √
Saturated fats	4g	√
Vitamins	*Good source of:*	
	A, B₁, C	
Minerals	*Good source of:*	
	Ca, Cu, Fe, Mg, Zn	

Illustrated on page 153

BAKED
•TOFU CHEESECAKE•

INGREDIENTS

For the base
50 g (2 oz) butter or sunflower margarine
10 ml (2 tsp) concentrated pear and apple spread
50 g (2 oz) porridge oats
50 g (2 oz) wholewheat flour

For the filling
rind and juice of 1 orange
4 ripe bananas
594 g (21 oz) silken tofu
Garnish
grapes and orange segments
Serves 6-8

1 Preheat the oven to gas mark 4, 180°C (350°F).
2 For the base: cream the butter or margarine and fruit spread together until smooth. Stir in the oats and flour and mix well.
3 Spread the mixture over the base of a lightly oiled 18 cm (7 in) spring mould. Bake for 10 minutes.
4 For the filling: liquidize the orange rind, orange juice, bananas and tofu until smooth. Pour over the baked base.
5 Bake for about 45 minutes until just set.
6 Leave to cool in the tin before removing. Decorate with grapes and orange segments. Chill before serving.

• CRANACHAN •

This high-fibre dessert can be varied according to the fruit in season.

NUTRITIONAL PROFILE	*per portion*	
Total calories	450	
Protein	16g	√√
Fibre	9g	√√√
Polyunsaturated fats	4g	√√
Saturated fats	3g	√√√
Vitamins	*Good source of:*	
	B1, B2, B6, C, E, FA	
Minerals	*Good source of:*	
	Ca, Fe, Mg, Zn	

Illustrated opposite

INGREDIENTS

75 g (3 oz) hazelnuts, roughly ground
75 g (3 oz) medium oatmeal
300 ml (½ pint) hung yogurt and 150 ml (¼ pint) low-fat yogurt or 450 ml (¾ pint) home-made low-fat hung yogurt

225 g (8 oz) black grapes, halved and deseeded
225 g (8 oz) strawberries, sliced
Garnish
a few small whole strawberries
Serves 4

1 Preheat the oven to gas mark 4, 180°C (350°F).
2 Mix the hazelnuts with the oatmeal and place in a shallow oven-proof dish or on a baking sheet. Toast in the oven for 10-15 minutes until golden.
3 Using 4 wide tumbler glasses, make layers of the yogurt, fruit and oatmeal mixture. Finish with a layer of yogurt and decorate with whole strawberries. Serve chilled.

CITRUS • CASTAGNE •

This high-protein pudding owes its unusual taste to tahini and sesame.

NUTRITIONAL PROFILE	*per portion*	
Total calories	150	
Protein	12g	√√√
Fibre	2g	√
Polyunsaturated fats	5g	√√√
Saturated fats	2g	√√
Vitamins	*Good source of:*	
		C
Minerals	*Good source of:*	
		Fe, Mg

Illustrated opposite

INGREDIENTS

100 g (4 oz) dried chestnuts, soaked overnight in 225 ml (8 fl oz) orange juice
30 ml (2 tbsp) lemon juice
10 ml (2 tsp) carob powder
60 ml (4 tbsp) tahini

175 g (6 oz) quark
12 drops almond essence
10 ml (2 tsp) maple syrup
Garnish
grated carob chocolate
Serves 4

1 Place the chestnuts and their soaking juice in a saucepan. Bring to the boil, cover and simmer for 35-40 minutes or until soft. Drain.
2 Liquidize the chestnuts with the remaining ingredients.
3 Pile into 4 glasses and chill. Decorate with grated carob.

• GOLDEN SALAD •

In a healthy diet fruit salads come into their own — naturally sweet and fat-free.

NUTRITIONAL PROFILE	*per portion*	
Total calories	120	
Protein	2g	√
Fibre	6g	√√√
Polyunsaturated fats	0.5g	√
Saturated fats	0.5g	√√√
Vitamins	*Good source of:*	
		A, C
Minerals	*Good source of:*	
		—

Illustrated on page 156

INGREDIENTS

1 mango
1 ugli or pink grapefruit
2 passion fruit
1 pomegranate

8 fresh dates
6 yellow plums
5 ml (1 tsp) lemon juice
15 ml (1 tbsp) white grape juice
Serves 4

1 Peel the mango and chop the flesh into bite-sized pieces.
2 Peel the ugli fruit or grapefruit and segment the flesh.
3 Halve the passion fruit and pomegranate and scrape out the seeds, taking care to remove the bitter white pith from the pomegranate.
4 Stone the dates and plums and chop into bite-sized pieces.
5 Mix fruits together with the juices. Leave for 2-3 hours.

It takes time to adjust to eating sugar-free fruit. Pick ripe fruit for the best flavour and used dried fruit—in this case sultanas—to add extra sweetness. This pie is high in most vitamins, iron and zinc.

NUTRITIONAL PROFILE	*per portion*	
Total calories		385
Protein	11g	√ √
Fibre	8g	√ √ √
Polyunsaturated fats	1g	√
Saturated fats	5g	√ √
Vitamins		*Good source of:*
		A, B₁, B₂, B₁₂, C, D, N
Minerals		*Good source of:*
		Fe, Mg, Zn

Illustrated opposite

• FRESH FRUIT PIE •

INGREDIENTS

450 g (1 lb) dessert pears (Williams or Comice)
3 medium peaches, skinned
50 g (2 oz) sultanas
150 ml (¼ pint) white wine or apple juice
2.5 ml (½ tsp) ground coriander
12 cardamom seeds
5 ml (1 tsp) arrowroot
1 quantity of yeasted pastry (see page 40)
1 egg, beaten
Serves 4-6

1 Coarsely chop the fruit. Place in a saucepan with the sultanas, wine or apple juice, coriander and cardamom seeds. Cook, uncovered, over a gentle heat for 15-20 minutes. Remove the cardamom seeds.
2 Preheat the oven to gas mark 6, 200°C (400°F).
3 Dissolve the arrowroot in a little water and add to the fruit. Bring to the boil, stirring, and simmer for 2-3 minutes.
4 Divide the pastry dough in half.
5 Roll out one portion and use to line a 20 cm (8 in) pie plate. Spoon in the fruit. Moisten the pastry edges with water.
6 Roll out the remaining pastry for the lid. Seal and crimp the pastry edges. Brush with beaten egg.
7 Bake for 25-30 minutes or until the pastry is cooked.

In this high-fibre, low-fat dessert an apricot purée is used to make a sweet pancake batter. This is a thick mixture best cooked in small amounts rather like drop scones. Once the bubbles have burst the pancakes should be turned over. Keep the pancakes hot in a warm towel until ready to eat.

NUTRITIONAL PROFILE	*per portion*	
Total calories		240
Protein	7g	√ √
Fibre	6g	√ √ √
Polyunsaturated fats	3g	√ √ √
Saturated fats	1g	√ √ √
Vitamins		*Good source of:*
		B₆, C, E
Minerals		*Good source of:*
		Fe

Illustrated opposite

• BAKED BANANA •
WITH APRICOT PANCAKES

INGREDIENTS

4 large bananas
5 ml (1 tsp) lemon or lime juice
25 g (1 oz) pecan nuts, chopped
For the pancakes
40 g (1½ oz) dried apricots
1 egg
5 ml (1 tsp) sunflower oil
100 g (4 oz) wholewheat flour
pinch of salt
Garnish
slice of lemon or lime
Serves 4

1 Preheat the oven to gas mark 5, 190°C (375°F). Bake the bananas in their skins for 15-20 minutes or until soft.
2 Split the skins, scoop out the flesh and mash well with lemon juice and pecan nuts. Divide in 4 portions.
3 For the pancakes, cook the apricots in water to cover for 15-20 minutes until soft. Liquidize the apricots and liquid. Make up to 300 ml (½ pint) with water.
4 Add the egg and oil and liquidize again.
5 Add the flour and salt, then liquidize until a smooth batter.
6 Use 15 ml (1 tbsp) of the mixture to make each small pancake (see page 107). Keep them hot, wrapped in clean tea-towel.
7 Serve each person with a portion of banana and a plate of pancakes.

Clockwise from the top: **Date and orange frazzan** *(see page 158)*; **Golden salad** *(see page 155)*; **Fresh fruit pie**; **Baked banana with apricot pancakes**

Sweet, without added sugar, these fruit slices should follow high-protein, low-fat dishes.

NUTRITIONAL PROFILE	per portion	
Total calories	215	
Protein	5g	√
Fibre	3g	√ √
Polyunsaturated fats	0.5g	√
Saturated fats	6g	√
Vitamins	Good source of:	
	B2, B12, C, D	
Minerals	Good source of:	
	—	

Illustrated on page 156

• DATE & ORANGE •
FRAZZAN

INGREDIENTS

100 g (4 oz) dried stoned dates, chopped
5 ml (1 tsp) orange rind, grated
300 ml (½ pint) orange juice
40 g (1½ oz) butter or sunflower margarine
25 g (1 oz) wholewheat flour
2 eggs, separated
Serves 4

1 Place the dates in a small saucepan.
2 Add the orange and orange rind and cook for 10-15 minutes or until the dates are soft.
3 Meanwhile, preheat the oven to gas mark 4, 180°C (350°F).
4 Melt the butter or margarine in a large saucepan and stir in the flour until smooth. Stir in the date mixture, bring to the boil and simmer for 2-3 minutes, stirring. Cool.
5 Beat the egg yolks into the date mixture.
6 Beat the egg whites until stiff, then fold into the mixture.
7 Spoon into a lightly oiled ovenproof dish and bake for 30 minutes.

Patience is called for when making rice puddings from whole rice and this high-protein, high-fibre, low-fat pudding is no exception. It's best to use a short-grain rice and to stir the mixture frequently, thus breaking the grain down. Accompany with sharp, stewed fruit such as black-currants, gooseberries or apricots.

NUTRITIONAL PROFILE	per portion	
Total calories	145	
Protein	8g	√ √ √
Fibre	9g	√ √ √
Polyunsaturated fats	0g	√ √ √
Saturated fats	0.5g	√ √ √
Vitamins	Good source of:	
	B2, B12, C	
Minerals	Good source of:	
	Ca	

Illustrated opposite

• NORWEGIAN •
RICE CREAM

INGREDIENTS

40 g (1½ oz) short-grain brown rice
600 ml (1 pint) skimmed milk
5 ml (1 tsp) agar
60 ml (4 tbsp) orange juice
1 large dessert apple
5 ml (1 tsp) honey (optional)
25 g (1 oz) quark
15 ml (1 tbsp) skimmed milk
For serving
350 g (12 oz) stewed fruit (blackcurrants, gooseberries or apricots)
Serves 4

1 Place the rice and milk in a saucepan. Bring to the boil, cover and gently simmer for abour 2 hours, stirring frequently, until the rice is completely soft. The consistency should be fairly thick.
2 Dissolve the agar in the orange juice in a small pan. Bring to the boil, then mix into the cooked rice.
3 Peel and grate the apple. Mix into the rice, adding honey if liked.
4 Beat the quark with the 15 ml (1 tbsp) skimmed milk until the consistency of double cream. Stir this into the rice.
5 Put the mixture into a lightly oiled 600 ml (1 pint) mould or 4 individual dishes. Leave to cool.
6 Turn out, if in a mould, and serve with stewed fruit.

Clockwise from the top: **Iced cashew cream** *(see page 160)*; **Red and white salad** *(see page 160)*; **Norwegian rice cream**; **Mango and orange sorbet** *(see page 160)*

With the fruits used here the dish is high in vitamin C.

NUTRITIONAL PROFILE	per portion	
Total calories		80
Protein	2g	√
Fibre	4g	√√
Polyunsaturated fats	0g	√√√
Saturated fats	0g	√√√
Vitamins	Good source of:	
		C
Minerals	Good source of:	
		—

Illustrated on page 159

◆ RED & WHITE SALAD ◆

INGREDIENTS

350 g (12 oz) lychees   15 ml (1 tbsp) Kirsch
225 g (8 oz) red fruit (strawberries,   *Serves 4*
cherries or raspberries)

1 Peel the lychees. Using a small sharp knife, cut in half and remove the stone. It's easier to try to find the top of the stone and work down towards the stem end, splitting open the fruit.
2 To prepare the red fruit: hull and slice the strawberries, stone the cherries but leave the raspberries whole.
3 Mix the fruits together in a bowl and toss in the Kirsch. Leave to stand for 2 hours before serving.

It is best to use a liquidizer to break up the frozen purée of this sorbet so the egg white is well incorporated.

NUTRITIONAL PROFILE	per portion	
Total calories		110
Protein	2g	√
Fibre	2g	√
Polyunsaturated fats	0g	√√√
Saturated fats	0g	√√√
Vitamins	Good source of:	
		A, C
Minerals	Good source of:	
		—

Illustrated on page 159

◆ MANGO & ORANGE ◆
SORBET

INGREDIENTS

2 mangos   15 ml (1 tbsp) Cointreau (optional)
juice of 1 orange   1 egg white, beaten
5 ml (1 tsp) orange rind   *Serves 4*

1 Peel the mangos and cut the flesh away from the stone, remembering that the stone is flat and oval in shape.
2 Put the mango flesh, orange juice and rind into a liquidizer or food processor and blend until smooth. Transfer to a freezerproof container and freeze for 1-2 hours.
3 Remove from the freezer and liquidize again until well broken up.
4 Beat the egg white until stiff and fold into the fruit purée. Freeze again for 2-3 hours.

The richness and flavour of this ice cream come from the nuts and fruit.

NUTRITIONAL PROFILE	per portion	
Total calories		230
Protein	5g	√
Fibre	1g	√
Polyunsaturated fats	4g	√√√
Saturated fats	3g	√√
Vitamins	Good source of:	
		C, E
Minerals	Good source of:	
		Mg

Illustrated on page 159

◆ICED CASHEW CREAM◆

INGREDIENTS

100 g (4 oz) cashew nuts   15 ml (1 tbsp) rum (optional)
150 ml (¼ pint) soya milk (unsweetened)   15 ml (1 tbsp) sunflower oil
10 ml (2 tsp) honey   ½ medium pineapple, diced
2.5 ml (½ tsp) vanilla essence   *Serves 6*

1 Grind the cashew nuts in a grinder, liquidizer or food processor until very fine powder.
2 Liquidize the milk, honey, vanilla essence, ground nuts, rum if using and oil together until quite smooth.
3 Add the pineapple and liquidize briefly again so that the pineapple still provides some texture.
4 Transfer to a freezerproof container and freeze for about 2 hours until the cream is firm.

CAKES
·& PASTRIES·

A delicious idea that can be made with a variety of toppings according to season. These slices can be served to complement low-fibre, low-vitamin dishes.

NUTRITIONAL PROFILE	*per portion*	
Total calories		380
Protein	8g	√
Fibre	9g	√√√
Polyunsaturated fats	2g	√√
Saturated fats	7g	√
Vitamins	*Good source of:*	
	A, B1, C, D, E	
Minerals	*Good source of:*	
	Ca, Fe, Mg	

Illustrated on page 163

· BRAMBLE ·
SLICE

INGREDIENTS

For the base
50 g (2 oz) butter or sunflower margarine
30 ml (2 tbsp) concentrated pear and apple spread
75 g (3 oz) porridge oats
75 g (3 oz) wholewheat flour
25 g (1 oz) soya flour
3 drops almond essence

For the topping
350 g (12 oz) dessert apples, preferably Cox's
225 g (8 oz) blackberries
15 ml (1 tbsp) concentrated apple juice
5 ml (1 tsp) arrowroot
Garnish
15 g (½ oz) toasted flaked almonds
Serves 4-6

1 Preheat the oven to gas mark 4, 180°C (350°F).
2 Cream the butter or margarine and fruit spread together in a large bowl.
3 Mix in the oats, flour, ground almonds and essence and work to a stiff dough.
4 Press into a 20 cm (8 in) flan ring and bake for 15 minutes. Leave to cool.
5 For the topping, dice the apples neatly, leaving the peel on. Mix them with the blackberries, concentrated apple juice and 15 ml (1 tbsp) water. Stew very gently for about 10-15 minutes until just softened.
6 Dissolve the arrowroot in 15 ml (1 tbsp) water, then mix into the fruit. Bring to the boil and simmer until the mixture thickens, stirring.
7 Spoon the topping on to the base and leave to set. Serve cold, decorated with toasted flaked almonds.

This version of the classic pastry is slightly less rich, being virtually sugar-free. As it is high in fibre it is ideal to serve after a low-fibre main course. Breadcrumbs are used here to absorb some of the fruit juices to prevent the pastry from becoming soggy.

NUTRITIONAL PROFILE	*per portion*	
Total calories		410
Protein	8g	√
Fibre	7g	√ √ √
Polyunsaturated fats	3g	√ √
Saturated fats	2g	√ √ √
Vitamins	*Good source of:*	
		B1, E
Minerals	*Good source of:*	
		Ca, Cu, Fe, Mg

Illustrated opposite

• APPLE STRUDEL •

INGREDIENTS

1 quantity of strudel pastry (see page 41)
For the filling
15 g (½ oz) butter
50 g (2 oz) wholewheat breadcrumbs
450 g (1 lb) crisp dessert apples
100 g (4 oz) raisins
50 g (2 oz) flaked almonds

10 ml (2 tsp) ground cinnamon
5 ml (1 tsp) grated lemon rind
5 ml (1 tsp) maple syrup
little melted butter
For the glaze
5 ml (1 tsp) malt extract
5 ml (1 tsp) concentrated apple juice
Serves 6-8

1 Melt the butter in a pan and gently fry the breadcrumbs for about 3 minutes until very lightly toasted.
2 Preheat the oven to gas mark 6, 200°C (400°F).
3 Finely slice the apples and mix with the raisins, flaked almonds, cinnamon, lemon rind and maple syrup.
4 Pull out the dough very thinly on a floured cloth to form a rectangle.
5 Sprinkle over the breadcrumbs. Cover with the apple filling to within 1.5 cm (½ in) of the edges.
6 Brush the edges of the dough with melted butter. Fold in the long side edges over the filling so that they meet in the centre. Roll up the strudel like a Swiss roll.
7 Put on a lightly oiled baking sheet. Brush the top with a little melted butter. Bake for 45-50 minutes.
8 Remove from the oven. Mix the malt extract and concentrated apple juice together and brush over the strudel.

More fruit than cake, this high-fibre recipe is also high in essential vitamins and minerals. Other fruit combinations could be used according to season.

NUTRITIONAL PROFILE	*per portion*	
Total calories		490
Protein	11g	√
Fibre	10g	√ √ √
Polyunsaturated fats	3g	√ √
Saturated fats	14g	√
Vitamins	*Good source of:*	
		A, B1, D, E
Minerals	*Good source of:*	
		Ca, Fe, Mg, Zn

Illustrated opposite

• PLUM CAKE •

INGREDIENTS

450 g (1 lb) plums, stoned and chopped
50 g (2 oz) sultanas
50 g (2 oz) almonds, chopped
5 ml (1 tsp) ground cinnamon
15 ml (1 tbsp) concentrated apple juice
100 g (4 oz) butter or sunflower margarine
15 ml (1 tbsp) concentrated pear and apple spread

150 g (5 oz) wholewheat flour
5 ml (1 tsp) baking powder
1 large egg or 15 ml (1 tbsp) soya flour mixed with 15-30 ml (1-2 tbsp) water
Garnish
6 whole blanched almonds
For serving
yogurt or smetana
Serves 6

1 Preheat the oven to gas mark 4, 180°C (350°F).
2 Mix the plums, sultanas, almonds, cinnamon and apple juice.
3 In a separate bowl, cream the butter with the fruit spread. Sift in the flour and baking powder, adding the bran left in the sieve. Beat in the egg or soya flour mixture.
4 Grease an 18 cm (7 in) cake tin. Spread two-thirds of the cake mixture in the base of the tin. Cover with the fruit filling. Spread the remaining cake mixture on top. Decorate with the whole almonds.
5 Bake for 50-60 minutes. Serve warm with yogurt or smetana.

Clockwise from the top: **Plum cake; Apricot & gooseberry savarin** (see page 164)**; Apple strudel; Bramble slice** (see page 161)

The texture of this savarin, which is light and airy, proves that high fibre doesn't mean dense and heavy. Keep the water that you stew the apricots in for juice or to flavour stocks and sauces.

NUTRITIONAL PROFILE	*per portion*	
Total calories		275
Protein	10g	√ √
Fibre	11g	√ √ √
Polyunsaturated fats	1g	√
Saturated fats	5g	√
Vitamins	*Good source of:*	
	A, B12, C, D	
Minerals	*Good source of:*	
	Ca, Fe	

Illustrated on page 163

·APRICOT·
& GOOSEBERRY SAVARIN

INGREDIENTS

75 ml (5 tbsp) warm water
5 ml (1 tsp) honey
15 g (½ oz) fresh yeast or 10 ml (2 tsp) dried yeast
100 g (4 oz) wholewheat flour
15 ml (1 tbsp) soya flour
pinch of salt
2 eggs

25 g (1 oz) margarine
For the filling
100 g (4 oz) Hunza apricots, soaked overnight
450 g (1 lb) gooseberries
15 ml (1 tbsp) honey
Serves 8

1 Mix the water and honey together, then add the yeast. Leave in a warm place for 10 minutes until frothy.
2 Mix in 25 g (1 oz) of the wholewheat flour and the soya flour, cover the batter and leave for 30 minutes.
3 Add the remaining flour, salt, eggs and margarine. Beat very well.
4 Pour into a lightly buttered 900 ml (1½ pint) savarin mould and leave to prove for 30 minutes.
5 Meanwhile, preheat the oven to gas mark 6, 200°C (400°F).
6 Stew the apricots in their soaking water for about 15-20 minutes. ▶

7 Bake the savarin for 20 minutes.
8 Turn out, cool slightly. Replace in tin and prick top.
9 Drain the apricots and pour 150 ml (¼ pint) juice over the savarin. Leave to soak for 2-3 hours.
10 Gently cook the gooseberries with the honey and a little water for about 10 minutes.
11 To serve the savarin, turn out, fill the centre with gooseberries and top with yogurt or smetana.

· CHRISTCHURCH ·
TEA RING

Based on a bread dough, this impressive-looking tea bread is high in fibre but low in saturated fats. The predominant flavour comes from the prune purée.

NUTRITIONAL PROFILE	*per portion*	
Total calories	235	
Protein	8.5g	√√√
Fibre	9g	√√√
Polyunsaturated fats	5g	√√
Saturated fats	2g	√√√
Vitamins	*Good source of:*	
	A, B1, B2, B6, C, E, FA, N	
Minerals	*Good source of:*	
	Ca, Fe, Mg, Zn	

Illustrated opposite

INGREDIENTS

10 ml (2 tsp) dried yeast or 15 g (½ oz) fresh yeast
30 ml (2 tbsp) malt extract
150 ml (¼ pint) warm water
100 ml (4 fl oz) yogurt
1 egg, beaten
450 g (1 lb) wholewheat flour
15 ml (1 tbsp) ground cinnamon
10 ml (2 tsp) ground ginger
2.5 ml (½ tsp) grated nutmeg
pinch of salt
30 ml (2 tbsp) sunflower oil
350 g (12 oz) prunes
150 ml (¼ pint) orange juice
5 ml (1 tsp) grated orange rind
2.5 ml (½ tsp) vanilla essence
50 g (2 oz) raisins
For the topping
15 ml (1 tbsp) malt extract
15 ml (1 tbsp) concentrated apple juice
Serves 10-12

1 Cream the yeast with the malt extract and warm water. Leave in a warm place for about 5 minutes until frothy.
2 Mix in the yogurt and most of the egg, reserving a little for glazing the dough.
3 Sift the flour, spices and salt together in a large bowl, adding the bran left in the sieve.
4 Pour in the yeast mixture and oil. Knead well.
5 Put the dough in a clean bowl, cover with polythene or a damp cloth and leave to rise for 1 hour or until double in size.
6 Gently stew the prunes in the orange juice for about 20 minutes until soft. Stone them, then liquidize to a stiff purée adding the orange rind and vanilla essence. Leave to cool.
7 Knock back the dough, knead in the raisins. Roll out to a 30.5 x 45.5 cm (12 x 18 in) rectangle.
8 Spread on prune purée and roll up the dough from the long side.
9 Form into a ring and make 12 deep slits in the dough so that the ring will rise evenly. Twist each portion slightly so that the cut side faces upwards. Leave to prove for 15-20 minutes.
10 Preheat the oven to gas mark 6, 200°C (400°F).
11 Place the tea ring on an oiled baking sheet. Brush with beaten egg. Bake for 20-25 minutes.
12 Mix together the malt extract and concentrated apple juice and use to brush the tea ring while still hot.

Left: Christchurch tea ring; Spicy orange muffins *(see page 166)*

With their moist, chewy texture, these low-fat muffins make an excellent alternative to cake.

NUTRITIONAL PROFILE		*per portion*
Total calories		220
Protein	6g	√√
Fibre	5g	√√
Polyunsaturated fats	3g	√√√
Saturated fats	1g	√√√
Vitamins		*Good source of:*
		B1, B6, C, E, FA
Minerals		*Good source of:*
		Ca, Fe, Mg, Zn

Illustrated on page 164

• SPICY ORANGE •
MUFFINS

INGREDIENTS

175 g (6 oz) wholewheat flour	100 g (4 oz) dried figs
175 g (6 oz) oatmeal	15 g (½ oz) sunflower seeds
10 ml (2 tsp) baking powder	225 ml (8 fl oz) orange juice
10 ml (2 tsp) ground mixed spice	1 egg, beaten
pinch of salt	30 ml (2 tbsp) sunflower oil
	Makes 9

1 Preheat the oven to gas mark 6, 200°C (400°F).
2 Mix the flour, oatmeal, baking powder, spice and salt together in a bowl.
3 Remove the stalks from the figs and chop the flesh thoroughly. Add to the dry ingredients with the sunflower seeds.
4 Mix together the orange juice, egg and oil. Beat well.
5 Pour this liquid over the dry ingredients and stir in thoroughly. Add a little more fruit juice if necessary, as the mixture should be fairly soft.
6 Spoon into lightly greased deep bun or muffin tins. Bake for 25-30 minutes. Once cooked, they should come out of the tin easily. Cool on a wire rack. Eat warm or cold.

This recipe is not low in calories, but compared with standard high-fat and high-sugar snacks it is a nutritious alternative.

NUTRITIONAL PROFILE		*per portion*
Total calories		315
Protein	7g	√
Fibre	11g	√√√
Polyunsaturated fats	2g	√√
Saturated fats	1g	√√
Vitamins		*Good source of:*
		B1, E
Minerals		*Good source of:*
		Ca, Fe, Mg

Illustrated opposite

• FRUIT & NUT •
BARS

INGREDIENTS

50 g (2 oz) apricots	50 g (2 oz) hazelnuts
50 g (2 oz) dates	110 g (4 oz) porridge oats
50 g (2 oz) figs	15-30 ml (1-2 tbsp) lemon juice
50 g (2 oz) sultanas	15 ml (1 tbsp) concentrated apple juice
50 g (2 oz) sunflower seeds	*Serves 4*

1 Preheat the oven to gas mark 4, 180°C (350°F).
2 Finely chop or mince the fruit and nuts, and mix thoroughly with the other ingredients.
3 Press into a lightly greased 18 cm x 18 cm (7 in x 7 in) square tin. Bake for 15 minutes. Cut into slices whilst still warm.

On rack, clockwise from the left: **Fruity oatcakes** *(see page 168)*; **Fruit and nut bars**; **Carob digestives** *(see page 168)*

These iron-rich biscuits are easy to make, and the use of a purée instead of sugar means that they have a fruity flavour.

NUTRITIONAL PROFILE	*per portion*	
Total calories		130
Protein	2g	√
Fibre	5g	√ √
Polyunsaturated fats	0.5g	√ √
Saturated fats	4g	√
Vitamins	*Good source of:*	
	A, B₁	
Minerals	*Good source of:*	
	Fe, Mg	

Illustrated on page 167

FRUITY
· OATCAKES ·

INGREDIENTS

100 g (4 oz) butter or sunflower margarine 100 g (4 oz) wholewheat flour
50 g (2 oz) date or apricot purée 100 g (4 oz) porridge oats
Makes 12

1 Preheat the oven to gas mark 4, 180°C (350°F).
2 Cream the butter or margarine and fruit purée together in a large bowl until light. Mix in the flour and oats and beat to a stiff dough.
3 Press or roll out the dough and cut into small rounds—making about 12.
4 Bake for 15 minutes or until just firm and lightly browned. Cool on a wire rack.

These simple, low-fat biscuits have a good texture and subtle flavour, naturally sweetened by dates.

NUTRITIONAL PROFILE	*per portion*	
Total calories		130
Protein	3g	√
Fibre	2g	√
Polyunsaturated fats	4g	√ √ √
Saturated fats	1g	√ √ √
Vitamins	*Good source of:*	
	B₁, E, FA, N	
Minerals	*Good source of:*	
	Fe, Mg	

Illustrated on page 167

CAROB
· DIGESTIVES ·

INGREDIENTS

50-75g (2 -3 oz) dates 5 ml (1 tsp) cinnamon
50 g (2 oz) unsalted peanuts 15 ml (1 tbsp) carob powder
10 ml (2 tsp) aniseed 1 small egg
10 ml (2 tsp) sesame seed *For the topping:*
100 ml (4 fl oz) olive or sunflower oil 1 egg white
rind and juice of 1 orange 25 g (1 oz) finely chopped peanuts
225 g (8 oz) flour *Makes 18*

1 Preheat the oven to gas mark 4, 180°C (350°F).
2 Cook the dates gently in a little water until soft, drain and beat to a stiff purée with a fork.
3 Grind the peanuts, aniseed and sesame seeds, and place in a large bowl.
4 Slowly mix in the oil, then add the orange rind and juice, and puréed dates.
5 Add the flour, cinnamon and carob powder. Stir again.
6 Beat in the egg and mix to a stiff dough.
7 Turn onto a floured work surface. Roll out and cut into biscuit shapes, or divide the mixture into walnut-sized pieces and press into individual rounds.
8 Brush with egg white and scatter with peanuts.
9 Bake on a greased tray for 25-30 minutes.

CHOOSING
A
·BALANCED·
DIET

CHANGING TO
·A HEALTHY DIET·

*Eat less fat, less salt and less, if any, sugar. Eat more fibre and
complex carbohydrate, especially from whole grains,
pulses, fresh fruit and vegetables.*

This is the message from nutritionists. These guidelines sound straightforward, but if it were simple to follow them, I am sure that we would all be healthy tomorrow. Change is not easy. People become rooted in their eating habits, and cannot believe that what is being suggested can really improve their health and general well-being. However, if you approach change gradually, the transition to good health can be relatively painless! It will also give you time to change to a new shopping and cooking routine. Remember, while it's important to aim for meals that relfect the low fat, low salt, low sugar, high protein, high fibre principle (see page 6), don't worry if every dish doesn't contain the perfect balance. What counts is your average intake of nutrients over a week.

How to change over

Look carefully at your present diet. Ask yourself: do I eat enough fresh foods? Do I eat a lot of fats? Do I eat too much tinned or processed food? Only you can decide what changes need to take place. Then start to think about which of the foods you normally buy could easily be replaced with something more healthy. First steps might be to replace whole milk with skimmed milk; butter with polyunsaturated margarine; and to eat wholewheat bread and pasta, and brown rice instead of polished white rice.

Foods for a healthy diet should be wholesome and nutritious, supplying the body with energy and nutrients but containing no dangerous chemicals or additives. The term "wholefoods" applies to foods to which nothing has been added and nothing taken away. The benefit of these types of food is that they retain nutrients that would be lost in refining or food processing. For example, a wholewheat product contains fibre, protein, vitamins and minerals, most of which would be lost in the refining process that produces a white flour product.

Nowadays, wholefoods are not restricted to health-food shops. Many supermarkets produce a range of products that are largely additive-free, using good-quality, natural ingredients. There is a range of wholewheat products—flours, breads, pastas, biscuits and cereals—as well as preservative-free yogurts and fruit juices, and unrefined oils.

Next, start looking at the labels on any processed food that you buy—look particularly for the sugar, salt and fat content. Start buying sugar-free breakfast cereals, watch out for sugar in savoury products such as canned soups and baked beans and note the salt content in canned vegetables—and some frozen ones. In fact, try to cut down on canned food altogether. Think about some of the processed foods that you buy and consider making them yourself. Mayonnaise, sweet and savoury sauces, muesli and soups can all be made quite easily at home, and by doing this you can be sure there are no unwanted additives.

Consider, also, the quality of the fresh food you are eating. If you are lucky enough to be able to grow your own fruit and vegetables, you can eat really fresh produce which has been cultivated without chemical sprays and pesticides. To help you with this there are a number of organizations that can give you advice on organic growing methods. If you cannot grow your own fruit and vegetables, do choose quality produce; go to a reputable shop, preferably one supplying organic fruit and vegetables, which will be relatively free from chemicals.

Think about your meals

Once you have the correct ingredients, small changes to your menus can make huge differences to your diet.

Breakfasts Make your own muesli or choose a sugar- or fat-free cereal. If you prefer a hot breakfast, try porridge, home-made muffins, home-made baked beans or grilled tomatoes or mushrooms on whole-wheat or rye bread. Drink unsweetened fruit juices and coffee substitutes or herbal teas (see page 177).

Lunch and supper There is a wide range of staple foods for you to draw from. Cereals and pulses should be eaten for their carbohydrate, fibre, protein, vitamin and mineral content; nuts and seeds for proteins and fats—remember they have a high fat content; fruit and vegetables for their fibre, vitamins and minerals. Within these groups different foods have different nutritional values (see pages 16-28).

Change the emphasis slightly so that the main part of your meals is unrefined carbohydrate, which is satisfying and provides energy—do not rely on high calorie, low nutrient processed foods to fill you up. Alter the way you cook your meals: grill or bake instead of frying, and steam or stir-fry your vegetables.

Try to include some raw fruit or vegetables in at least one of your main meals to obtain maximum nutritional benefit. This could be a salad starter or main course—there are plenty of ideas in the book to choose from that are a far cry from lettuce and tomato. You could also serve a fresh fruit salad instead of a sticky pudding—just as satisfying and nutritionally far better for you.

Snacks Fresh vegetables and fresh fruit make nourishing snacks. Replace sweets with dried fruit, and savoury nibbles with nuts and seeds. Eat sugar-free or low-sugar biscuits or cakes until you can give up sweet snacks and try wholewheat bread spread with miso for a savoury snack.

Eating out

Healthfood restaurants are burgeoning and they generally have a good range of dishes to choose from. Eating in a conventional restaurant is sometimes more difficult. I find the starters more imaginative than the main courses and order several plus a salad. Select vegetables that have been steamed rather than fried.

Eating in other people's houses is more difficult because there may not be a choice. Just remember that no food is completely forbidden, it is just up to you to balance your diet on a weekly basis.

Meals for children

If your children have always eaten wholefoods at home, problems start only when they go out or go to school. It is up to you to make sure that the rest of their diet is balanced. If you're changing to a wholefood diet yourselves, your children may be more resistant to change, but again it is a question of doing it gradually. Remember to let them have a treat occasionally as well.

Main courses are relatively easy because most children like pizzas, pastas and grain dishes, particularly rice and millet. For puddings try the *Trifle, Cranachan* or *Fruit pie.* Many children love yogurt with fresh fruit.

If you are making packed lunches for school or picnics, vary the type of bread you use and fill sandwiches with imaginative spreads such as quark, *Golden tofu pâté* or *Sweet tahini spread.* The latter two are especially good for children because they are high in protein, which is essential for their growth and development. Make pasties with a light yeasted pastry or use a shortcrust wholewheat pastry for flans and tartlets.

Snacks are a particular problem with children because raw fruit and vegetables do not have the same appeal as a bar of chocolate or a sticky cake. However, dried fruit can make a good substitute for sweets, and there are several recipes in the book for sugar-free cakes and biscuits, for example, *Christchurch tea ring* and *Fruit and nut bars.* Avoid giving very young children small nuts and seeds because they can easily choke, and avoid fruit squash, which is high in additives—offer fruit juices mixed with sparkling mineral water instead.

• HEALTHY ALTERNATIVES •

This section is intended as a guide to the foods to avoid or cut down on,
with suggestions for alternatives to help you ease into a new and
healthier way of eating without really missing the old way.

• FATS •

There was a time when only the rich could afford rich foods, which largely meant foods high in fat. Fats are now the cheapest form of calories available. This is because weight for weight they contain almost twice as many calories as carbohydrates and proteins. In 1800 fat accounted for about 10 per cent of the calories in our diet. Nowadays it accounts for around 40 per cent of the calories in most Western diets.

Fats and disease

There are now clear links between fat and various so-called Western diseases. Too much fat can make you fat, leading to obesity. This brings a greater likelihood of diabetes, arthritis, gall bladder disease, high blood pressure and heart trouble. Even without obesity there are clear links between fat consumption and heart disease, and because high-fat diets tend to be low-fibre diets, they are thought to a be a factor in cancer of the bowel.

Reduce consumption

We urgently need to cut down our consumption of fats to less than 30 per cent of our total calorie intake. Although we need some fat in our diet for energy and to supply essential fatty acids and fat-soluble vitamins, on average an adult needs to eat less than 85g (3oz) per day.

Saturated vs unsaturated fats

It's not just a matter of how much fat we eat but also the type of fat (see page 15). Saturated fats can cause fatty deposits on artery walls. These fatty deposits are largely cholesterol, a normal component of most body tissues, supplied only by animal and dairy fats. The deposits may build up and block the arteries, thus obstructing the flow of blood, a process called atherosclerosis. If this occurs in a heart artery it can cause a heart attack. Blockage in other regions can cause strokes, angina or other circulatory problems. Low blood cholesterol levels reduce the risk of heart attacks and it is known that cholesterol levels fall when less saturated fat is eaten.

Unsaturated fats are thought to offer some protection against atherosclerosis by lowering blood cholesterol levels. However, the best protection is to eat less fat altogether— particularly saturated fats.

Avoiding fats

In practical terms, this means cutting down on animal-derived products such as lard, eggs, butter, hard cheese, cream and full-fat milk. This can be very hard to do unless you make everything you eat so that you can see exactly what goes into things. Processed foods may be loaded with unsuspected fats and the only way to tell is by reading the labels: they should give the fat content, if not the type. Generally, ingredients are listed in descending order of weight, so it should be possible to get some idea of the proportion of fat. This particularly applies to oils and margarines.

The percentage of fat on a label is given by weight, sometimes, wet weight. Thus, in sausage, for example, which is fatty meats, cereals and water, the overall fat content may appear to be only 25 per cent. Because water has no energy value, the actual percentage of calories coming from the fat is nearer 70 per cent.

Blended oils should be avoided as they may well be made from a mixture of palm or coconut oil (both containing saturated fats) and an unsaturated oil such as sunflower. Buy the unmixed, unsaturated oils such as corn, sunflower and safflower, and get them cold-pressed

How to cut down on fat

- Eat more vegetarian meals.
- Have fresh fruit salads, fruit compotes or yogurt instead of puddings.
- Use yogurt as a salad dressing instead of oil.
- Grill or bake rather than fry.
- Use non-stick pans so you use less oil.
- Use gentle heat when cooking because high temperatures change unsaturated fats into saturated fats.
- Use polyunsaturated oil and margarine in place of butter and lard.
- Use fresh herbs on food instead of butter.
- Change from full-fat milk to skimmed milk.
- Moisten sandwiches or crispbreads with salad or savoury spread rather than butter.
- Avoid blended oils made partly with saturated fats; use cold-pressed oils instead.
- Have cakes, pastries, chocolate, crisps, biscuits and ice-cream rarely, even home-made low-fat ones.
- Avoid food where fat is high on the label.

if possible because the heat used in other methods of processing can destroy some of the nutrients they contain, such as lecithin and vitamin E.

Many margarine manufacturers start with cheap ingredients such as beef suet and whale oil and rely on extensive processing, colouring and additives to produce palatable results. Moreover, they use the process of hydrogenation to solidify the fat, thus turning unsaturated fats into saturated fats. The best margarines are made with cold-pressed, unsaturated oils that have not been hydrogenated, and can be found in healthfood shops.

◆ DAIRY PRODUCTS ◆

About a third of our fat intake comes from meat and a third from dairy products. Together, these make up about 40 per cent of our saturated fat intake, so it makes sense to cut down on these products or use less fatty alternatives. Dairy products do contain high proportions of proteins, vitamins and minerals, but we can make do with less of them because all these nutrients can be found in other sources.

There are, however, other reasons, apart from a high fat content, for cutting down on dairy products. Milk contributes to a number of complaints and milk allergies are common. There are two types of milk allergy: some people are allergic to milk protein, which can result in breathing difficulties, catarrh or eczema; others have an enzyme deficiency known as lactose intolerance that hinders the breaking down of milk sugars in the body. Lactose is one of the milk sugars and it is broken down in the body by an enzyme called lactase. If lactase is not present, the milk sugar accumulates in the intestine, ferments and causes cramps and diarrhoea.

After chocolate, the most likely causes of migraine headaches are cheese and other dairy products. They also cause the formation of mucus and may contribute to sinus problems and bronchitis.

Alternatives
There are many ways in which you can cut down on your consumption of dairy products. Start by using skimmed milk. If you cannot drink cow's milk, try goat's milk or soya milk.

Skimmed milk
Whole, full-fat milk is about 3.8 per cent fat; skimmed milk is only 0.1 per cent. Semi-skimmed milk contains about half as much fat as whole milk. The advantage of skimmed milk is that only the fat and fat-soluble vitamins are removed. Skimmed milk does taste different and it can take time to get used to it, but when you become adjusted, whole milk will seem too rich.

Goat's milk and soya milk
Those allergic to cow's milk can substitute goat's milk or soya milk. Goat's milk has a higher phosphate, copper and magnesium content than cow's milk but beware, because it also has a much higher fat content and it is very difficult to obtain low-fat goat's milk. Soya milk also has a higher fat content than skimmed milk. Both soya and goat's milk are available in powdered form.

Low-fat milk products
It is easy enough to cut down on fatty dairy products. I have listed some of the low-fat ones below. Some of the products have high-fat versions, or versions containing water and salt, so it is important to check the labels carefully.

Cottage cheese Similar to curd cheese but made from skimmed milk so it is low in fat, yielding about 30 calories per 25 g (1 oz). Some varieties contain salt and preservatives, so check the label carefully.

Curd cheese Made from the separated curd of whole cow's or goat's milk, so it is about 11 per cent fat and gives 40-45 calories per 25 g (1 oz).

Quark Another soft, white cheese but it is made from semi-skimmed milk, and does not contain salt. The fat content is generally low but can be up to 40 per cent, so it is wise to check the label.

Smetana Looks like cream and tastes similar to sour cream but it is made from low-fat dairy products. Its fat content varies from 5-10 per cent. Check the label if you buy it or make your own (see page 34).

Yogurt This can be made from skimmed or whole milk but is acidic enough to break down milk protein into a more easily digested form. You can make your own (see page 33).

How to cut down on high-fat dairy products

- Use skimmed milk instead of whole milk.
- Serve yogurt as a pudding.
- Use yogurt or smetana instead of cream in cooking.
- Make yogurt-based dressings for salads.
- Soak muesli in fruit juice instead of milk.
- Try herbal teas instead of milky drinks.
- Sprinkle vegetables with herbs instead of butter.
- Use a good-quality margarine made from polyunsaturated fats instead of butter.
- Avoid butter in sandwiches; moisten the bread with tahini, yeast extract or a similar savoury spread.

◆ SALT ◆

We need less than 4 g of salt per day and we can get this from whole, fresh foods, yet we add salt to our food and take in about ten to twelve times as much as we need. There are links between intake of salt and high blood pressure, a condition which can lead to other circulatory problems such as heart disease and strokes.

Salt is sodium chloride. Sodium and potassium together help to regulate the body fluids and the balance is delicate (see page 14). Too much salt can upset the balance and cause fluid to be retained. The kidneys also have to work harder to get rid of the excess salt.

Avoiding salt

Most of the salt we eat comes from processed foods. Canned vegetables, for example, may have 200 per cent more sodium than fresh ones, so it is not just obvious things like crisps that you have to watch. High-salt foods include many canned and packet soups, pickles, sauces, butter and margarine, as well as plenty of unexpected ones such as breakfast cereals. Many additives are sodium-based.

The best strategy is to cut out all processed foods and, when cooking, simply leave salt out of a recipe, or use one of the alternatives. Give your taste buds a chance to get the flavour of a dish. Adding salt at the table is often just a habit, sometimes an addiction; reduce the amount you add gradually if you find it easier.

Alternatives

There are several flavourings that can be used instead of salt and there is even a way to reduce the salt content in baking by making a low-salt version of baking soda.

Low-sodium salt
Half sodium salt and half potassium salt, this is helpful in making the transition between using salt and not using it.

Herb salt
This is salt with herbs. Whilst it is just as salty, it has more flavour and will therefore help you use less salt.

Gomasio
A mixture of toasted, crushed sesame seeds and salt.

Miso
A seasoning made from soya beans fermented with salt and wheat or barley, which has the consistency of a dense spread. There are several varieties available (see page 186). It can be stored for several months but should not be subjected to extremes of temperature.

Shoyu and tamari
Dark liquids with a salty taste (see page 186-187), they can be added to any savoury dish. Shoyu is made from soya beans, wheat, salt and water. Tamari should be made without wheat. Shoyu and tamari will keep indefinitely.

Low-sodium baking powder
This is a useful substitute for baking soda, which has a high salt content. Mix equal parts of rice flour or arrowroot, cream of tartar and potassium bicarbonate.

How to cut down on salt

- Use a low-sodium salt.
- Use gomasio or herb salt instead of ordinary salt.
- Sprinkle vegetables with fresh herbs, spices or lemon juice instead of adding salt during cooking.
- Use miso as a savoury spread.
- Use miso, shoyu or tamari to flavour soups and stews.

◆ SUGAR ◆

We know that refined sugar can make us fat, rot our teeth and that it is linked with diabetes. So why do we eat on average 1 kilo (2 lb) of refined sugar a week each? Is sugar addictive? The culprit is sucrose in the form of white or brown sugar. The way nature packages sugar, with fibre, vitamins, minerals and water, as for example, in fruit and vegetables, ensures that we don't eat too much. Refined sugar, on the other hand, gives no nutrients, only calories.

Whatever we eat raises the level of blood glucose (blood sugar). Provided glucose is released slowly and steadily during digestion, the blood sugar level is maintained within normal limits, sustaining mental and physical ability, helping us to concentrate and keeping emotions balanced. All goes well when unrefined, high-fibre carbohydrates (both starches and sugars) are eaten because these are digested slowly, but a concentrated supply of refined sugar is absorbed quickly and raises blood sugar to high levels. The pancreas sends insulin to lower the sugar level, causing a rapid fall, which leaves a craving for more sugar. It is a vicious circle, causing bursts of energy followed by fatigue and moody ups and downs. Refined sugar does not leave you satisfied, and in excess amounts can make you fat. In addition, if the pancreas can't cope with so many sudden demands for insulin, this may lead to diabetes.

The acid-producing bacteria that attack our teeth love sugar, because it reacts with saliva to produce just the environment the bacteria need.

Sugar is also a drain on nutrients, especially B vitamins and calcium, which are used in metabolizing sugar. Naturally sweet foods like dates often contain enough of the B vitamins to compensate, as do unrefined carbohydrates. Refined sugar, which lacks nutrients, draws more nutrients away from the body's supplies.

There appear to be links between sugar intake and hyperactivity in children, and heart disease. Too much sugar also increases the level of triglycerides (fats) in the blood, and increase in fats may be associated with circulatory disorders such as atherosclerosis.

Sugar consumption cannot be measured in packets. Packet sales have in fact fallen in recent years, while sugar consumption has not. This is because as much as three quarters of the sugar we eat is found in manufactured foods, and not just obvious ones like Coca-Cola, which has as much as 35 ml (7 tsp) sugar in one glass. A surprising number of savoury foods contain sugar, among them soups, sauces, pickles, ready-made salads and canned vegetables.

Alternatives

It is perfectly possible to avoid packet sugar altogether. You simply use unrefined natural sweeteners instead.

Honey
This contains fructose and glucose. It has slightly fewer calories than sucrose and is sweeter so you use less. It contains traces of vitamins and minerals. Honey can be used as a sweetener in drinks, on food such as yogurt, or in cooking.

Molasses
The residue left after extracting sugar from cane or beet, it contains minerals, especially calcium and iron, and vitamins. It is sucrose, not fructose, but it has a strong flavour so you do not need to use very much.

Maple syrup
This is not as sweet as honey and is largely sucrose but it does contain calcium and potassium.

Malt extract
A product of beer-making, malt extract contains maltose, which is far less sweet than sucrose. It has a strong flavour and contains iron and some of the B vitamins. Other grain syrups have a similar taste.

Fruit juice concentrates
Undiluted, these can be used instead of sugar in cakes and cereals. In the refrigerator they will keep undiluted for 3-5 weeks.

Dried fruit purées
These make excellent sugar substitutes in baking—the sweetest is date purée. To make fruit purée, chop the fruit finely, cover it with water and simmer for 10-15 minutes, until soft enough to mash. Cream it in with the fats as you would sugar. I find 25-50 g (1-2 oz) dates is equal to about 25 g (1 oz) of sugar.

How to cut down on sugar

- Do without sugar in hot drinks.
- Buy sugar-free breakfast cereals or make your own.
- Drink unsweetened fruit juice or mineral water.
- Use less sugar than called for in recipes.
- Eat ice-cream and sweets only rarely.
- Replace puddings with fruit, low-fat cheese or yogurt.
- Eat dried fruit, fresh fruit and raw vegetables.
- Avoid processed foods as much as possible.
- Buy sugar-free or reduced-sugar jams or switch to savoury spreads such as miso (see page 186).
- Check labels on processed foods.

◆ ADDITIVES ◆

Nutritionists caution against too much fat, salt and sugar but these are not the only "baddies". High on the list of substances to cut down on or avoid are additives. Mostly non-nutritive substances, additives are added to food to prolong shelf life, assist in processing and cosmetically improve the taste and appearance of food. They are now so commonplace that it is almost impossible to avoid them, yet many are suspect and unnecessary.

Additives include flavourings, flavour-enhancers, thickeners, stabilizers, emulsifiers, colourings, preservatives, bases, antioxidants, sweeteners, bleaches and glazing agents. Different countries have different laws governing the use of additives in food. The general rule is that they must be safe and not used in greater quantities than necessary.

The testing of a new additive is not necessarily foolproof. Results of tests on animals may or may not be valid on humans, and little is known about the long-term effects. Some additives may cause cancer but it is hard to trace the cause of a disease that takes years to develop. Studies are needed to see if harmful effects are being passed from one generation to another. As yet we know almost nothing about how additives interact with other chemicals in food.

When an additive comes into common use, it may be consumed in large quantities from several different sources, so a permitted safety limit set for any one food is irrelevant. We need more information, and unfortunately food labels are not much use. Firstly, because, in the U.K., flavourings do not have to be listed. Secondly, even when additives are listed, they are generally referred to by their "E" numbers, so unless you are a chemist it is like a foreign language.

Avoiding additives
The best way to avoid additives is by eating as many whole, fresh foods as possible. However, it may be

difficult to avoid buying some processed foods: even wholewheat bread, for example, may contain emulsifiers.

Antioxidants

Vitamins C and E are natural antioxidants. Artificial antioxidants are substances normally used to keep fats from going rancid and to prolong shelf life. BHA (E320, butylated hydroxyanisole) and BHT (E321, butylated hydroxytoluene), when tested on animals, were found to cause abnormalities and poor growth in the young. BHA affects intestinal muscles of humans. BHT has caused liver and kidney damage, balding, raised cholesterol levels and altered brain chemistry in animals, while human effects include asthma and other allergies. Both substances are found in butter, margarine, cooking oils and bakery products containing fats. Other antioxidants to watch out for are: E310 (propyl gallate), E311 (octyl gallate) and E312 (dodecyl gallate) found in oils, fats and breakfast cereals. They can cause asthma and skin complaints.

Artificial sweeteners

These are used to add sweetening without calories. Saccharine, the best known, is used in ever-increasing amounts. Reported ill-effects include tumours in old animals, and digestive and blood clotting disorders and skin allergies in humans. Saccharine is banned in several countries.

Bleaching agents

Used to whiten flour, bleaching agents destroy most of the nutrients not already removed in refining, particularly vitamin E. Chlorine (925) and chlorine dioxide (926) are powerful irritants and their use is banned in every EEC country except the U.K. Potassium bromate (924) has been shown to cause nausea and diarrhoea.

Colourings

These are the least justifiable additives, because they are purely cosmetic. They are increasingly used to make cheap food look appealing, although the actual number of permitted colourings is likely to be reduced, due to doubts about their safety. The main ones to watch out for are coal tar dyes, which are made synthetically and, in particular azo dyes. Coal tar dyes causing cancer in animals have already been banned. These dyes have been implicated in hyperactivity in children. About a fifth of those sensitive to aspirin also react to azo dyes; other reactions include asthma, rashes and gastric upsets. Watch out for colourings particularly in soft drinks, packet soups, sweets, canned fruits and vegetables, cake mixes, biscuits, smoked fish, salad cream and jam. The following are azo dyes: E102 (tartrazine), E110 (sunset yellow FCF), E122 (carmoisine), E123 (amaranth), E124 (ponceau 4R), E128 (red 2G), 154 (brown FK), 155 (chocolate brown HT), E151 (black PN), E180

(pigment rubine). The following are other types of coal tar dyes: E104 (quinoline yellow), E127 (erythrosine BS), E131 (patent blue V), E132 (indigo carmine), and E133 (brilliant blue FCF).

E150 (caramel) is both a colouring and a flavouring additive which, when made with ammonia, can cause vitamin B_6 deficiency in rats. There are several varieties of caramel and they are found in a wide range of foods.

Flavourings

These comprise the largest group of additives. Few have been tested and there are no permitted lists so manufacturers can use what they like. Glutamates, including monosodium glutamate or MSG (621), enhance flavour and side-effects of eating food containing them include headaches, dizziness, palpitations and chest pains. Glutamates are banned in baby foods.

Glazing agents

Used to give food a protective or shiny finish. Mineral oil (905), used on some dried fruits, prevents the body absorbing fat-soluble vitamins.

Preservatives

Considered the most justifiable additives because they prevent spoilage and let us enjoy out-of-season foods. E220 (sulphur dioxide), the preservative most commonly used in the U.K., is also an antioxidant and a bleach.

Sulphites help preserve vitamin C but in the process destroy vitamin B_1 and E. They are not supposed to be used in foods that contain significant amounts of vitamins B_1. They are dangerous to all asthmatics and can cause allergic reactions. Sulphur dioxide is suspected of triggering genetic mutations because it affects nucleic acids, the building blocks that pass our characteristics on to our offspring. You will find sulphites in fruit juices, wine, jam, sugar, dried vegetables, canned fruits, flour and bakery products.

Other sulphite preservatives used are: E221 (sodium sulphite), E222 (sodium hydrogen sulphite), E223 (sodium metabisulphite), E224 (potassium metabisulphite), E226 (calcium metabisulphite), E227 (calcium hydrogen sulphite) and 513 (sulphuric acid).

Nitrates and nitrites turn meat pink and prevent micro-organisms from growing. In the digestive system nitrates can turn into nitrites, and these can prevent the blood from carrying adequate supplies of oxygen around the body. Allergic reactions, arthritis and an inability to store vitamin A are other side-effects. Most worrying is evidence that nitrates or nitrites can be turned into nitrosamines during digestion. Some nitrosamines have been shown to cause cancer in animals. They are found in ham, bacon, delicatessen meats and in some cheeses. E252 (potassium nitrate) is saltpetre but watch out, too, for E250 (sodium nitrite) and E251 (sodium nitrate).

Benzoates preserve food by preventing mould growth. Their presence can cause rashes and other allergic reactions, may numb the mouth, and contribute to hyper-activity in children. The benzoates to avoid are: E210 (benzoic acid), E211 (sodium benzoate), E212 (potassium benzoate), E213 (calcium benzoate), E214 (ethyl 4-hydrobenzoate), E215 (ethyl 4-hydrobenzoate sodium salt), E216 (propyl 4-hydroxybenzoate), E217 (propyl 4-hydroxybenzoate sodium salt) and benzyl peroxide (no number).

How to avoid additives

- Avoid all processed foods.
- Wash fresh fruit and vegetables to get rid of any sprays or coatings that have been used.
- Buy organically produced food where possible.
- Look out for new additive-free products in health-food stores and supermarkets.
- Use wholewheat flour, which, by law, must not contain additives.
- Buy bread from shops you know do not use additives, or make your own.
- Read food labels carefully.

◆ DRINKS ◆

Drinks are another potential problem area. Fizzy drinks, squashes and mixers contain additives and sugar, whilst tea and coffee contain caffeine and tannin.

Caffeine and tannin

I have never heard of a caffeine death but the lethal dose is said to be about 10 gm. To take in 250 mg, the point at which caffeine qualifies medically as a stimulant, you would need to drink 19 cups of cocoa, four to six cups of tea or instant coffee, three to five 341 ml (12 fl oz) bottles of Coca-Cola or only one to two cups of fresh ground coffee. Caffeine makes the heart beat more rapidly and irregularly. It makes you feel more alert when you drink it, but too much can cause anxiety, restlessness and sleeplessness. It raises blood pressure and levels of fats in the blood. It makes the pancreas produce more insulin, which lowers blood sugar levels, and makes the stomach more acid.

Sensitivity to coffee and tea varies from one person to another. Caffeine is suspected of preventing iron from being properly used and of causing deficiencies of certain B vitamins. It may also reduce the absorption of other vitamins and minerals. Unexplained allergic reactions including rashes and migraine sometimes stop when caffeine is excluded from the diet. As well as caffeine, tea contains tannin, which tends to cause constipation.

Alcoholic drinks

A little alcohol may not be a bad thing because it acts as a tranquillizer or relaxant and may lessen the likelihood of heart disease. Alcohol is not, as some people think, a stimulant. Alcohol-tolerance is related to size so women can take less than men, for whom a safe amount is either a pint of beer, two glasses of wine or sherry or a double measure of spirits per day.

Too much alcohol causes dehydration, puts a strain on the liver, and exhausts supplies of B vitamins. Heavy drinkers can suffer malnutrition because alcohol, like sugar, offers no nourishment, only calories. Pregnant or lactating women should be wary of alcohol because it crosses the placenta and also passes into breast milk.

Alternatives

If you want to cut down on your intake of additives, sugar, caffeine, tannin or alcohol, try one of the drinks below.

Decaffeinated coffee and low-tannin tea
Available as beans or instant coffee, decaffeinated coffee contains minute traces of caffeine—no more than 3 mg per 100 gm jar. However, it can cause digestive disorders. Low-tannin tea is made in the same way as ordinary tea but, as the name implies, has a lower tannin content.

Cereal coffees
These are made up of roasted grains such as wheat or barley, and sometimes dandelion or chicory, all of which are good for the digestion.

Herbal teas
These come in a vast range and are best drunk without milk or sugar. You can add lemon juice or sweeten them with fruit juice concentrate or honey if you prefer.

Carob
A cocoa substitute, this makes a good hot or cold milky drink when flavoured with cinnamon and honey. Make it with skimmed milk.

Yogurt drink
To make a refreshing drink, beat yogurt until frothy, then dilute with water or orange juice and garnish with mint.

Fruit juices
Available from a wide variety of fruit; look out for those made with organically grown fruit, but if you cannot find them, make sure you buy pure, unsweetened juices.

Mineral water
This can be bought either carbonated or still, and makes a refreshing drink. Mix it with unsweetened fruit juice.

BUYING &
· PREPARATION ·

Eating a well-balanced diet is not, unfortunately, the whole story.
Much depends upon the quality of food you buy and how you prepare it.
Aim to serve food that has been adulterated as little as possible so
that nutrients are preserved and undesirable additives are avoided.

You should buy fresh, unrefined, organically grown ingredients. To get the best from your ingredients you should know how to choose, store and prepare them.

Why buy organically grown foods?

There is increasing concern about modern farming methods and the intensive use of chemicals to boost crop yields or animal growth. New chemicals are constantly being introduced, more drugs are being added to animal feeds and more poisonous insecticides are being sprayed on crops. Some of the insecticides, such as DDT and Aldrin, have already been banned or severely restricted in some countries yet they are still in use elsewhere.

It is claimed that up to a third of our foodstuffs are now contaminated. Vegetable crops such as leeks may receive up to eight or nine spray treatments during growth; 25 per cent of all main crop potatoes are sprayed with a chemical when they go into storage to prevent them sprouting if the temperature changes.

Most worrying is the increasing use of chemical fertilizers, particularly nitrates, a new form of inorganic nitrogen. It was discovered during the 1940s that nitrates could be added to the soil to boost crop yields dramatically. Most crops grown by intensive farming methods are now subjected to high concentrations of inorganic nitrogen. Whereas organic nitrogen is essential to plant life and many plants absorb it straight from the soil, inorganic nitrogen causes the plant tissues to become more watery and more susceptible to attack by fungus or insects, which then need to be treated again.

The effectiveness of the fungicides, pesticides and insecticides is decreasing because they are so commonly used, so the chemical needs to be up to 20 times stronger now than five years ago to do the same job. Apart from the health of the plant, human health is at risk from these chemicals, particularly the nitrates. Recent research studies have linked high-nitrate foods with gastric cancer (see page 176).

Organic farming is a means of combating this. It is a system whereby a fertile soil is maintained and replenished with the use of organic matter instead of chemicals. It seeks to produce good-quality foods with natural systems. Vegetables produced by organic farming methods may not be as evenly sized as those found in supermarkets but they are relatively free from chemicals.

· PULSES & GRAINS ·

These are the meat in a vegetarian diet because, used together, pulses (beans) and grains make high-quality protein (see page 12). Apart from soya beans, no one pulse or grain has all the amino acids in sufficient amounts to make a high-quality protein by itself but when grains and pulses are eaten together, what's lacking in one can be made up by what's in the other.

Of the grains, wheat, millet and oats are the richest sources of protein but all unrefined grains also provide fibre, carbohydrate, minerals and vitamins, especially the Bs. Dried beans and peas, too, are good sources of protein, fibre, carbohydrate, minerals and vitamins. They may lack vitamin C but all you have to do to get that is sprout them. Vitamin content increases dramatically with sprouting (as much as 600 times for C) and, depending on the pulse, you can also use sprouts as good sources of A, B, D, E and K.

Soya beans are higher in calories than other beans because they have a higher fat content. They also contain some carbohydrates, calcium and B vitamins. Tofu (or bean curd), made from soya beans, is a cheap, nourishing food from the Far East. It is tasteless so it needs to have flavour added. The firmest kind, which is like white cheese, is often eaten like a piece of meat with a tasty sauce over it, or it may be added to main course vegetable dishes. Softer custard-like kinds are used to enrich and thicken, much as we use cream or yogurt. Tofu keeps for a month in a vacuum pack but once opened it should be used within a week. Store it in water (changed daily) in the refrigerator.

Shops with a higher turnover are more likely to have the freshest foods, and even when you are buying grains and beans, freshness matters. The older they are the longer they take to cook. Stored in airtight containers, whole grains will keep for a long time. Flours and flakes should be used as soon as possible or within two months, because the milling process exposes the oils contained in the wheat-germ, so that the oils go rancid and the vitamin E content is lost. Unstabilized wheat-germ, that is wheatgerm that has not been heat-treated to remove the most volatile oils, should also be kept in the refrigerator. Stabilized wheatgerm keeps longer. Pulses will stay in good condition for six months in dry, dark, airtight conditions. The freshest are plump and unwrinkled, with colour that hasn't faded.

To prepare either whole grains or pulses, first wash them to get the dust off and pick out any grit. To save cooking time, beans and peas are usually soaked overnight, but you can get the same effect by boiling them hard for three to five minutes, then letting them stand in the water for an hour (see page 45). Cooking times vary. Lentils cook quite quickly and do not need soaking—red lentils cook in about 15 minutes, continental lentils take slightly longer—but kidney beans need an hour or more after soaking. Pressure cooking takes a third as long, but timing needs to be precise. With ordinary cooking, soya beans need to boil hard for the first hour, and all but lentils and split peas need an initial ten minutes of fast boiling to destroy toxins found in the skins. Then they are simmered until soft enough to eat. Whole grains take longer to cook than polished or cracked grains, (see page 46).

• VEGETABLES •

The most nutritious way to eat vegetables is raw because the more a food is processed the greater the loss of nutrients. Of course some vegetables, such as potatoes, are unpalatable unless cooked but there are ways of cooking which minimize nutrient losses.

Overcooking is one of our commonest sins. Peeling is another because so many nutrients lie just under the skin. The water-soluble vitamins, such as vitamin C, are destroyed most readily by cooking and other processing. See what happens to the vitamin C in a 3 oz (100 gms) serving of peas:

fresh or frozen, uncooked	25 mg
fresh or frozen, boiled	15 mg
canned garden	9 mg
canned processed	trace only
freeze dried	trace only

Even if left untouched at room temperature, leafy vegetables can lose half their C in a day, and light destroys half their B_2. Cutting exposes more surface to destructive contact with light and air and cooking can have a devastating effect. This is what happens to the most important vitamins in spinach when prepared:

	B_1	C	folic acid
raw, shredded	no loss	30% loss	25% loss
steamed	30% loss	50% loss	75% loss
boiled	total loss	total loss	total loss

Holding on to nutrients is a struggle that starts well before the preparation stage. Unless you are lucky enough to be able to pluck food straight from the garden, what is available is bound to have deteriorated somewhat. Make the best of it by buying first thing in the morning.

If you want vegetables grown organically without artificial fertilizers or sprays, expect to pay a little more. They may be smaller and less perfectly shaped but that's nothing compared to their superior flavour and nutritional value. For vegetables grown the usual way, find a good greengrocer who will let you select the freshest—go for plumpness and good colour. Nutrients are lost in storage no matter what precautions you take so it's best to use vegetables as soon as possible.

A growing number of exotic vegetables are available and, if you haven't already tried them, I urge you to sample three in particular. Radicchio rosso which is a kind of chicory eaten raw as a salad vegetable; Chinese leaves, a cross between celery and greens; and mangetout, young peas in their shells, eaten shells and all.

As soon as you get vegetables home, wash, dry and refrigerate them. This applies to all but salad vegetables and vegetables with skins thick enough to protect against light and air. The point of washing and refrigerating is to stop enzyme action. Enzymes help synthesize vitamins during plant growth but once the plant is gathered or overripens, enzymes become destroyers. Enzyme action thrives at room temperature but is inhibited by cold or heat, or lack of light or oxygen. Acid retards it but alkali encourages it.

Be sure not to soak when washing. Water leeches out sugars, vitamins and minerals, so foods should be exposed to as little as possible, whether by soaking or cooking. Apart from destroying vitamins, a mere four minutes' boiling of whole vegetables will cause 20 to 45 per cent of the mineral content and 75 per cent of the sugars to go the same way. With cut and peeled food it's even worse. Unless the water is used in soups and sauces all those nutrients go down the drain.

Oil-soluble vitamins such as A are less likely to be lost in cooking but they, too, are sensitive to heat and oxygen. Left at room temperature, green and yellow vegetables slowly lose their A, B_2 and C vitamins.

Peeling and scraping do almost as much damage as water, especially to root vegetables, so spare yourself all that tedious peeling and your health will benefit. Peel only when the skin is tough or bitter; if it's edible I simply scrub gently with a vegetable brush.

You may not realize how delicious uncooked vegetables can be until you try, say, a bit of raw turnip or cauliflower. Raw plants are such important sources of fibre, minerals and vitamins (especially C) that salad should be on the menu every day. Green ones are best because deep green leaves have higher concentrations of nutrients than most fruits and other vegetables. Cooked greens are good but they do lose nutrients so how, without salads, would we manage? Salad foods must be kept dry, chilled and uncut until soon before serving. Toss them in dressing to keep oxygen from surfaces once they have been cut.

Steaming is a way to hold on to nutrients because if little water is used, if there is a tight-fitting lid, and if heat is kept so low that no steam gets out, nutrients that escape into the steam are reabsorbed into the food by the time it's cooked. If you use a pressure cooker, time it carefully.

Coating with oil is another way to avoid contact with oxygen. Frying is not good for the health but stir-frying and sautéeing are different because so little oil is used — 10 ml (2 tsp) oil is enough to coat the vegetables and keep juices in while cooking. Make sure the food is dry or the oil won't cling, and stir it into hot oil. Cover the pan, lower the heat once food is heated through, and it will cook in its own moisture.

You can also coat with milk. Milk covers the surfaces as oil does and food cooks in its own juices, keeping its colour beautifully. The taste is sweeter and milder than cooking with water, and the milk is lovely in soup.

Vegetables can be baked or grilled but oil them first to stop oxygenation and loss of vitamin C, aggravated by long, slow heating. It is a good idea to steam vegetables first so that heat foods through quickly and enzyme action is stopped. When using a casserole, get both it and the oven hot before adding vegetables with hot liquid. Unless liquid covers the food, keep the casserole covered.

Preparing and cooking vegetables

Washing vegetables
- Clean quickly in cold water. Never soak.
- Brush root vegetables. Don't scrape.
- Dry thoroughly.
- Store in vegetable compartment of the refrigerator.

Preparing vegetables
- Cut food while still chilled.
- Peel only when you absolutely have to.
- Save peelings for soup.
- Save tops (for example, radish and carrot tops) for soups or salads, or to cook as a vegetable.
- Toss cut foods in a little lemon juice or vinegar to prevent discoloration and preserve nutrients.

Cooking vegetables
- Don't cook in copper or iron pans.
- Never add soda.
- Add a drop of vinegar to hard water.
- Steam if possible. Otherwise, boil very little water, add food, return to boil. Cover pan tightly, then simmer.
- Cook until barely tender.
- Save water for soups, sauces or the next lot of cooking.

Vitamin C destruction continues in cooking even after enzymes are inactivated, and it's made worse by alkali. Hard water is alkaline and so is soda, which is why you should never add soda to prevent discoloration of vegetables. Instead use a drop of vinegar to acidify the water. Salt draws out nutrients and is not good for you so avoid that, too. Iron and copper destroy C totally and at once, so don't cook in either of those metals. Because B_2 is destroyed by light, always cover your pans.

Most B vitamins disappear when the temperature is above boiling, as in frying or pressure cooking, but E and K seem to survive. Aromatic oils which give foods flavour are lost in proportion to how long the cooking takes, so serve vegetables firm, not mushy.

◆ SEA VEGETABLES ◆

Most seaweeds are like salty rubber but there are, surprisingly, around 70 edible species. We would do well to know about them because they provide an excellent, cheap, seemingly inexhaustible supply of protein, vitamins and minerals. As a source of B vitamins they are unusual in having B_{12}, not often found in vegetables. They are hard to beat for minerals, supplying all we need, and are particularly rich in calcium, potassium, sodium, iodine and iron.

We eat some seaweed without knowing it — is is used in manufactured vegetable gelatines, ice cream, salad dressing, soups, sauces and sausage skins. Those who eat it knowingly are the Celts, Chinese and Japanese. A variety eaten in Wales is red seaweed called laver, which smells like cabbage and looks like spinach.

In the Far East kelp, or brown seaweed, is particularly popular, used as a garnish for rice or as a seasoning. Nori, intensively farmed in Japan, is similar to laver and usually sold in sheets. As a salad ingredient it needs rinsing and boiling for 15 minutes, or you can avoid softening and simply crumble it over a salad.

Kombu, valued and cultivated in Japan, is eaten both raw and cooked. The flavour is sweet and it is used to enhance stocks and soups (see page 46). The Japanese think so highly of it that it is even given as presents, but Westerners may find it an acquired taste.

If you're not sure about seaweeds, wakame is the first to try because it is closest in taste to green vegetables. It can be served as salad after soaking or as a hot vegetable after ten minutes' simmering, but first cut out the central vein.

Broad-leafed arame is usually sold finely shredded and is similar to hijiki, which is shredded more coarsely. Both can be steamed, sautéed or eaten as salad. Arame is another good introduction to seaweeds because its mild taste goes well with other flavours.

Two other seaweeds that are quite widely available are dulse and carrageen. Dulse, dark and leafy with a sweet, tangy flavour, is good with cooked cabbage.

Ireland, New England, Iceland and parts of Canada know about it and make good use of it. Carrageen or Irish moss, is still enjoyed in Ireland, where most often it is used in carrageen mould or blancmange. It is useful for savoury moulds and fruit puddings. Agar, in flakes or powder, is a kind of gelatine made from seaweed, used instead of animal gelatine. Make a delicate jelly by dissolving 10 ml (2 tsp) of agar powder in 600 ml (1 pint) boiling liquid.

To buy seaweeds already cleaned, dried and packaged, turn to a healthfood shop. They keep for years if unopened and up to four months in an airtight container once opened. A five minute soaking is needed to soften most seaweeds unless they are going straight into soup. Dulse needs a ten minute soak but carrageen needs only a rinse.

◆ FRESH FRUIT ◆

It seems a shame to do anything to fruit because most of it is so good just as it comes. But if you must, cook it according to the same rules that apply to vegetables. Cook in the shortest possible time and serve in its own liquid to get nutrients that dissolve into the water. Very few need sweetening. Skins should be eaten when possible.

Choose firm, plump fruit without any bad spots. Fruit with stones is best when neither squashy nor very hard. Melons are ripe when they smell ripe and are a little soft at the stalk end. Pineapples should be more golden than green, with leaves that pull off without much struggle. Mangoes, paw paws (papayas), kiwi fruit and figs should be soft but if you buy them hard they will ripen at room temperature. Ripe passion fruit has wrinkled skin. Kumquats, like tiny oranges, are ripe when they become quite yielding to touch. Lychees are ripe when they turn red.

Fruits with good protective skins, such as citrus fruit, apples and bananas, can be kept at room temperature but others should go in the refrigerator as soon as they ripen to avoid destruction of vitamins A, B_2 and C. Once fruit is overripe, and especially if it's bruised, these vitamins quickly disappear. Guavas lose four-fifths of their vitamin C content in a day when overripe.

Soft fruits like strawberries should go into the refrigerator without washing or stemming because handling can bruise, and bruises increase enzyme action and vitamin losses. If strawberries are handled when well chilled, and only just before serving, damage is minimized. Firm fruit, which is less likely to bruise, can be washed before chilling, but avoid soaking and dry it well.

Fruit salad should be prepared at the last moment because cutting exposes more surface to the harmful effects of air, and discoloration and vitamin losses result. Toss cut fruit in lemon juice to prevent discoloration.

I think all fresh fruit should be washed before being eaten. Even it it's organically grown, how can we be sure it's free of pollutants such as lead from petrol fumes? I also think it's wasteful to buy more ripe fruit than can be refrigerated, frozen or otherwise preserved, or eaten right away. Exceptions are apples and citrus fruits, which can be stored for a long time in a cool place. Soft fruits need to be eaten as soon as possible.

◆ DRIED FRUIT ◆

Dried fruits are a concentrated form of sugar so they are relatively high in calories, but they are also better for you than sweets because minerals and vitamins are concentrated, too. There is less likelihood of over-indulging because, being full of fibre, they fill you up. Dates are about two-thirds sugar and figs about half, while prunes come out best with about two-thirds the calories of most dried fruits. Prunes and figs are useful natural laxatives, too. Dried fruits can be reconstituted for use in puddings (see page 45).

Sultanas, currants and raisins are all dried grapes which have a lot of iron but, sadly, it's in a form the body does not absorb well. Peaches, on the other hand, are an excellent source. The highest protein content is found in apricots, which are also good for vitamins A and C, but apples are better for C because they lose none in the drying process. Figs have a lot of minerals, protein and B vitamins. Dates, like most dried fruits, are rich in B_3 (niacin) and also have carotene, B_1 (thiamine), B_2 (riboflavin) and B_6.

Apples and dessert pears are fairly easy to dry at home. You halve the pears and peel, core and cut the apples into rings, then put them on racks in a slow oven. Leave for several hours at gas mark 2, 60°C (150°F) or with the door open a little.

Buy plump dried fruit rather than anything that is really hard. It will keep up to a year in an airtight container but after six months it is a good idea to add some orange or lemon peel to keep it moist. Frozen dried fruit also lasts a year but if the fruit is reconstituted and then frozen, it will keep for only two or three months.

Sulphur dioxide is often used as a preservative in dried fruit to slow down browning and prevent spoiling. It helps keep vitamin C but destroys B_1 and is suspected of being a factor in genetic mutations, a serious cause for alarm (see page 176). Figs and dates are free of it and some shops carry other dried fruits which have not been sulphured. The pale fruits are very likely to have been sulphured. The shiny appearance of some dried fruit may be due to a coating of mineral oil, something else to avoid if possible. Mineral oil in large quantities can interfere with absorption of calcium and phosphorus in the body; it also picks up oil-soluble vitamins (A, D, E, K) as it passes through the body, which are then excreted. Oestrogen and the adrenal hormones also dissolve in mineral oil and are lost in the faeces.

· BALANCED MEALS ·

If you've just changed to a vegetarian diet, or you don't want to work out a
daily nutritional plan, try using these menus, which illustrate the
high-protein, high fibre, low-fat principle of the book.

LIGHT MEALS

NUTRITIONAL PROFILE		per portion
Total calories		620
Protein	29g	√√√
Fibre	34g	√√√
Polyunsaturated fats	9g	√√
Saturated fats	5g	√√√
Vitamins		Good source of:
		B, C, N, A, E, K
Minerals		Good source of:
		Ca, Mg, Fe

NUTRITIONAL PROFILE		per portion
Total calories		505
Protein	23g	√√√
Fibre	22g	√√√
Polyunsaturated fats	4g	√√
Saturated fats	5g	√√√
Vitamins		Good source of:
		A, C, B1, B2, N, E, B6, FA
Minerals		Good source of:
		Mg, Fe, Cn, Zn

NUTRITIONAL PROFILE		per portion
Total calories		795
Protein	35g	√√√
Fibre	33g	√√√
Polyunsaturated fats	10g	√√√
Saturated fats	6 g	√√√
Vitamins		Good source of:
		B12, D, A, C, B1, N, FA
Minerals		Good source of:
		Mg, Ca, Cu, Zn, Fe

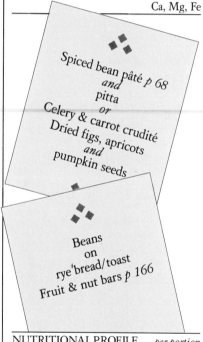

Spiced bean pâté *p 68*
and
pitta
or
Celery & carrot crudité
Dried figs, apricots
and
pumpkin seeds

Beans
on
rye bread/toast
Fruit & nut bars *p 166*

Yorkshire pasties *p 96*
Tomato &
Apricot relish *p 145*
Natural yogurt
and
soft fruit

Date and tahini sandwiches
Cottage cheese
and
watercress
Colourful leaf salad *p 128*

Minestrone *p 58*
Soho salad *p 121*
Radicchio salad *p 128*
Tropical trifle *p 152*

Austrian pancakes *p 110*
Broccoli
&
sunflower sauce *p 146*
Green bean julienne *p 132*

NUTRITIONAL PROFILE		per portion
Total calories		690
Protein	27g	√√√
Fibre	32g	√√√
Polyunsaturated fats	5g	√√
Saturated fats	2g	√√√
Vitamins		Good source of:
		C, B1, E, FA
Minerals		Good source of:
		Fe, Ca, Cu, Zn, Mg

NUTRITIONAL PROFILE		per portion
Total calories		535
Protein	28g	√√√
Fibre	12g	√√√
Polyunsaturated fats	6g	√√√
Saturated fats	3g	√√√
Vitamins		Good source of:
		C, B1, B2
Minerals		Good source of:
		Ca

NUTRITIONAL PROFILE		per portion
Total calories		420
Protein	18g	√√√
Fibre	18g	√√√
Polyunsaturated fats	10g	√√√
Saturated fats	4g	√√√
Vitamins		Good source of:
		B1, B2, E, B6, C
Minerals		Good source of:
		—

MAIN MEALS

NUTRITIONAL PROFILE		*per portion*
Total calories		520
Protein	19g	√√√
Fibre	9g	√√√
Polyunsaturated fats	3g	√√
Saturated fats	2g	√√√
Vitamins		*Good source of:*
	A, B₂, B₆, FA, C, E, B₁, N	
Minerals		*Good source of:*
	Cu, Mg, Zn, Fe	

American hot pizza p 106
Spinach salad p 128
Fresh fruit salad

NUTRITIONAL PROFILE		*per portion*
Total calories		780
Protein	32g	√√√
Fibre	29g	√√√
Polyunsaturated fats	16g	√√√
Saturated fats	4g	√√√
Vitamins		*Good source of:*
	B₆, FA, C, A, B₁, E	
Minerals		*Good source of:*
	Mg, Fe, Cu, Zn	

Bean burgers p 76
and
Wholewheat bread p 31
Crunchy green salad p 128
Choice of fruit

NUTRITIONAL PROFILE		*per portion*
Total calories		670
Protein	31g	√√√
Fibre	20g	√√√
Polyunsaturated fats	4g	√√
Saturated fats	2g	√√√
Vitamins		*Good source of:*
	C, FA	
Minerals		*Good source of:*
	Ca	

Baked potatoes
and
chilli bean sauce p 139
Crunchy green salad p 128
Low-fat cheeseboard
and
celery
and
fresh dates

Sweet red pepper soup p 54
Horiatiki p 124
Pitta bread
Fresh peaches

Leek & tomato terrine p 65
Hungarian pie p 97
Sharp mushroom sauce p 146
Roasted buckwheat
Steamed cauliflower
Crunchy green salad p 128
Cranachan p 155

Aubergine dip p 60
and
Wholewheat bread p 31
Nasi Kunyit p 18
Ankake sauce p 145
Courgette &
broad bean salad p 131
Tofu cheesecake p 154

NUTRITIONAL PROFILE		*per portion*
Total calories		425
Protein	19g	√√√
Fibre	9g	√√√
Polyunsaturated fats	5g	√√√
Saturated fats	7g	√√
Vitamins		*Good source of:*
	B₂, FA, N, C, B₁, A	
Minerals		*Good source of:*
	Fe, Ca, Cu, Zn	

NUTRITIONAL PROFILE		*per portion*
Total calories		1670
Protein	60g	√√√
Fibre	44g	√√√
Polyunsaturated fats	15g	√√√
Saturated fats	16g	√√√
Vitamins		*Good source of:*
	N, C, E, B₁, B₂, B₆, FA	
Minerals		*Good source of:*
	Cu, Mg, Fe, Zn, Ca	

NUTRITIONAL PROFILE		*per portion*
Total calories		1115
Protein	41g	√√√
Fibre	23g	√√√
Polyunsaturated fats	10g	√√√
Saturated fats	15g	√√
Vitamins		*Good source of:*
	C, A, B₁, B₂, B₆	
Minerals		*Good source of:*
	Mg, Zn, Fe, Cu, Ca	

·GLOSSARY·

Some of the major recipes call for ingredients that you may not have come across before. I have included some definitions to help you identify them and give you an idea of how they can be used and what they taste like.

◆ BEANS, PEAS & LENTILS ◆

Aduki beans
Also called adzuki beans, these are very small, dark red beans with a sweet, fairly strong taste. Native to Japan and very popular in the Far East, aduki beans are used in rice dishes, soups and desserts. They are rich in protein and sometimes ground into flour.

Black-eye peas
Sometimes known as cowpeas, these are small, whitish beans with a distinctive black and yellow "eye". These beans are native to Central Africa and are very popular in the southern states of America. They are useful in casseroles because they absorb other flavours. The immature pods can also be eaten whole, either cooked or raw.

Cannellini beans
A creamy white variety of haricot bean. They have a fluffy texture and can be used in soups or served cold in salads.

Chick peas
Also called garbanzos, these are small, sandy-brown beans which resemble small hazelnuts. They are highly nutritious and are frequently used in Mediterranean, Middle Eastern and Indian dishes. They are also ground to make flour.

Dutch brown beans
A variety of haricot bean, these are small, brown beans, sometimes used to make Boston baked beans.

Flageolet beans
A pale green variety of haricot beans with an unusually delicate and subtle taste; popular in France and Italy.

Ful medames
Also known as Egyptian brown beans, these are small, dark brown beans popular in the Middle East, particularly Egypt.

Haricot beans
There are many varieties of haricot beans: the most well known and widely available are small, white and round. These beans are used to make Boston baked beans. Haricot beans are also known as navy beans or Great Northern beans.

Kidney beans
These are quite large, kidney-shaped beans, hence the name. The red variety is Mexico's chilli bean, and the sweeter black one is used all over Latin America.

Lentils
Small, flat beans that, unlike all the above beans, do not need soaking before cooking. They are useful in soups, and because they cook quickly they make excellent purées. There are several varieties available: the small, red lentil, sometimes sold split, and the larger continental, or green, lentil are the two most common ones.

Mung beans
These are very small, round, bright green beans with a small "eye". They are native to the Far East. Generally used for sprouting, they can also be eaten whole as a vegetable.

Okara
This is a by-product of tofu-making and looks like wheat bran. Although it is not normally available in the shops, you can obtain it by making tofu (see page 36).

◆ DAIRY FOODS & SUBSTITUTES ◆

Curd cheese
A soft cheese made from the separated curds of whole cow's milk; it is usually set without using rennet. It has a slightly acidic taste (cottage cheese is a mild curd cheese).

Feta cheese
A moist, white, crumbly cheese from Greece with a slightly salty taste. It is made from goat's or sheep's milk and is ripened in brine or in its own whey.

Hung yogurt
Yogurt which has been strained through a piece of muslin to make it thicker (see page 34).

Mozzarella cheese
A soft, moist, unripened curd cheese originally made from buffalo milk but now made mostly from cow's milk. It has a slightly rubbery texture and a mild, creamy taste. It is normally sold swimming in its own milk or water.

Quark
Similar to curd cheese but sharper and more acidic; it is low-fat when made with skimmed milk.

Ricotta
Smooth, mild, unripened Italian cheese made with the whey of cow's milk. It is soft and moist in consistency, with a mild, creamy taste.

Smetana
A substitute for cream or sour cream and like a cross between the two. It is lower in fat because it is made with skimmed milk and cream. There are two types available, smetana and creamed smetana.

Soya milk
This is milk made from soya beans. It tastes sweeter than cow's milk and because it is easier to digest, it is used as a substitute for those with milk allergies.

Tofu
Low-fat, nutritious, bland-tasting bean curd made from soya beans, which looks a bit like white cheese. It has a particularly high protein content. Tofu is available in three forms: silken tofu is the softest, rather like junket in consistency and made from lightly pressed bean curd; firm tofu is made from heavily pressed bean curd and is like a firm cheese; soft tofu has a texture between the two.

◆ FLOURS ◆

Buckwheat flour
A strong, savoury flour made from roasted buckwheat; often used to make pancakes.

Rice flour
Usually made from polished rice but useful for those on low-gluten diets. It is often used to thicken sauces.

Rye flour
A low-gluten flour used to make the black breads of Europe.

Soya flour
Made from soya beans, it is used as a thickening, or, mixed with ordinary flour, as a nutritious supplement in baking.

Wheatmeal flour
This flour is made with wheat grains that have had most of the bran and some of the wheatgerm removed but because it contains some of the germ and bran, it is still a good source of fibre and vitamins and far more nutritious than white flour. It is available stone-ground or roller-milled.

Wholewheat flour
Flour in which the whole grain is ground to make the flour. Always buy the stone-ground variety—it is slightly coarser than ordinary flour but will contain all the nutrients.

◆ FRUITS ◆

Kumquat
A small, oval, orange tree fruit. It has a sweet skin and a rather bitter flesh and is eaten whole.

Mango
A green, pink, or yellowish Indian fruit, mangoes vary in size; some are as large as melons, others are as small as apples. The flesh of a ripe mango is normally pinky-golden and the fruit contains a large, flat, oval stone. Mangoes have a slightly fibrous texture and taste like a cross between a peach, apricot and melon.

Paw paw
Sometimes called papaya, this is an avocado-sized fruit with yellow-orange flesh and small black seeds. It tastes rather like a melon.

◆ GRAINS ◆

Alfalfa
Also called lucerne, it is exceptionally nutritious, being a good source of vitamins, especially A, B and E. Alfalfa is also a natural diuretic. The leaves can be used to make tea; the tiny seed can be ground for flour or sprouted.

Buckwheat
This is the seed of a plant related to rhubarb and dock. Thought to have originated in China, it is now a staple in Russia and Poland. Buckwheat is generally roasted, then cooked and served like rice or added to soups. It has a high mineral content, especially iron, and contains all the B vitamins and rutin.

Bulgar wheat
Also know as burghul, this comes from wholewheat berries which have been cracked, then hulled, steamed and roasted. It needs little or no cooking so is ideal for use in salads.

Couscous
Made by cracking wholewheat berries with rollers so that they cook fairly quickly. When combined with chick peas, it makes the North African dish of the same name.

Millet
This grain has a delicate flavour which may seem bland at first. Millet can be used instead of rice. It is extremely nutritious, being a good source of iron and B vitamins.

Pot barley
This is the whole barley grain minus the husk, so, unlike pearl barley, it still contains the bran, germ and vitamin B. It is low in gluten and has a slightly nutty taste.

Rice
There are two main types of rice: long-grain and short-grain. Long-grain stays dry, separate and fluffy when cooked and is generally used in savoury dishes. Short-grain tends to be moist and the grains cling together. Brown rice is unpolished, complete with nourishing bran.

Wheatgerm

The heart of the wheat grain, the germ contains many of the nutrients, notably B vitamins and vitamin E.

Wild rice

The seed of a water grass native to North America, wild rice is not actually related to rice but it looks like dark, thin long-grain rice. It has a subtle flavour similar to that of artichokes. Wild rice is difficult to harvest so it is expensive.

Wholewheat berries

These are the unrefined grains of wheat, and the most nutritious form of wheat complete with bran (the outer covering), which contains vitamins, minerals, fat and fibre, and the wheatgerm, a concentrated source of B vitamins and vitamin E. When cooked, the berries have a chewy texture and are ideal in salads.

✦ NUTS & SEEDS ✦

Anise seeds

Also called sweet cumin, these are the dried seeds of a plant native to Egypt and Greece. Anise tastes rather like licorice and is used in puddings and baking. The seeds can be used whole, or ground into a fine powder.

Pine kernels

The seeds of various pine trees in the Mediterranean, mainly the Stone pine. Pine nuts can be eaten like nuts or used in cooking. They are also called pigñolas or Indian nuts.

✦ OILS ✦

Olive oil

An oil made from olives, a good source of monounsaturated fat. Always buy a cold-pressed variety, sometimes called "virgin-quality"—heat used in other forms of processing destroys the nutrients and makes the oil a saturated fat.

Sesame seed oil

This is oil made from toasted sesame seeds. There are two, main varieties: a thick, dark aromatic oil which is used in Chinese cooking, and pale, odourless sesame oil used in Indian cooking. Sesame oil is a polyunsaturated oil and particularly useful because it does not easily turn rancid.

Safflower oil

A pale-coloured oil with a delicate taste. It is a poly-unsaturated oil and is ideal for salad dressings.

Sunflower oil

Made from sunflower seeds, this is probably the best all-purpose oil. It has almost no flavour so can be used in cooking and in salads. It is high in linoleic acid.

✦ SEAWEEDS ✦

Agar

This is a vegetarian substitute for animal gelatine. It is obtained from different seaweeds and is sold in flake or powder form. It is sometimes called Japanese or Ceylon Moss.

Arame

A broad-leafed, mild-tasting seaweed, arame is normally sold shredded into hair-like threads. It is highly nutritious, being particularly rich in iron. It can be steamed or sautéed and eaten hot or eaten cold. It is mild tasting and mixes well with other vegetables.

Kombu

Much cultivated by the Japanese, kombu has a sweet flavour. It comes in long, flat, finger-shaped strips and can be eaten raw or cooked or added to stocks and soups.

✦ SEASONINGS & FLAVOURINGS ✦

Fresh root ginger

The knobbly root of a plant native to South East Asia, with a juicy and firm, yellowish flesh. It should be peeled before use. Fresh ginger is normally grated or sliced and has much more flavour than dried or ground ginger.

Garam masala

An aromatic mixture of spices such as cardamom, cumin, coriander, chilli, and black pepper. It is often added to dishes near the end of cooking time or to the finished dish as a garnish. You can buy it ready-made or make up your own.

Gomasio

Also known as sesame salt, this is crushed and toasted sesame seeds mixed with salt. Gomasio is used as a salt substitute to cut down on sodium intake.

Miso

A salty paste made from soya beans and fermented with grains, water and salt. It is used in soups, stews and as a savoury spread. It has a consistency rather like peanut butter. There are several different varieties but the main ones are: hatcho miso, made from pure soya beans; mugi miso, made from soya beans and barley grains; and germai miso made from soya beans and rice. They are all fairly salty but the lighter coloured misos, such as germai miso, contain slightly less salt.

Shoyu

This is pure soya sauce made with soya beans, salt and barley or wheat. It has a slightly salty taste and is used as a flavouring instead of salt. Check labels carefully because commercial soy sauces often contain additives.

Tahini
A paste made from ground sesame seeds, used frequently in Middle Eastern cooking. It has a similar taste and texture to a fairly smooth peanut butter.

Tamari
Like soy sauce, but with a stronger flavour. Pure tamari should not contain wheat so is suitable for anyone on a gluten-free diet, but unfortunately it is still not widely available.

◆ SWEETENERS ◆

Apple juice concentrate
Used as a sweet flavouring for fruit salads, sauces and cereals instead of sugar — it is too strong to eat on its own. It can be combined with other sweetening such as honey.

Carob
Carob powder is made from the seeds of the Mediterranean carob tree. Similar to cocoa powder but nutritionally superior, it contains some vitamins but no caffeine, and has a lower fat content.

Creamed coconut
This is coconut flesh which has been dried and compressed into blocks.

Malt extract
Also known as barley syrup, this is the soluble part of barley which has been extracted and evaporated. It is not as sweet as sugar. It is used as flavouring in baking and hot drinks.

Molasses
A thick, dark, strongly flavoured syrup which comes from sugar cane. It is a by-product of sugar making but it is not as sweet as sugar. Molasses contains useful amounts of minerals. Black strap molasses in particular contains some B vitamins, calcium and iron.

Pear and apple spread
A fruit purée that can be substituted for sugar in baking. Available in healthfood shops.

◆ VEGETABLES ◆

Beansprouts
Many beans can be sprouted to use in salads or cooked dishes. Beansprouts are highly nutritious because the shoot has a high vitamin C content, which increases dramatically as it grows. They are also high in other vitamins, minerals and protein. Mung bean sprouts are the most well known; soya beans, aduki beans, lentils and wheat grains are all suitable for sprouting.

Chinese leaves
A type of celery cabbage that comes from Eastern Asia and China in particular, hence the name. It is about the size and shape of a cos lettuce but has very tightly packed leaves, each of which has a large white rib down the centre. It has a crunchy texture and tastes like a combination of celery and cabbage. Chinese leaves can be eaten raw in salads or stir-fried with other vegetables.

Endive
Also known as curly endive, this is like a large, open lettuce but it has narrower, wavy or curly leaves that are white in the centre and green on the outside. It has a distinctive bitter taste and is best eaten in salads, although it can be cooked. Endive contains many vitamins, folic acid in particular, and minerals.

Lamb's lettuce
Also called corn salad, this has soft-textured, tongue-like green leaves. Very popular in France where it is called mâche, it makes a useful winter salad, although it can be cooked and eaten like spinach.

Mangetout
Tender young peas eaten pod and all. They are flatter than garden pea pods and the pods do not have a tough inner skin, which is why they can be eaten whole. They have a delicate, slightly sweet taste and are sometimes known as sugar peas.

Mouli
Related to the radish, this is a long, white root vegetable with a distinctive peppery taste. It is particularly good in salads.

Okra
Also called lady's fingers or gumbo, this is a young seed pod of an African plant in the hibiscus family. Unlike a pea pod, okra has ribbed sides. It has slightly sticky flesh and contains small edible seeds. It can be eaten as a vegetable or it can be used to thicken soups and stews.

Oyster mushrooms
These are wild mushrooms with a blue-grey cap, much favoured in France.

Radicchio
A kind of chicory from Northern Italy with crisp red leaves. It looks like a very small cabbage but with slightly more open leaves. It has a peppery taste and is delicious in salads.

Sweet potatoes
The roots of a tropical vine, not true potatoes. Usually elongated with reddish-brown skin, and yellowish-white flesh, they are sweet and can be served in the same way as potatoes; they are particularly good baked.

· ACKNOWLEDGMENTS ·

Author's acknowledgments
I would like to thank, in particular, Ian
Burleigh for all his invaluable help in
preparing and testing recipes; Chris
Glazebrook for typing the original draft;
Barbara Croxford for checking the
recipes, and Fiona MacIntyre for bringing
the whole project together so efficiently.
My thanks to my friends and staff at
Sarah Brown's, Scarborough. Also to
Pauline Ashley, Phil Cook, Nicolas Cressey,
Harriet Cruickshank, Michael Hunter
and David Sulkin, all of whom have given
me so much encouragement and support.

Dorling Kindersley would like to thank:
Barbara Croxford for all her work on
the recipes; Jemima Dunne and Michael
Upshall for their editorial work on Choosing
a Balanced Diet and Good Sources of
Nutrients; Dr Michèle Sadler for her work
and advice on the nutritional aspects of
the book; Cheryl Picthall for design
assistance; Fred Gill for proof-reading;
Richard and Hilary Bird for the index;
Andy Butler, assistant to Philip Dowell and,
finally, The Scottish Merchant, David
Mellor, Covent Garden Kitchen Supplies;
Boda and Neal's Yard.

Photography
Philip Dowell   Graeme Harris(p. 140)
David Bradfield(p. 6-10)   Tom Dobbie (p. 3)

Stylist: Carolyn Rusell

Food preparation
Jane Suthering   Joyce Harrison
Lisa Collard   Pete Smith
Anne Hildyard   Jacki Baxter

Illustrator: Barbara Wardle

Typesetting: Modern Text Typesetting

Reproduction: A. Mondadori, Verona